A man who is not afraid of the sea will soon be drowned, he said, for he will be going out on a day he shouldn't. But we do be afraid of the sea, and we do only be drowned now and again.

—John Millington Synge

The Aran Islands

Derek:

To Hélène

Wayne:

To Derek Charles Hutchinson, with thanks for your inspiration

THE COMPLETE BOOK OF
SEA KAYAKING

SIXTH EDITION

DEREK C. HUTCHINSON
REVISED BY WAYNE HORODOWICH

Guilford, Connecticut

An imprint of The Rowman & Littlefield Publishing Group, Inc.
4501 Forbes Blvd., Ste. 200
Lanham, MD 20706
www.rowman.com

Falcon and FalconGuides are registered trademarks and Make Adventure Your Story is a trademark of The Rowman & Littlefield Publishing Group, Inc.

Distributed by NATIONAL BOOK NETWORK

British Library Cataloguing in Publication Information available
Library of Congress Cataloging-in-Publication Data available

ISBN 978-1-4930-2423-0 (paperback)
ISBN 978-1-4930-2424-7 (e-book)

♾™ The paper used in this publication meets the minimum requirements of American National Standard for Information Sciences—Permanence of Paper for Printed Library Materials, ANSI/NISO Z39.48-1992.

Printed in the United States of America

Note: All units of measurement in the following text are imperial. A conversion table may be found on p. 270. Individual paddlers are referred to as 'he'; this should, of course, be taken to mean 'he' or 'she' where appropriate.

The authors and The Rowman & Littlefield Publishing Group, Inc. assume no liability for accidents happening to, or injuries sustained by, readers who engage in the activities described in this book.

CONTENTS

Derek Hutchinson in his early years

FOREWORD

I was first introduced to sea kayaking in 1990 while I was studying Outdoor Education at Prescott College. My first sea kayaking expedition was to the Sea of Cortez, an amazing journey I will never forget. From that point on I was hooked; I wanted to find out as much about the sport as I could. First stop, the college library, where the first book I found was Derek Hutchinson's *Sea Canoeing*. I tore through the dog-eared edition that only fed my new-found kayaking addiction. Each page was filled with descriptions and drawings of kayaking history, techniques, and anecdotes. The more I read, the more I realized the potential for what I could do and where I might explore in a kayak. That was the start of my career in paddle sports.

I left Prescott with my then friend and now wife, Samantha Ladd. We traveled seasonally, guiding climbing and backpacking trips, but we both were drawn to the water. Sam had a background in sea kayaking, canoeing, and rafting, and in '95 we started guiding kayaking tours for the Sakonnet Boat House in Tiverton, Rhode Island. Shortly thereafter, Sam learned that Derek Hutchinson was touring the East Coast, giving talks on his expeditions and teaching classes. She got in touch with him, and our relationship with Derek started. We were his local knowledge and assistants on the water, not that he needed our help. At this point neither Sam nor I had any real training as kayak instructors or coaches, just guiding and expedition experience. When the weekend was over, Derek approached us and encouraged us both to pursue coaching and teaching paddle sports. We didn't know it at the time, but this was the launching point for our careers as professional kayakers.

In the years that followed, Derek became a close personal friend and our home became his base camp whenever he was teaching in New England.

When Derek was on the West Coast, he traveled and taught with his longtime friend and kayaking colleague, Wayne Horodowich, the founder of the University of Sea Kayaking. Wayne spent many years traveling up and down the coast with Derek, teaching clinics and presenting at symposia. Wayne produced an instructional video featuring Derek teaching his famous "Beyond the Cockpit" clinic as part of the USK Instructional Video series. Towards the end of Derek's life, Wayne captured many of Derek's stories in a DVD called *North Sea Crossing & Yarns from the Cockpit*. These videos capture Derek at his best, humorously recalling kayaking friends, innovations, and adventures. They became fast friends and family to one another, working together until Derek's untimely departure in 2012.

It was Derek who introduced Wayne to Sam and me sometime in the late '90s, when Sam and I were starting up our own paddle sport school, Osprey Sea Kayak Adventures. Naturally, we invited Wayne to be a guest instructor over the years and we also became fast friends, sharing our stories of Derek and his antics.

Wayne knew and respected Derek more than any of the other paddlers I know. He also learned a lot from Derek's wealth of experience. I can't think of anyone better suited to continue Derek's work and to inspire future generations of kayakers.

Please sit back and enjoy this edition of *The Complete Guide to Sea Kayaking* by Derek Hutchinson, edited and updated by Wayne Horodowich. Have fun exploring.

—Carl Ladd
Owner, Osprey Sea Kayak Adventures
ACA Level 5 Instructor and Level 4
Instructor Trainer

LETTER TO DEREK

To my friend and mentor,

Derek, I write to you as a representative of your many students. I've been honored to share many hours with you, on and off the water, as my friend and mentor. What may have been a brief moment in your life was a significant part of mine.

Some of our most important lessons in life come when we least expect them. Mine came in the quiet moments with you off the water. Our discussions of love, life, and stories of mistakes made along the way were highlights I'll never forget.

As your student, I've taken away many lessons. The one on back-paddling through the surf has saved my butt more times than you'll ever know.

I have so many great memories of the smiles you handed out and the confident, but humble students you created.

If we are lucky, we have one person that will grace our lives and who leaves an impact so great we are changed forever. For myself, and paddlers all over the world, you were that person. On behalf of myself and all the other paddlers you infected and corrupted, thank you.

Love always,
Bob
(Bob Burnett)

ACKNOWLEDGMENTS

Derek

For a book of this nature, it is inevitable that the material will have been acquired over many years and from many sources. Much of this particular book has grown from experience shared with paddlers whose skill, courage, and opinions I value highly.

It would therefore be impossible to mention all those to whom I owe my gratitude. However, I feel I owe special thanks to the following: the late Brian Barton, of the BCU Lifeguards; Duncan Winning, for his generous information about Scottish kayaking; Mike Clark of *Canoeing Magazine*, for his ready help in tracing specific photographs and other research; Mr. Graham, Curator of the Whitby Museum; Mr. Tynan, Curator of the Hancock Museum, Newcastle; the Chief Librarian, Public Library and Museum, South Shields, for permission to draw and study their kayak; Chris Hare and Chris Jowsey for their help in some of the historical research; Frank Goodman, who knows about plastic kayaks; Stewart Cameron and the staff of Metromedia; Bill Gardner, who is an expert on talk balloons; Kevin Danforth of the British Canoe Union; Alistair and Marianne Wilson of Lendal Paddles; Chris Cunningham of *Sea Kayaker Magazine*; John Nixon of HM Coastguard; and Denis Ball of the BCU Surf Committee.

Special thanks must go to my daughter, Fiona, for her tireless modeling of hand positions; my wife, Helene, for her unfailing encouragement and help in a thousand different ways; and Mike Hanson, who said, "Why don't you write a book?"

For their help with the racing stroke, I am indebted to Barney Wainwright, the Sports Science Officer of the British Canoe Union; Imre Kemecsey, racing coach and Silver Medalist at the Rome Olympics; Greg Barton, four-time Olympic Gold Medalist; and Debra Moore, Archivist, Hudson's Bay Company Archives.

Wayne

In addition to those mentioned above by Derek in the previous edition, I want to thank the following people for their help with this new edition: Karen Komenko for her patience in reading copy, Barb and George Gronseth for getting me paddlers for the new photos, Carl Ladd for the foreword, and Bob Burnett for his letter. It should be noted the following paddlers braved the freezing northwest waters for the winter photo shoot: Bonnie and Edward Alm, Larry Grove, and Wade Johnson and his son Myles.

I owe a special thanks to Clive Hutchinson, Derek's son, for the chance to edit this book.

Most of all I want to acknowledge all my students and the instructors and guides I have worked with over the years, because all that I know and share with others is a result of the time we spent together.

INTRODUCTION

In 1976 A. & C. Black Ltd. published the very first book on sea kayaking, written and illustrated by Derek Hutchinson. The fifth edition of that book was published in 2003. To celebrate the fortieth anniversary of Derek's first book, the publisher wanted to produce a new edition. Unfortunately Derek is no longer with us in body, so a suitable replacement needed to be found

Cover of Sea Canoeing, *the first book on sea kayaking. "Canoeing" was the term originally used in the UK for kayaking.* WAYNE HORODOWICH

to edit the sixth edition. Knowing my close ties with Derek, his son Clive suggested the publisher contact me. While I can never replace Derek, I spent considerable time teaching and traveling with him, which gives me a good perspective of Derek's style, his teaching philosophy, and his values on and off the water. I happily accepted the challenge of editing Derek's book because I wanted to keep the soul of his work intact.

Updating this book has been difficult, but it needed to be done. As you peruse this edition, there are times you will be reading "I did this" or "I believe this." I did my best to indicate when Derek was speaking. If no reference is made to Derek, then assume it is me doing the talking. It is important to note that there is rarely only one correct way of doing things, especially in sea kayaking. Our opinions are based upon our experiences. With that in mind, there are times when I present differing opinions to Derek's. As with all the information in this book, it is up to you to decide what you use and how you use it.

Since everyone has his or her own way of organizing stuff, I took the liberty of rearranging the chapters in addition to adding a few new ones. I also updated techniques to reflect those being used today as opposed to the original ones Derek knew and loved. I kept some of the earlier techniques for historical purposes.

Philosophically Derek and I were about 95 percent on the same page regarding skills needed for paddling and shared a strong sense of safety concerns, risk assessment, and the self-sufficiency needed by those who paddle on the sea. We did differ at times with respect to equipment, which is no surprise since Derek was a designer and I am not. In addition, I am 6 feet 7 inches and Derek was somewhere around my chest level. Since we spent so much time together, we were often referred to as the "giant and the gnome." That size difference also translated to differences in equipment and technique priorities. Therefore, almost all of the equipment references and opinions are still Derek's.

My goals for this new edition were to update techniques and show some of the new equipment on the market, while maintaining Derek's personality and style, and to pay tribute to all he has done for the sport of sea kayaking. I also added stories about Derek so the reader can get a better sense of his playful nature, which was often missed by those who didn't take the time to know him. Derek was often his own worst enemy by the way he delivered his strong beliefs regarding equipment and training. Unfortunately his message was often disregarded, with the focus instead on his misunderstood English humor and curt delivery. Yes, Derek was tough at times, but his goal was to get the most out of his students. He was not brought up with the philosophy of "catching more flies with honey."

I added new photos for some equipment and capsize recovery techniques. I kept as many of Derek's hand-drawn illustrations as possible because they are still accurate and demonstrate Derek's artistic ability. Some of Derek's humor can be seen in a couple of his drawings. If you wonder why there are few faces in his illustrations, Derek once told me, "I am terrible at drawing faces."

I also have to say it has been difficult to remember that this is Derek's book and my job is to edit it. It is not my book even though my name will be on it with Derek's. If I wrote my own book, it would be different. Not better or worse, just different.

I will be happy to answer any questions you may have regarding this new edition and can be reached at study@useakayak.org.

Now that I have tried to clarify my involvement in this book, it is important to understand why Derek wrote the original book in the first place. Back in the early 1970s when Derek was introduced to sea kayaking, there were no books on the subject. Knowledge was learned from experience (trial and error) and word of mouth. Most of the equipment was homemade or from some basic kits, which the paddler had to assemble. Unlike the United States, where there are many protected large bodies of water, the majority of the United Kingdom is surrounded by cold and often unforgiving waters. A simple capsize had a high chance of fatality due to the environment and the lack of adequate immersion clothing, not to mention inadequate training. Those homemade kayaks did not have any bulkheads, so a capsize meant a completely flooded kayak, which often ended up sinking into the depths.

As an educator and someone who fell in love with the sport, Derek decided to write down the accumulated knowledge and experiences of the time and organize it into a book. He took a big chance because he dared to put his name on a book that could educate and inspire current and future paddlers or send some unprepared folks to their deaths. It turned out to be a huge success and an inspiration to innumerable paddlers who dared to take to the sea because of the skills and experiences included in his book. That first book became the foundation and a template for instruction and future books on sea kayaking.

One of the many passions Derek and I shared was a fascination with and appreciation of the original kayakers. Derek spent countless hours researching Arctic history for designs and the techniques used by the native paddlers. He felt it was important to honor the past as the sport moved forward. Derek also knew that there were hundreds and hundreds of years of experience that should not be ignored. As a result, he not only dedicated an entire chapter to Arctic origins of the sea kayak, but also incorporated the full use of the paddle into his teaching with his extended paddle techniques.

As a side note, I had the opportunity to see Derek's original manuscript for the first book. It was handwritten, not typed. When he had to correct a passage, he glued a strip of white paper (pre–correction fluid) over the error and then penned in the corrected copy. As I write this on my computer, I can only imagine the number of tedious hours Derek must have spent writing and illustrating to get to the final copy, all while working and supporting his family.

Derek did not stop with the first book. Aside from updated editions of *Sea Canoeing*, he also wrote books about touring, expeditions, and even one on rolling. His books were published all over the world, which meant he had a global influence on the sport of sea kayaking.

Concerned for the safety of paddlers, Derek used his design training to develop and improve the equipment being used. Having a reliable and high-performing sea kayak was an endless pursuit for him. Derek felt his greatest contribution was developing a reliable (watertight) hatch system, which then allowed for the safe installation of bulkheads. His ideas led to the first commercially produced kayaks in the UK that had bulkheads and reliable hatches. As a result of these trapped air spaces, kayaks could not completely flood during a capsize. It also meant the gear being stored had a better chance of staying dry, which was important for overnight trips and long expeditions.

His experiences and creativity led to deck lines being added to kayaks, added features on PFDs, new paddle designs, and clothing and equipment enhancements. Derek Hutchinson influenced the development of most of the kayaks and equipment you can buy today.

Derek's greatest contribution to the sport was how he inspired countless generations of paddlers. Aside from his writings, he was a superb storyteller. Anyone who ever heard Derek speak or saw his graceful on-water demonstrations could not wait to get into their kayak and have an adventure. When he gave his famous talk about his North Sea crossing, he held his audience captive. He did it without any visual aids and the only prop he had was a small telescoping wand, which he used to point into thin air and draw imaginary pictures while he spun his yarn. At the end of his talks, the audiences did not rush out the door. In fact, they sat there asking questions and demanding that he tell more stories. The most common complaint I heard from audiences over the years was "I don't want to miss a word, but I need to go to the restroom." Fortunately, Derek agreed to have his talks recorded for posterity. *North Sea Crossing & Yarns from the Cockpit* is a two-disc DVD that features Derek telling his tales and includes interviews with him in his home. If you never heard him speak, this is a must-have for your video library.

The best way I can describe Derek's feeling for sea kayaking is in his own words:

> Contrary to first impressions, this book is not simply a textbook on how to progress in a particular sport. Rather it is a record of one man's discovery of a very special kind of freedom. Through the ages, man has always pursued his quest for personal freedom and has always sought to satisfy his tremendous longing to explore the unfamiliar and the unknown.

Many of the more popular rock climbs are now worn smooth by countless grasping fingers and chafing boots. Hill walks, which were once a real adventure, are now well-trodden scars on the grass and heather. The kayak, however, cuts no groove and leaves no scar. The same stretch of water can be paddled every day but the surface may never be the same twice.

The sea provides the unfamiliar, the unworn and the unexpected. Sea kayaking gives a person the opportunity to venture on to a wild, unpredictable expanse in a craft that moves solely by the strength of their arm, directed by their experience and knowledge. Facing the challenge of the sea in this way causes a paddler to journey into the genuine unknown, the unknown and untried areas of his own soul. The sea kayaker depends on neither wind nor engine; he shares his craft and responsibility with no one. The kayak man challenges the sea in what appears to be the most diminutive and delicate of crafts, even more fragile in appearance than the smallest sailing dinghy. Nevertheless, the man who paddles the kayak well is the master of one of the finest, most seaworthy crafts in the world. It can lay beam on to a breaking sea many times its own height. The fastest and most dangerous of waters, which are treacherous terrors for even the largest sailing boat or motor craft, can be conquered by the shallow-draughted kayak. It can hop from bay to bay seeking shelter and passages where no other boat can or dare go, and it can avoid the roughest water by hugging the shore. It can capsize and be righted by a dexterous paddler without him ever having to leave the security of the kayak.

Paddling in areas such as this, one is dwarfed by the tremendous power of the water; yet the advanced paddler can feel confident and secure in what must be the only small boat capable of coping with it.

As you read this fortieth anniversary edition of the first book on sea kayaking, I hope you appreciate that the information included within began with one man taking the chance to write it down and share it with the world. I also hope you get to know a little more about Derek through some of his stories. Little did he know how big this oak tree would grow from the little acorn he planted.

—Wayne Horodowich
President, University of Sea Kayaking

"Native Paddler with Bird Dart" ORIGINAL ARTWORK BY DEREK HUTCHINSON

CHAPTER 1
EQUIPMENT

Having the proper equipment is essential in any sport, but it could mean the difference between life and death in the sport of sea kayaking. When you take to the sea, you are entering a wonderful yet challenging world that can be very unforgiving. The goal of this chapter is to make you aware of the equipment that is used and the items that can enhance your experience while reducing the risks that can occur. I said reduce, not eliminate. You can never eliminate risk. However, if you are properly prepared and well trained, you can find an acceptable level of risk for your own personal adventures.

As you read about all the different equipment options, keep in mind you will eventually decide what is best for you. There will be some trial and error. However, this chapter will give you a good foundation from which to start.

Kayaks

A kayak, by historical definition, is an enclosed boat with a hole in the center for the paddler. Kayaks were developed as a means of hunting and transportation (Photo 1.1). They were also designed to handle the unforgiving environmental conditions of the Arctic. These marvelous crafts were made specifically to fit the paddler and were constructed with whatever materials were available, mainly driftwood, animal skins, sinew, and bones.

The skills of the paddlers had to be well honed to survive the sometimes-treacherous conditions in which they paddled. Not only did the paddlers have to deal with the water and weather, they also had to face possible attacks from the prey they hunted while in their kayak. Having reliable and functional equipment meant life or death to the native paddlers.

Today kayaking has become a sport. As in all sports, having the proper equipment, which is well made and well designed, is important. Just for the record, there are numerous watercrafts being marketed as kayaks that should be called paddle crafts because they are not closed-deck boats with that hole for the paddler.

Photo 1.2 shows Derek's first successful sea kayak design. Even though his kayak was made of fiberglass, you can see the similarities between Derek's kayak and the ones used by the native paddlers in Photo 1.1. Since the construction of modern-day sea kayaks and equipment is no longer bound by scarce materials, numerous options are available to today's paddlers with respect to their kayak and paddling equipment.

The Anatomy of a Sea Kayak

A sea kayak must be seaworthy in that it must be watertight, able to withstand the effects of salt water, wind, rain, and the forces of the environment in which it travels. The kayak should be

Photo 1.1 *East Greenland kayaks ready for the hunt. These kayaks from Angmagssalik are fully equipped and ready to go for a seal hunt. With a width of only 20 inches and a length of 19½ feet, they were fast and sleek, but with their low freeboard, they gave little protection and if the seas were rough, a paddler could expect water to break over the decks.* JOHN PATERSEN, COURTESY OF THE DANISH NATIONAL MUSEUM, DEPARTMENT OF ETHNOGRAPHY, COPENHAGEN

Photo 1.2 *The "North Sea" kayak was Derek's first successful design. As he explained, "It was a stormy day and I had been doing some rolling, so I was wearing my nose clip and a neoprene hood under my helmet. The paddles were made from a plywood kit and glued into an aluminum shaft. In order to carry small items, I stitched a pocket on the cover of my life jacket. I had fixed some elastics on the rear deck for my spare paddles and two across the foredeck for my chart and compass. However, lifting toggles and deck lines were yet to come. The white disc on the foredeck is not a hatch cover but a number disc. In my very first sea race, I would draw number 13—and win."* DEREK HUTCHINSON

long enough to bridge the smaller wave troughs and should have a straight keel to enable the craft to track well (maintain a course) in a head, beam, following, or quartering sea. The rocker (Figure 1.1), or the curve of the keel upwards fore and aft, enables the kayak to maneuver. In sea kayaks the rocker must be limited, or else the boat becomes difficult to manage in a quartering sea.

Since relaxation is important for prolonged periods of time spent in the cockpit, stability is absolutely vital. This is mainly governed by the kayak's width and hull shape. Generally speaking, wide boats are stable; narrow ones are less stable.

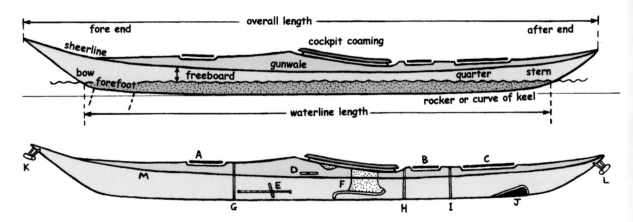

Figure 1.1 *Parts of a sea kayak. A: Front hatch. B: Day hatch, leading into the smallest compartment; this is the only hatch that is safe to remove out on open water. C: Rear hatch, giving access to the widest of the storage compartments; some room is taken up by the skeg box, but this is only really important when one is packing with supplies for more than a couple of weeks. D: Sliding control, which raises and lowers the skeg; it is usually positioned on the right side. E: Adjustable footrest; the tracks should be rinsed and kept clear of sand. F: Seat and cockpit coaming, which are usually all in one piece, enabling the seat to be "slung" from the coaming without touching the bottom of the hull; sometimes the seat is cushioned underneath by a small block of foam fitted between it and the hull. G: Front bulkhead separating the cockpit area from the front watertight compartment; for tall people, many manufacturers will alter the position of the bulkhead and in some cases a specially strengthened front bulkhead can be fitted and used as a footrest. H: Bulkhead immediately behind the seat; this allows the kayak to drain almost completely when the boat is lifted bow first and held upside down. I: Bulkhead separating the day compartment from the main rear storage space; this is accessed by a much larger hatch than the other compartments. J: Skeg box, which is the sleeve into which the skeg is retracted; it should be rinsed and kept clear of small stones. K and L: Carrying or towing toggles; they should not be able to trap the fingers and should allow the kayak to rotate in the hand of anyone swimming and pulling the boat. M: Seam line where the two halves of a composite boat are joined together; on the inside, the joint should be finished smooth with no jagged edges; this line also forms the gunwale.*

Hull

The V-shaped, or chine, hull (Figure 1.2), the traditional shape of many Eskimo kayaks, gives directional stability as long as the amount of rocker is not excessive. However, with such a hull it is unfortunately almost impossible to maintain fast forward speeds because as the speed increases, the boat tends to plane on the flat chines. The kayak thus retards itself on its own bow wave. Despite this, as long as the bottom V is not too acute, these boats can be extremely stable and comfortable. In rough steep seas their movements are predictable, increasing confidence and allowing more relaxation than some other boats. Figure 1.3 is an example of how hull designs are depicted from the front and rear views.

The round hull is the traditional shape of the Aleutian Islands kayaks. It is a faster shape than the chine hull because it offers less harsh resistance in the water, and it gives a softer ride in beam seas. The true round hull is basically very unstable and requires skill in handling. Modern sea kayaks have a modified round hull, which gives speed without the unsteadiness.

Many recreational boats have been bought with flat bottoms and wide beams under the mistaken idea that this type of stability is also seaworthy. In a flat sea the kayak does sit flat on the water, but because the hull shape also follows the wave slope (Figure 1.4 A), it is unsuitable for anything but a flat, calm sea. The round and V-shaped hulls, on the other hand, can

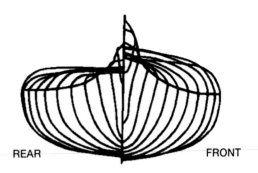

REAR   FRONT

Figure 1.3 *This modern compromise incorporates the best qualities of the basic cross-sections in Figure 1.2. What you see are the "lines" of a Gulfstream sea kayak. This line drawing is simply the various cross-sections of the hull and deck taken at fixed intervals from the bow to the stern and then depicted in sequence superimposed one upon the other. The gunwale line, or join line, can be seen separating the deck from the hull. The bilge (side of the hull as it leaves the gunwale) is gently rounded. It is the careful configuration of these soft chine curves that gives the hull its stability and speed. These cross-section lines are always covered by copyright.*

Flat bottomed boat thrown over by wave

Rounded hull can be leant into wave

Figure 1.4 *Behavior of different hull shapes on waves*

round shape   V-shape or hard chine   U-shape (flat bottom)

Figure 1.2 *Hull shapes in cross-section*

compensate for the wave slope, the shaped bottom enabling the occupant to lean into the wave (Figure 1.4 B) for the necessary bracing stroke.

A sea kayak needs a high bow, the hull approach to which should be an acute V to slice through oncoming waves. Some fullness in width, however, should be retained near the bow if possible. Extremely fine and narrow bows, although elegant in appearance, cause the kayak to plunge into the waves and thus submerge the fore end and throw spray over the paddler.

The amount of freeboard (Figure 1.1) should be small so as to provide little to be caught by beam winds, although the after end may have to be raised to compensate for the high bow.

Rocker

Rocker is the term applied to the curve of a hull fore and aft. This rockering tends to govern directional stability, making the kayak easier to turn. The amount of rocker in sea kayaks has to be limited, as it causes stern drag, hence a reduction in forward speed. The shape and degree of the rocker is important, as a beam wind can use the deepest part of the rockered hull as a pivot on which to spin the boat.

Skegs and Rudders

Sea kayaks are designed to run straight. Unfortunately, in strong beam winds nearly all kayaks have a tendency to "weathercock"; i.e., their bows tend to swing into the wind, causing the paddler to make tiring corrective strokes on the upwind side. Think of a kayak as a weather vane on the water. A weather vane has a fixed pivot point placed so the vane turns into the wind. A kayak does not have a fixed pivot point, but it is near the middle of the kayak. The purpose of a skeg (fin) or a rudder is to change the pivot point on

the kayak. The primary function of both the skeg and rudder is to keep the kayak tracking straight. However, the rudder also has the ability to steer the boat. A skeg can only react to the forces of the wind; it cannot steer the kayak if there is no wind.

Skegs

The Eskimos were aware of this problem, and many traditional Greenland kayaks had a temporary skeg (fin) fastened to the underside of the hull. In some cases the skeg was built into the frame during construction. Some modern designers have improved on this idea, and a number of sea kayaks are now fitted with retractable skegs as part of their integral construction.

The controls, which work the skeg, should be positioned within easy reach. These controls usually take the form of a sliding toggle, held in a recess at the side of the cockpit. When the skeg is not needed, it can be pulled up into its boxed housing inside the rear compartment. When needed, the skeg is simple to operate and effective in use.

If the fin is in the "up" position, the kayak will follow its natural tendency and "weathercock" into the wind (Figure 1.5 A). In the "down" position, the fin will grip the water and allow the bow to be blown downwind (Figure 1.5 B). The paddler can gradually drop the skeg until it reaches a position where the influence of the wind is cancelled out completely (Figure 1.5 C). Only occasionally may it be necessary to "fine-tune" the controls in order to compensate for any major changes in the wind speed. A good way to remember this is as follows: skeg up = kayak goes upwind; skeg down = kayak goes downwind; skeg in the middle = kayak stays on course.

The drag created by the skeg through the water is hardly noticeable. The mechanism is

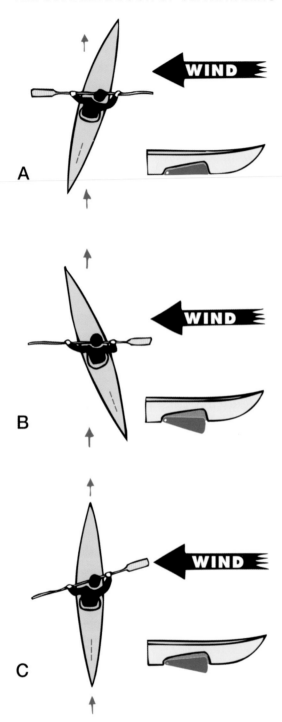

A

B

C

Figure 1.5 *Effects of a drop-down skeg*

easy to repair. A pebble jamming in the skeg box caused the only problem I have ever had. If the fin is made of plastic, it can snap if struck sideways by rocks. Those made of aluminum will bend, but they can always be bent back or knocked reasonably straight again. Skegs that are raised and lowered by means of a concealed steel cable deploy in a more positive manner than those that are operated by a stretchable rope, which extends back along the rear deck.

Many paddlers with skeg boats drill a small hole at the tip of the skeg and attach a small piece of cord to it. If the skeg gets jammed, your partner can reach down and pull on the cord to lower the skeg while you are both still on the water. The drag created by the string is insignificant.

Rudders

A rudder is another mechanical means of maintaining a course in awkward seas. Thin wires lead in from the rudder mechanism, through the deck either behind or to the side of the cockpit. These wires are then connected to foot-operated pedals. Pressing on a foot pedal will turn the rudder, which will cause the kayak to turn. Press right to go right and left to go left.

While rudders have the added advantage of steering a kayak, they also pose some added concerns for the paddler. Rudders are metal or plastic blades attached to the stern of your kayak, with thin wires also attached. These wires and blade can be a safety issue if you are in the water next to them, especially in rough seas.

Concerns regarding rudders:

- Avoid your rudder and cables in rough seas.
- Cowboy recoveries are not recommended (see Chapter 2).

- Rear-deck-mounted towlines can get snagged on a rudder.
- If you have to grab the end of your kayak to pull it through the water, you need to pull the bow.
- Rudder mechanisms may get hooked on the deck lines of another kayak.
- Older rudder pedals were spongy, but new designs allow steering with a solid foot pedal.

Just like the skeg, the rudder is a mechanical device, which can malfunction and/or break. Don't become lazy. Learn how to maneuver your kayak in all kinds of conditions without depending on these devices.

Spray Skirt

A spray skirt, or spray cover or spray deck (Figure 1.6), makes the sea kayak one of the most seaworthy crafts on the water, because if the boat flips over, it does not fill with water. If the captain of this vessel is skilled enough, he or she can right the kayak and continue on his or her way. Since the paddler sits in the only open hole in the boat, almost filling it, wearing a shaped skirt with an elastic around the hem effectively seals the opening when the cover is pulled over the cockpit coaming.

Skirts made of thin neoprene material are probably the most watertight. Derek used one with a very long funnel, which helped to keep him warm and could be rolled down in warm weather. For calm summer paddling, he preferred one made of neoprene-covered nylon with an adjustable elastic waist fitting. He found it did not cause condensation around his waist, and if it got really warm, he could slacken the waistband. A spray cover must have a release strap, loop, or toggle so that its removal can be quick and trouble-free.

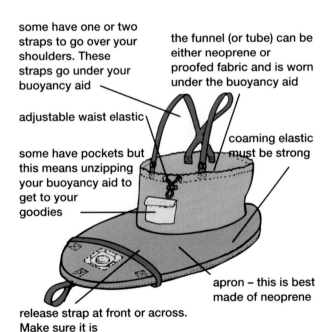

some have one or two straps to go over your shoulders. These straps go under your buoyancy aid

the funnel (or tube) can be either neoprene or proofed fabric and is worn under the buoyancy aid

adjustable waist elastic

some have pockets but this means unzipping your buoyancy aid to get to your goodies

coaming elastic must be strong

release strap at front or across. Make sure it is worn on the outside

apron – this is best made of neoprene

Figure 1.6 *Spray cover, or spray skirt. Derek preferred a high tube made from proofed nylon linked to a tight-fitting neoprene apron. Some paddlers like their compass fastened onto the apron, either with Velcro or in an open-sided neoprene pocket.*

Seats and Foot Braces

Since kayaking involves sitting, comfortable and supportive seating is essential. Part of maintaining good paddling posture involves having foot braces.

Seats and foot braces will be discussed later in this chapter. For now, understand that sea kayaks come with both.

Kayak Flotation

Floatation was a big concern for Derek and his peers when watertight hatches did not exist for kayaks, which meant bulkheads could not be installed. If you wet-exit your kayak or do not attach your spray skirt on a rough day, water will enter your kayak. Without adequate floatation in the front and rear compartments, a kayak can sink. Derek has shared numerous stories of kayaks drifting off to King Neptune's used kayak lot. Without airtight compartments, other means of floatation had to be used.

Bulkheads (Sealed Air Compartments)

You create sealed compartments by installing bulkheads. One is usually in front of the footrest and the other is behind the seat. The watertightness of these compartments depends upon the method of securing the bulkheads and on the effectiveness of the hatch covers. Leaking hatch covers are a serious safety concern and therefore a liability.

Even if your cockpit completely floods, watertight bulkheads with reliable hatches will keep air trapped in the enclosed compartments. Many sea kayaks today have a third bulkhead, which creates a day hatch just behind the cockpit. The only hatch one should ever open while on the water is a day hatch. Day hatches are small enough that flooding one will not cause your kayak to sink as long as the other two (air-filled) compartments are intact. That small flooded hatch may cause instability, but will not sink you.

Some kayaks have a sloping bulkhead. The top of the bulkhead almost touches the rear of the cockpit coaming and the bulkhead then slopes at an angle. Paddlers who prefer the sloping bulkhead do so because when the boat is upside down in the water, lifting the bow will cause the cockpit to become an almost self-draining unit.

Flotation Bags and Foam

The two early means of flotation were air bags or long vertical blocks of polystyrene foam called "pillar flotation." When these items displace enough of the flooding water, the kayak remains afloat.

Waterproof bags filled with equipment, properly sealed and secured inside your kayak, will provide ample flotation. Any large spaces around the bags can be filled with items such as empty water containers, small blocks of foam, or indeed anything that is light and buoyant and will not float out in a capsize.

The Deck Layout

Photo 1.3 is an example of the features found on the deck of a kayak.

Deck Lines

These are the grab lines. They can be run round the outside of the foredeck, rear deck, or both. Situated just above the gunwale line, they have various uses. They can be used for assisting during recues, for hauling and pulling the wet slippery kayak, or for holding onto in the water. Deck lines are there for safety. They should not be a liability with respect to entrapment or

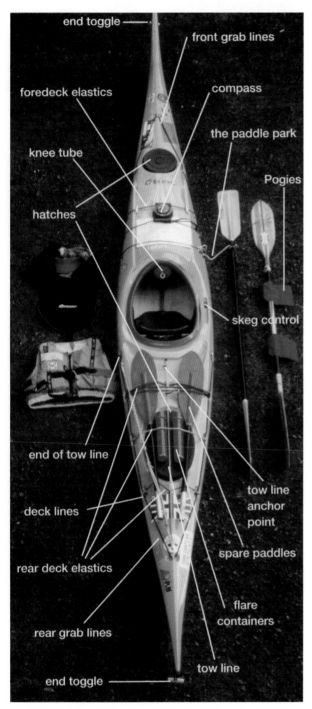

end toggle

front grab lines

foredeck elastics

compass

the paddle park

knee tube

Pogies

hatches

skeg control

end of tow line

tow line anchor point

deck lines

spare paddles

rear deck elastics

flare containers

rear grab lines

end toggle

tow line

Photo 1.3 *A sea kayak showing equipment and deck lines.* DEREK HUTCHINSON

entangling. These lines should not be allowed to sag or become too slack, but still allow a swimmer to grab them.

The most efficient and up-to-date method of securing deck lines is by means of the recessed deck fitting. UV light causes the lines to weaken. Inspect them and replace as needed.

Deck-Mounted Towline

When Derek started kayaking, the accepted method of towing involved deck-mounted tow systems. Currently the favored towing methods use tow belts, which are worn around the paddler's waist. While deck towing was effective, there are many more advantages to using tow belts. Towing will be discussed in detail in Chapter 12.

Hatches

The round black rubber hatch on the foredeck and the larger oval hatch on the rear deck are used to access the fore and rear watertight compartments. These compartments are formed by two bulkheads, one just in front of the footrest, the other either immediately behind the cockpit or about 2 feet behind it, to allow more space behind the paddler for items that need to be instantly accessible (such as first-aid and repair kits).

Hatches that allow access into the main compartments should never be removed out on the open sea. Hatches can blow away or get dropped overboard accidentally. Boats can swamp, and in anything but a calm sea, this can be a major disaster. Most good-quality kayaks now come with a small day hatch situated on the rear deck, directly behind the cockpit. This allows access to a small, enclosed compartment that is isolated from the rest of the interior. You will find that there is enough room in here to carry all those immediate items that you may need on the water.

Whether or not a hatch is watertight often depends on its shape. Round is always watertight. Oval is usually watertight (if you place the lid in exactly the right place on the rim). Hatches in other shapes and securing systems mean that you take your chances.

Remember that "watertight" and "waterproof" are concepts the manufacturers strive to achieve. However, there almost always seems to be water seeping into a compartment or into a so-called dry bag. Therefore, do the best you can and check your compartments and bags regularly.

Beware of those hatches that have lids over neoprene seals. People naturally remove the rubber seals during storage, but they then forget to replace them before going out onto the water. Check inside the hatch rim to see if the rim has been fitted properly and that the finish is smooth. You should not be able to feel any ragged edges. Be careful when you do this.

All hatch covers should be tethered to the boat in some way to prevent them from blowing back out to sea while you are unloading gear on the beach. Yes, they really do blow away!

While on the subject, if your flexibility and balance are not good, forget about trying to secure the hatch cover on your day hatch. They come off fairly easily but can be difficult to reattach, especially when in rough water. I have seen numerous paddlers ask their partner to reattach their day hatch cover.

Bungee Cords (Foredeck Elastics)

These elastics, configured in many different ways, are used to hold your chart and compass. Feel free to change the configuration of your deck elastics to fit your specific needs. Also,

replace your elastics as they wear. Derek felt very strongly that you should resist the temptation to store your hand pump, paddle float, sunglasses, water bottle, sunscreen, VHF radio, hat, cellphone, and medications under the elastics. These items will certainly inhibit you from using your paddle at a low angle and might make it difficult for you to perform a number of the more advanced bracing and directional paddle strokes.

While I appreciate Derek's concern for crowding the front deck with items that inhibit your strokes, I believe there are certain items that should be on your front deck. I store my pump, paddle float, spare paddle, charts, and compass on my front deck. The compass and paddles are far forward. My inflatable paddle float is secured under the cords and lies flat. My pump is still within reach, but does not interfere with any of my strokes.

A paddler needs to be able to access and re-stow his or her equipment while on rough seas. Storing in the cockpit is out because taking the spray skirt off of the coaming in rough seas is not wise. As for my back deck, I would capsize in a second if I had to reach around to get something or re-stow it if my kayak were bouncing around.

Spare Paddle

Every paddler should be a self-contained unit. Having a spare paddle is a necessity because paddles do break and can float away. In addition, having a second paddle in a different shape could be useful if you need more power or less strain on your body.

There are devices that allow paddles to be securely stored on your front deck and not be in your way. You can make your own or look at PaddleBritches from North Water.

Here is Derek's take on storing spare paddles: "Spare paddles are usually carried on the rear deck and are held in place by shock-cord elastics. I have never considered carrying paddles on the foredeck because any water that swills down the deck is then often deflected up your nose. Their presence would also clutter my view from the 'bridge,' a situation, which as a purist, I would find quite unacceptable."

Paddle Leash

A paddle leash, also known as a paddle park, is a way to secure your paddle to your kayak or wrist. There are numerous designs and methods of attachment. Of all the leashes out there, I have found Derek's design the most versatile (Figure 1.7).

The leash is made from a piece of thin shock-cord elastic with a loop and some kind of toggle or ball at either end. One of these ends is fastened to the paddle. If I wish to rest or take part in a rescue, the little ball on the end can be tucked under a deck elastic, which allows you to have both hands free and not lose your paddle. The leash can be pulled free of the boat with one hand because there is no knot or clip fastening. In rough or windy weather, one loop is held over the wrist of the controlling hand. I have my leash about 26 inches long so that, if necessary, I can hold my paddle in the extended position. When my wrist leash is not being used, it can be wrapped round my paddle shaft and kept out of the way until I need it. (See Photo 1.3. Notice the tiny red ball near the neck of the wooden Toksook paddle.)

Never fasten the paddle you are using permanently to your kayak. It needs to be detachable. Always disconnect your leash in the surf zone. A capsize when landing in surf or in any rough

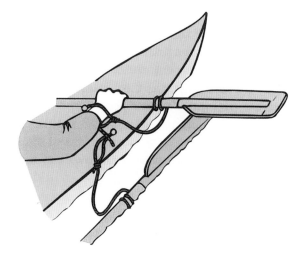

Figure 1.7 *The paddle leash, or paddle park*

water could cause you to find yourself irrevocably tethered to a tumbling sledgehammer.

End Toggles (Grab Loops)

The toggles at the bow and the stern are the handles used for lifting and carrying the kayak when empty. You can also hang on to them when you swim your kayak ashore after capsizing. As lifting a fully loaded kayak puts a lot of strain on the toggles and their anchors, I recommend carrying loaded boats from under the bow and the stern.

Towing a kayak in surf is not easy, and your boat will sometimes twist over and over again while you are trying to maintain your grip. For the best results, you should have small-diameter toggles, as close to the ends of the kayak as possible with the cord holes about three-quarters of an inch apart. These will allow your boat to rotate without the tourniquet effect of a twisting loop damaging your fingers, or without the end of the kayak thrashing your forearm and wrist. If you are ever towed by another kayak, the assister's towline may be attached to your toggle loop or deck lines. You should therefore inspect the cords holding the toggles regularly, and renew them when necessary.

Leaders should inspect the toggles of all their group's kayaks. This is especially necessary when people are using their own kayaks and equipment. I used to carry about 9 inches of thin strong cord just in case someone in my group had a frayed or weak toggle loop.

Learn to splice! It makes a neat job of lines and loops.

Pumps

During your ventures on the sea, you will eventually need some method of removing accumulated water. In other words, you will need to bail out the boat. A small plastic cup or container can come in handy, but for larger quantities of water, you will need some kind of pump. There are a number of varieties from which to choose; for example, portable, foot-operated, hand-operated, and electrically driven. Everyone should carry a sponge to remove the water left after pumping.

Portable Pumps

The cheapest and most popular pump is the handheld type (Figure 1.8). It can be carried on the deck when not in use. To remove water, you merely stick the suction end of the pump into the water that has accumulated in the bottom of the boat and slide the handle up and down, like a bicycle pump. The water will then gush over the side of the boat out of the nozzle at the top of the pump. Mechanically it is foolproof, and it will remove large quantities of water in a short period of time. In order to use the pump, however, you must break the seal of your spray skirt, which needs to be considered in choppy seas. Make sure

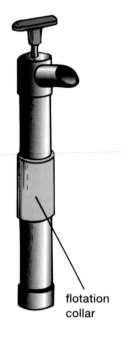

flotation collar

Figure 1.8 *Portable hand pump*

your hand pump comes with a flotation collar because it will end up in the water.

Deck-Mounted Hand and Foot Pumps

I have always favored the hand-operated deck pump. I have mine positioned on the rear deck, immediately behind my back. It can be a little awkward to operate, but then it is not often used.

I find foot-operated pumps are very useful. They are fixed either to a front bulkhead, although this would have to be reinforced, or to a wood crossbeam fixed in place above the footrest. The joy is that the spray skirt does not have to be removed nor is there any need to let go of your paddle.

Both of these pumping systems require a small outlet hole on the side of your kayak and tubes in the cockpit. In addition, your pump cannot be used to pump out another paddler's kayak easily, if at all.

Electric Pumps

Electric pumps, like deck-mounted pumps, require an exit hole in your kayak and tubes in the cockpit. Aside from the pump itself, they also have a battery and power switch. Since electronic equipment and salt water have additional challenges, reliable electric pumps were once hard to find and required a lot of maintenance. In recent years, reliable electric pumps with good battery life have become available. Being able to empty the water in your cockpit at the flick of a switch is a nice feature if you dislike manual pumping.

Regardless of your own fixed pump system, you should carry a portable hand pump somewhere on the deck. You can use this to empty out any kayak belonging to your group *without removing your own spray skirt*. The pump can also be passed around for others to use.

Modern Sea Kayaks

In tracing the history of the modern sea kayak, it becomes apparent that over the years many different types of boats have been used, but that few of these have been built specifically for use on the sea. Most of the individuals who explored the delights of sea kayaking made "one-off" boats. They then duplicated them for a few friends. Others paddled standard kayaks currently in use, sometimes adapting them. Many bought plans and built their kayaks in lath and fabric. The Tyne Single Kayak was very popular and so were some of the longer boats designed by Percy Blandford.

Derek's first kayak, designed by Blandford, is well worth a mention. Known as the PBK 10, Blandford's description of it reads: "This decked, kayak-type canoe is the smallest craft capable of carrying a man and camping kit on rivers and canals and the open sea in moderate conditions. Construction is simple and economical and well within the capabilities of the average practical boy or girl (several PBK 10 canoes are already in use by the girls who built them)." (Source: Percy W. Blandford, *Boat Building*, Foyles Handbooks, 1957)

The Rob Roy canoe (Figure 1.9), popularized by John McGregor, was often used for sea and estuary work and even surfing. It was built of overlapping wooden planks, which were fastened to the steam-bent frames by copper nails clinched home in the traditional clinker-built rowing boat style. These boats were very strong and heavy; whether they were true canoes in that they could be portaged by the one-man crew is debatable. Note the unfeathered paddle blades, the cockpit coaming with no provision for a spray cover, the hole in the foredeck to take a mast for a small lugsail, and the rather bizarre backrest. When under sail, the paddle was used to steer. (Source: O. J. Cock, *A Short History of Canoeing in Britain*, BCU, 1974)

In the old type of sea kayak (Figure 1.9), the bow and stern were reinforced by a brass strip extending about 1 foot along the bottom of the keel. The boats were either made rigid or with a folding frame and skin which fitted into two bags, one about 5 feet long for the frame, the other rather more square for the rubber-proofed canvas hull covering. The large press-studs illustrated around the cockpit coaming were used to secure the spray cover until it was found that they corroded and filled with sand, becoming quite useless.

Some firms started producing boats modeled very closely on Eskimo designs, but they demanded a very high degree of skill from the individuals paddling them. The Tyne Greenland, the Ottersports Angmagssalik (Figure 1.10), and the Klepper Eskimo were all of this type.

'Rob Roy' canoe (circa 1870)
clinker-built, approx. 15' x 28"

old-type sea canoe
'Tyne' single/PBK type
(lathe and canvas)
approx. 14½'x 26"

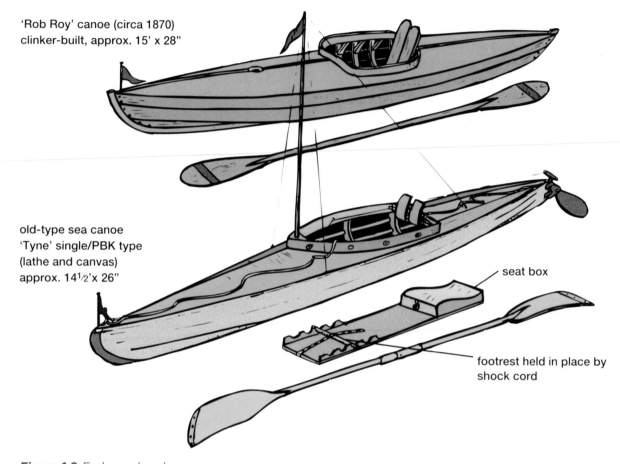

seat box

footrest held in place by
shock cord

Figure 1.9 *Early sea kayaks*

Scotland, with its wild, lonely offshore islands, has been a home of sea kayaking for many years and has consistently produced many good designs. In the 1930s John Marshal designed the Queensferry, which was still popular in 1955. Boats in this range were about 14 feet long with a beam of 30 inches. The hull was of hard chine form, the heavy frame covered in canvas. Another popular boat at that time was the Loch Lomond, designed by H. A. Y. Stevenson. This was light in build with more stringers (i.e., longitudinal laths), giving a rounder hull

form. A couple of years later came the Clyde Single (16 feet 3 inches by 25½ inches). A graceful kayak designed by Joe Reid, it was a hard chine form with a short V. Duncan Winning designed the Kempock and Cloch single kayaks. He and Joe Reid then joined to produce R. and W. Canoe Plans, the first being the 16-foot-long Gantock Single (Figure 1.11).

Ken Taylor, a fellow member of Derek's kayaking club with Duncan Winning, brought a kayak back from Greenland that inspired Andrew Carnuff to produce the Skua, approximately 15½ feet

Figure 1.10 *Angmagssalik (kit from Ganta Boats)*

Figure 1.11 *Gantock Single. Length: 16 feet; width: approximately 24 in. Plywood, joined at keel and chine with fiberglass. Watertight bulkheads fore and aft.*

long by 23 inches wide, which was then reproduced in fiberglass by John Flett and eventually found its way into the fields of education and coaching. The Ken Taylor kayak from Igdlorssuit was also to have its influence on kayak design much farther afield. Duncan Winning sent the drawings of his boat down to Geoff Blackford on the south coast of England. When Blackford later produced his Anas Acuta sea kayak, he succeeded in combining the hull design of the Ken Taylor kayak with a modified deck specifically aimed at accommodating a European adult.

Over the last few years, the popularity of the sport of sea kayaking has increased beyond all bounds, with the result that many new firms have sprung up to reap the benefit of an ever-increasing market. Sea kayaks are now being produced in large numbers commercially, and new models seem to appear at a bewildering rate. In the 1960s the sea kayaking world was a relatively small one, so that if a kayak came on to the market and had obvious faults, the word was passed around among paddlers by word of mouth. If the boat was a bad one, it usually fell by the wayside and was never heard of again. This is not so

today, and the bad designs stand next to the good in the retail stores—caveat emptor!

Derek Hutchinson's Contribution to Design

Before you read Derek's discussion of his designs, I want you to appreciate his first attempt at boat building when he was a young lad in England (Figure 1.12). Derek and his friend caught hell for the mess they made trying to waterproof the hull with tar. Derek drew this from his memory of that fateful day.

My venture into kayak design started at a time during the early '60s when there were no sea kayak designs on the market. It's hard to believe, but very true. So you see, I was driven to design my first kayak in a fit of desperation. I had been introduced to the sport of kayaking after signing up for an introductory course run by my local Education Authority. The affair was held on a local river and I took to the sport like a duck to water. Unfortunately, I happened to live right next to the sea

Figure 1.12 *Derek's first kayak as a kid*

and the idea of using a river kayak on the open North Sea did not seem the best way to go. The use of fiberglass had just been introduced onto the sporting scene, but only a few nondescript kayaks made of that material had began to appear on the market.

As I have mentioned earlier in this book, the handful of people who actually ventured out onto the sea did so in boats made from plywood or canvas stretched over a wooden frame. These boats tended to be wide and stable with huge, long cockpits. My own prized possession was a kayak just over 10 feet long and 36 inches wide. It was known as a PBK 10 after its designer, Percy Blandford. I sat on a wooden, box-type seat, which was loosely fixed to the bottom boards by two wooden turn-buttons. The support given to my behind could be compared to that given to a pea on a drum and in the event of a capsize and bail out, I would find myself swimming in the middle of a mass of floating debris; this would include the wooden plywood seat, its now loose cushion, together with the swivel wooden backrest, the bottom boards together, and the foot rest. The bailer, and any other valuable items, which had been placed strategically between my legs, such as my chart, compass, and lunch, would also have exited the boat. The various ropes and painters, which I had taken the care and time to coil up neatly on the bottom deck boards, would now be floating out in all directions. It was hardly a satisfactory state of affairs but if I wanted something more seaworthy, I would have to design and build it myself.

In the early '60s I had turned my back on the world of industry, and instead I taught Craft, Design, and Technology in a Secondary Modern School for boys. I suppose I was fortunate in that my design background included five years at the Marine and Technical College as well as two years at Art College. This meant that when I turned my attention to kayak design, besides being no stranger to a drawing board, I was also able to approach the challenge by looking at it more as a piece of sculptured kinetic art, rather than a technical exercise.

At this time, I was involved, with the enthusiastic aid of the older boys at my school, in the building of a modified river kayak design that could be used by my local Volunteer Lifeguard Club as a "rescue" craft close inshore and in surf. This grew out of the fact that I was spending two evenings a week, as well as weekends, putting the lifeguards through an intensive kayak handling program.

Meanwhile, back in my own garage, I began experimenting with various hull shapes all made of fiberglass. I coupled these hulls with decks of either plywood or wood and canvas. My results were anything but encouraging until I happened on a copy of *The Bark Canoes and Skin Boats of North America* by Adney and Chapelle. This delightful and informative book, together with the lines of the

Photo 1.4 *Derek in his Ice Floe. Turning is made much easier if you can take advantage of a wave passing underneath. The Ice Floe, which is a large-volume expedition kayak, has a capacity of 55 liters in the front compartment, 100 liters in the rear compartment, and 175 liters in the cockpit area. It was the success of the Ice Floe that twenty years later formed the basis for the Gulfstream.* ALAN AINSLIE

Oseberg Viking long-ship, which had been dug up some years previously, gave me plenty of inspiration. Amusingly, however, due to the length of my garage, any kayak I designed and built would have to finish up with a maximum length of 16 feet 10 inches. Not daunted by these limitations, I devoted myself totally to designing and building a kayak that would not only look the part but would also be at home on the open sea.

Basing my design loosely on the Mackenzie Delta kayak and the kayaks of West Greenland, I sculpted the "plug" (that's the full-size model) from a combination of plywood, cardboard, chicken wire, and plaster. I gave the rear end of the hull a cross-section very similar to that of the Viking long-ship. This gave the boat remarkable stability and the undercut leading to the rear part of the keel also prevented the stern from squatting at high speed. In plan view I made the hull "Swede Form"; i.e., the widest part of the hull was slightly behind the seating position of the paddler. This gave me speed and also stability to a narrow boat. Once the plug was polished and finished, I allowed it to "cure" (set hard) for a few days. It was then that I was able to make my first deck and hull.

My method of joining the deck and the hull together was primitive to say the least. Up until that time, I had joined the "Rescue" boats together by screwing in a wooden strip around the top edge of the hull on the inside. The deck was then fitted in place by using an exterior overlap, very like the lid on a tin. The overlap was then screwed into place. To make the joint watertight, I sealed the inside with strips of resin-impregnated, glass matt by using a brush on a long stick. The trouble was that in the long sea kayak I hadn't worked out a system of getting the "whetted out" glass strips into position up in the extremities of the bow and stern. I needn't have worried because the problem was solved for me. The deck would not fit into place over the hull, so in order to get the parts to meet together I was obliged to cut off an inch from the bow and stern. This created an inch-wide hole at both ends of the boat and I was able to use these holes to feed in the whetted glass draped round a wire coat hanger. To finish off the joint, all I had to do was stick a couple of tennis balls filled with glass and colored resin over the holes and wait for it to go hard. Then I merely peeled off the rubber and I was left with two colored ball ends. They protected what would have been sharp ends and gave me something to hold onto when carrying.

The kayak was fast, and, for a boat that was just over 20 inches wide, it was very stable (Photo 1.2). The slightly raised foredeck and the flat rear-deck, together with a pronounced sheer-line, gave the kayak a streamlined appearance. I made the cockpit small but not unpleasantly so. I called my new kayak "Kiska," after one of the Aleutian Islands, and I tested the new boat in rough seas and high winds in my local harbor. The boat handled beautifully and I delighted in the knowledge that I now possessed what I felt was a rocket ship. As far as the boat's speed was concerned, I decided to put my beliefs to the test and enter for an open-water kayak race. It was held on the sea from Sandsend to Whitby (the traditional home of Dracula) and I remember I drew number 13. The wind was strong, the sea was rough, and during the "Le Mans Start" I had trouble getting my spray skirt over the cockpit roaming. Nevertheless, in spite of my lack of experience and the fact I was competing against kayaks that had been designed for racing, I came in first place. My credibility as a kayak designer was established. It wasn't long after this that a local boat builder who wanted to build the North Sea Tourer on a commercial basis approached me.

The kayak was to be a very popular touring boat for many years, but in 1974 and in the light of what was now considerable experience, I felt that I could give the boat more stability and a little more room inside for long-legged paddlers. I also modified the seat and the cockpit. After listening to some bad advice, I also cut off some of the boat's graceful stern, so that a rudder could be fitted if the need arose, which it never did. To give the updated image a new name, I called the updated design the "Baidarka" in tribute to the Aleut kayaks that I admired so much. However, there was another big problem to overcome.

Fiberglass had become popular over a decade earlier, but to prevent this non-floating material from sinking, paddlers had been forced to fill their hulls with some kind of flotation. This was to prevent the very real danger of boats swamping and sinking after an accidental capsize. This internal buoyancy was usually in the form of inflatable bags of one kind or another (I used wine casks with a tube attached) or strategically placed blocks of closed-cell foam. The reality was that air bags were prone to puncture, valves had a habit of leaking, and foam floated out unless it was well fixed in place. Because of this, any deep-water rescue, no matter how well practiced, could swiftly become a drama. However, being something of an innovator, I felt I had the solution to this problem.

During rescues, it was customary to lift the bow first. I decided to fit a bulkhead behind the seat to form a watertight compartment. Access would have to be by means of some kind of watertight hatch. I settled on a design used on sailboats. It was large in circumference and locked into its frame with a quarter turn. I even designed a recessed molding in the rear deck of the Baidarka to accommodate this hatch. Sadly, after doing all that work, the hatch was nowhere near watertight, and I had to blank off the huge hole and look for a more suitable cover. I settled on the type, which I remembered having seen as a small boy on the lifeboats and life rafts, which littered my local beach immediately after the Second World War. After prying open these hatches we discovered that the goodies and Horlicks tablets (malted milk tablets) inside were still dry and fit to eat. I traced this hatch, which was still in production, and used it on the rear deck of the Baidarka. I tested the new kayak in the

Tyne Estuary on March 10, 1974. The day was memorable in another way because during the storm, a large vessel called the *Oregis* was blown onto the Black Midden Rocks with some loss of life. I sat and watched all this with water breaking over my decks while hanging onto my paddle. When I finally got to shore I discovered that the new hatch was totally watertight. It didn't take me long to cut out a hole in the foredeck and create a second watertight compartment at the front.

The result of all this effort was that I now had a fast, roomy, eminently seaworthy kayak. The next thing was to cast my restless eyes around for a suitable challenge. The North Sea was on my doorstep, so I decided to cross it and attempt to reach mainland Europe. After 34 hours on the water, my first attempt in the summer of 1975 almost finished in disaster. The following year, however, I launched from Felixstowe Ferry with two companions, all paddling Baidarkas (Photo 13.1). We set off at six o'clock in the morning and landed on the beach at Ostend 31 hours later.

In 1977 I modified the Baidarka even further. It was given more volume, the tip of the bow was extended up vertically,

and the cutaway stern was remodeled with a graceful upward sweep to balance any windage fore and aft. Thus the Baidarka Explorer took on its distinctive shape (Figure 1.13). All kayaks used for deep-sea work should behave well when they are paddled into oncoming seas. With its added buoyancy, the Explorer behaved exceptionally well. The boat's length, together with the narrow V section at the bow, caused the boat to rise gently to the waves so that very little water came over the bow. Straight running was assured by the integral keelson that ran the whole length of the boat.

The Baidarka Explorer was made even more famous in 1978 by the HTV film *Canoeing into the Past*. This was an account of the expedition I organized along the Aleutian Islands in 1978. We covered a distance of some 300 miles, during which time we were self-sufficient and lived off the supplies we carried inside the boats.

Not including his childhood design that messed up the backyard, Derek designed sixteen sea kayaks during his years as a designer and boat builder. His designs and safety features strongly influenced others in their designs. Many of the kayaks we see today can be traced back to Derek's skill and vision.

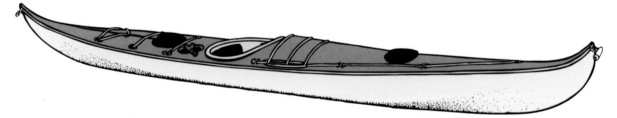

Figure 1.13 *The Baidarka Explorer. Length: 16 feet 10 inches; beam: 21 inches.*

Here are some of Derek's more popular designs.
It is important to note that his Gulfstream became
one of the most popular kayaks of its time.

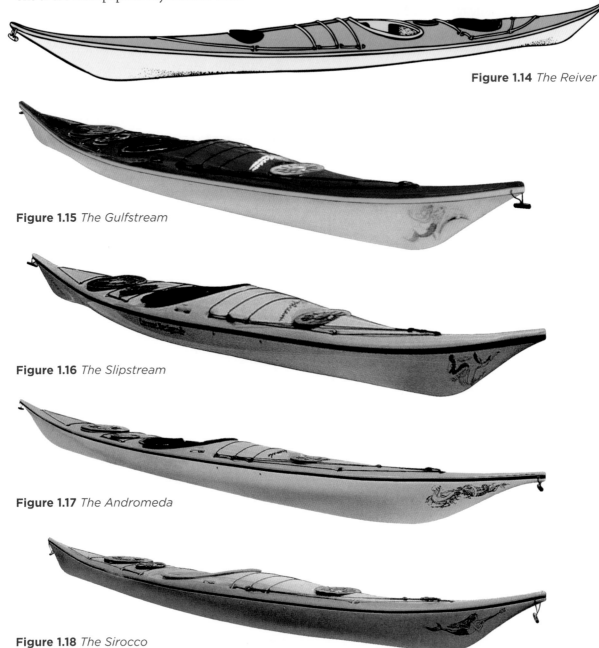

Figure 1.14 *The Reiver*

Figure 1.15 *The Gulfstream*

Figure 1.16 *The Slipstream*

Figure 1.17 *The Andromeda*

Figure 1.18 *The Sirocco*

Many people asked Derek why all his kayak designs have decals on the bow. He considered all of his kayaks to be true deep-sea craft in the traditional sense. Since he sculpted his kayaks to be things of beauty and grace, why not embrace tradition and have a figurehead!

Sea Kayaks: What Are They Made of and How Are They Made?

The modern solo kayak can be made from a wide range of materials, but they mainly fall into two categories. The most popular are those made from fiberglass "composite." Running a close second are the boats made from rotomolded polyethylene (plastic). In the past two decades, plastic sea kayaks may have outsold composite ones.

I remember when the first fiberglass kayaks came on the scene in the early 1960s, and it's a testimony to the material that many of these boats are still going strong today. If you are looking for a long-term investment, fiberglass is your best bet.

Composite Kayaks

Composite kayaks are made from layers of woven glass, graphite, or Kevlar cloth and are "laid up" in two female molds, one for the hull and one for the deck. After both of these molds have been prepared (i.e., waxed and polished), a coat of thick, colored resin gel is applied, giving the kayak its hard surface and shiny colored finish. Once the surface gel coat is dry, matting, precut to shape and made from any of the materials mentioned, is carefully laid inside a mold together with strategically placed reinforcing material, usually of Kevlar. Liquid resin is then forced into the fibers either by hand stippling with a brush or a roller, or by a process known

as vacuum bagging where the resin is sucked through the fibers with the aid of special machinery. Both of these methods bond the fibers together, before setting rock hard.

When the hull and deck have hardened or "cured," the two moldings are removed. The edges are then trimmed and joined together using fiberglass tape and resin or a shaped plastic extrusion. This jointing or gunwale line is then reinforced from the inside. Once this is hard, the kayak is ready to receive its cockpit, bulkheads, and hatch rims. All that is left to do then is the finishing process. This is when the boat receives all its necessary fittings, lines, and other additions that make it safe and seaworthy.

No maintenance is necessary. Leaving the kayak out in the sun for a few years may cause some gel coat colors to fade a little, and hatch covers that are made from a rubber composition have been known to degrade after a while if they are not protected. This does not seem to apply to pure rubber hatches. The joy of fiberglass is that kayaks can be cut, altered, customized and repaired very easily.

Fiberglass is an ideal material for small boats. It is lightweight, and the weight of individual kayaks can be controlled during manufacture. It is durable and rigid, and it will resist impact. If you are unfortunate enough to get a hole in your boat, it is not beyond any handy paddler to accomplish an invisible repair. Deep scratches to the surface gel coat will not affect the boat's performance to any extent, and they can easily be filled in and smoothed off, making the hull look as good as new.

Kevlar is another popular material for composite boats. This tremendously strong synthetic fiber is woven into a cloth and laid up with resin in the same way as fiberglass. It might be interesting to note that Kevlar is used in the manufacture of flak jackets and bulletproof vests. Because Kevlar is stiffer than the ordinary woven glass, kayaks can be made much lighter, with a weight saving of 5 to 10 pounds, yet still exhibit an incredible rigidity. The only problem with Kevlar is that it's dreadfully expensive, although this makes it a bit of a status symbol. Kevlar is also notoriously difficult to cut and repair, and it makes boats awkward to customize. Kevlar boats can be easily identified, as the cloth weave is golden brown, and some manufacturers exploit this by giving their Kevlar kayaks a coat of clear gel. If you have to haul your kayak about without assistance, Kevlar could be the material for you.

Plastic or Rotomolded Polyethylene

Note: This section is courtesy of the late Derek Hutchinson from the previous edition.
There was a time when the most serious paddlers of my acquaintance would not have contemplated changing to plastic. However, the vendor who watches the novice group dragging their kayaks over rocks and mussel beds, bouncing them against stone jetties, will be offering up a prayer of thanks to the scientist who invented polyethylene.

I have to admit that in the early days of plastic, I did not give these kayaks very good press. Because of the lack of stiffness, which was often due to poor design, I tended to think of them as an aesthetic nightmare. Since then, however, science and care on the part of some designers has solved many of the problems that haunted the earlier craft. Kayaks are now more rigid and also more resistant to UV sunlight, although they are still heavier than their composite counterparts.

Rotomolded kayaks are manufactured in huge, two-piece, heated metal molds. Pea-sized pieces of colored plastic are poured in. The mold is then clamped shut, heated, and then rotated and seesawed. This coats the whole of the mold with hot, liquid plastic. (This is why plastic kayaks are all one color.) The complete process takes about half an hour, and after some initial cooling, the finished kayak is removed from the still hot mold and placed in jigs to prevent it from warping and twisting as it cools. Once cooled, the kayak is finished off with hatches, bulkheads, cockpit furniture, deck fittings, and lines.

Kayaks are rotomolded from either linear or cross-linked polyethylene. Kayaks made from linear polyethylene do not scratch or gouge as easily as a cross-linked boat. The linear boat is more rigid and it is possible to repair damage by welding. At the end of its life, it can be sent back to the factory, recycled, and used again. Cross-linked boats have better impact resistance, but due to their increased flexibility, they need more support. It also takes an expert to execute a good weld. Cross-linked kayaks cannot be recycled and have to be disposed of as with so much trash.

Because rotomolded kayaks are heavier than composite boats, the question of weight might be an issue when it comes to carrying the boat or lifting it on top of your vehicle. However, this extra weight will have no bearing on the kayak's performance once it's afloat.

Polyethylene kayaks are very reasonably priced. They resist accidental impact like no other kayaks can, and they are certainly a godsend when landing on mussel beds or bouncing off rocky shorelines, or when hired out to careless members of the public. However, these boats do have a definite life span. When plastic boats are new, they resist impact damage very well. The newer the boat, the more kindly it receives the blows. After three to six years, depending upon how much your boat has been used and the amount of strong sunshine it has been exposed to, your kayak will start to chemically degrade. The ultraviolet stabilizers and plasticizers will begin to lose their effect. The color will start to fade; the boat will become less flexible and thus more susceptible to impact damage. Welding repairs will become much more difficult.

Plastic does soften with heat, so never fasten your rotomolded kayak down onto your roof rack by pulling it down tightly at both ends. It certainly won't enhance the boat's appearance even where the air is cool, and in hot climates your kayak may well finish up like a 17-foot-long, soft plastic banana.

To sum up, I would have to revise my thoughts on how plastic kayaks compare with those made of composites. If there is a weakness, it would be in the design of many plastic kayaks rather than the materials from which they are made. Poorly shaped decks still dent inwards during rescues, and many boats, although functional, still look as if a committee has designed them. Beauty appears to be a quality that some designers feel is unimportant so long as the boat floats and exhibits all the usual accoutrements. As a final piece of general advice to the potential buyer, I might suggest that you choose a plastic kayak that has already proved itself on the open sea in its composite form. As an example, the Sirocco (Figure 1.18) is my own contribution to the polyethylene scene and is the plastic version of my successful Gulfstream design.

Thermoformed

Thermoformed would seem to be the newest method of kayak construction, and as yet those that employ this method are in the minority. However, this could well change in the future.

Most people are familiar with polycarbonate as the material used in the manufacture of industrial eye-protection goggles. It has a more highly polished finish than polyethylene. It retains its rigidity, is more abrasion resistant, and from a distance it cannot be distinguished from one of its shiny composite cousins.

Polycarbonate is supplied from the manufacturers in sheet form and in a manner not dissimilar to the way composite kayaks are vacuum bagged; the polycarbonate sheets are vacuum shaped or pressed into separate hull and deck molds. Unlike plastic boats, the hulls and decks can therefore be in different colors. Polycarbonate kayaks can be slightly less expensive than composites. However, polycarbonate is still more expensive than polyethylene.

Polycarbonate is more resistant to destructive effects of UV sunlight. Even though thermoformed kayaks are the new kid on the block, they seem to be holding up well over time.

Folding Kayaks

Folding kayaks have been around for a very long time. Nautiraid, Tyne, and Folbot have all manufactured kayaks of excellent quality. Klepper, probably the most famous firm, introduced their first folding kayak before the First World War. Their most famous model, the Aerius, had inflated sponsons incorporated into the gunwales. This made the kayak unsinkable and left all the room inside for the stowage of equipment. The double version of this design gained immortality after the Atlantic crossings of Captain Franz Romer in 1928 and Hannes Lindemann in 1956. Kleppers are still beautifully made and can be supplied with a sail rig.

The early folding boats were beautiful craft, but assembling and maintaining these wide,

Figure 1.19 *The Feathercraft Kahuna*

stable, folding kayaks was something of an adventure. The canvas skins suffered abrasion. The brass fittings tended to corrode, and the wooden frames and stringers had their weaknesses and needed work with the varnish brush from time to time. However, when all is said and done, there is an undeniable appeal in being able to pack your kayak into a bag and backpack it or have it accompany you, even on a small airplane, to some remote paddling paradise.

The Canadian firm Feathercraft has certainly taken a more space-age approach to the manufacture of the folding kayak. As an example, the Kahuna (Figure 1.19) designed by Doug Simpson is a modern folding boat in the very best tradition of soft-skinned kayaks. Gone are the varnished wooden stringers and the plywood frames. The brass fittings are also a thing of the past. This kayak uses anodized aluminum tubing for its longitudinal stringers and heavy-duty polycarbonate for its frames. The fun in putting one of these boats together is that all the tubes are color-coded, and like tent poles, they all jump together with the assistance of thin, elasticized shock cord; however, care must be taken not to let sand get into the joints. The Kahuna has a rigid cockpit coaming, which gives the paddler the same rough-water dryness and rolling qualities that are enjoyed in a good-quality, rigid sea kayak. The Kahuna, like Feathercraft's other models, is covered with a specially formulated urethane material called Duratek, which is welded together with solid urethane reinforcing strips.

Like their other models, the Kahuna's rigidity comes from a stretch-and-lock lever system situated at the center, while the two inflatable sponsons, which are built into the gunwales, help to give the final tension to the skin. Optional extras include a rudder and hatches to the front and rear, which makes the positioning of equipment inside the hull much easier.

There are a few commonsense considerations regarding a folding boat's long-term storage. It is important to rinse the boat with freshwater after a long trip or before packing it away, in order to remove any residual salt. Remember to dry it completely before storing.

Stitch and Glue (Wood Kayaks)

One of the most popular, and probably the easiest, way to build your own kayak is by means of a plywood kit. There are plenty of imaginative and graceful designs to choose from. Even with the most basic of woodworking skills, success can be yours. You'll find that everything is supplied. The shapes you need are precut from top-grade marine plywood and all you have to do is follow the simple instructions and "stitch" the flat sections together using the wire provided. Once the kayak is sewn together, you merely reinforce and seal the seams with fiberglass and filler.

Kayaks made of wood (Photo 1.5) are usually finished with a coat of epoxy, paint, or marine varnish, and any damage that exposes the wood must be repaired immediately when the area is dry. Repairing boats of this kind means that you

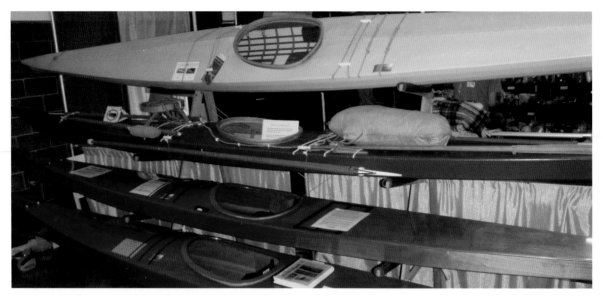

Photo 1.5 *Three wood kayaks and a skin-on-frame kayak* WAYNE HORODOWICH

will also restore the appearance as well as the hole. Getting wood repairs to look "invisible" can be a time-consuming process, but the result is well worth the effort. A finished and varnished plywood kayak is a joy to behold, but to get the best out of your kayak, it should be dried out thoroughly after use, stored in a dry place, and maintained by rubbing down and varnishing at least once every two years. The frequency of varnishing will depend on the amount of use your boat gets.

Skin-on-Frame Traditional Kayaks

We are now talking about kayaks that are built by what is called skin-on-frame or lathe and fabric construction (Photo 1.5). These boats are usually modeled on either Greenland-type kayaks or those from the Aleutian Islands. The ones I have seen all look as if they have been put together with the loving care of a gold watch. The wooden frames are delicately carved and the longitudinal

stringers are bound to them using waxed or synthetic twine (Photo 1.6). The covering is then stretched over the frame and sewn tightly. Instead of skins (which the native paddlers used), the outer fabric can be of fine glass cloth impregnated with a light coating of clear resin or a strong nylon fabric that is coated to become waterproof. These kayaks are extremely light and very strong and are works of art.

Choosing a Kayak

Choosing a kayak is a big decision. It is vitally important to choose a boat design with features that will allow you to do what you want to do with your kayak. However, at this stage of the game, you probably will have no idea what you want to do or the particular type of craft you want to do it in. If you don't mix with paddlers and don't have anyone to advise you, the real trouble starts in the kayak store. Here you will be assailed by all manner of shiny craft in

Photo 1.6 *The frame of my first skin-on-frame kayak, made of red and yellow cedar*
WAYNE HORODOWICH

flamboyant colors, which hang bewilderingly from the walls and ceilings. They all cry out for your attention (and your money). You will immediately notice that they come in a variety of lengths, widths, and colors, which range from weird to the absolutely impractical. I have to say that some of these craft will have originated from manufacturers with little or no experience of the sea.

Roughly speaking, the boats you see will fall into two categories: sea kayaks and recreational boats. Although both are used for touring, it is there that the similarity ends.

Recreational Boats

The short, stubby, little recreational (rec) boats with their huge, wide cockpits are not kayaks in the true sense of the word (Photo 1.7). Most have flat bottoms, which make them very stable on flat water but almost impossible to stabilize or maneuver in rough seas. They are slow and don't track (paddle in a straight line) very well. There will certainly be no support for your thighs or for your visible, unprotected knees.

Because of their "homely" qualities, recreational boats are very limited in the type of journeys they can undertake. On a calm day all the oceans of the world resemble the pool in your backyard, except they are much bigger. However, when conditions change, which can be at any moment, an oceangoing craft is required. Rec boats are not designed to be on the open sea and should be confined to protected and predictable waters.

To keep the price low, recreational boats are not fitted out with the basic safety features we have come to expect for boats built to travel open waters. These include watertight compartments and deck lines. Without proper flotation

Photo 1.7 *Recreational boat* WAYNE HORODOWICH

and watertight compartments, it is more difficult to recover these boats from a capsize (see Chapter 2). Because of their limited use, recreational boats rarely have options such as skegs or rudders.

Sea Kayaks

For the most part, sea kayaks are long, sleek, and straight-running, and you don't sit in them, you wear them. All good makes will have hatches and watertight compartments that make them unsinkable. They will have fixed deck lines for you to grab and toggles at both ends for carrying. The cockpit must be of a kind that can be sealed off with some kind of a spray cover when you are sitting on the seat. Sea kayaks are designed for open-water travel and are made to handle extreme conditions, with their greatest limitation being the experience of the paddler inside the kayak.

Testing Kayaks

If you think you would like to try kayaking, you should start by sitting in one and paddling it in a calm protected area while under some supervision. The best way to do that is either trying your friend's kayak or by attending a sea kayak symposium or "demo" day where various manufacturers line boats up along the beach for you to "test drive."

If you enjoy that experience and think you want to dive into this sport, I recommend taking a sea kayaking course. You will learn the basic skills needed for maneuvering your boat, but more importantly, the safety procedures needed to come back alive. In addition, you will be spending time in a kayak and learning about the different features needed in a kayak. After the course you will decide if the sport is for you. If not, you are only out the cost of the course and not the cost of buying a kayak and then not using it.

Now that you have a little bit of experience in a kayak, it is time to research different boats. Get opinions from other paddlers, but remember they are not you. You need to make a list of what you want from a kayak and where you intend to do most of your paddling. Once you have your checklist, it is time to test drive some boats.

Your first priority is to see how the boat feels when you sit in it. The seat should be nice and comfortable, with room for your thighs. This is a serious consideration because as you make progress, you will be sitting in your kayak for many hours at a stretch.

Next you need to test the primary and secondary stability of the hull. First you will need to adjust the footrest so that your legs are slightly bent and you can touch the thigh braces with your knee area when you press on the balls of your feet.

Sit in the kayak while you are on flat, calm water. Wiggle a bit in the seat. Does the kayak feel stable just sitting there? If yes, you have good primary stability.

Now get next to a low dock or use the bow of a friend's kayak positioned at right angles to you. What you are looking for is something solid to lean upon. Support the nearest hand lightly on the dock (or bow) and start lifting the outside knee. That knee, which will be the high side, should be bent upwards and hooked underneath the cockpit coaming. The leg nearest the dock should be straight and pushing down on the footrest. As you start to edge your kayak, you should feel some resistance before the kayak capsizes—it is almost like a stopping point. It should be easy to hold that edge. This is what is known as secondary stability. Suddenly there will come a

point where the boat will go over and you have to use your hand for support once again. This point is known as the moment-of-capsize.

As a little exercise, using only your hips, try wobbling the boat from side to side to the limit of its secondary stability. Keep your hand poised above the dock, just in case. Keep on doing this for a few minutes. Through repetition, the kayak's stability will be registered on your nervous system and the balance mechanism of your brain. Very soon your balance will be instinctive. A point to remember is that your stability will be affected by your center of gravity. If you are a paddler with a long torso and a good deal of upper body weight, you will be more unstable than a person of the same height but whose weight is spread lower down. You may wish to add some fixed ballast, which will be discussed later.

Your skill level will start to improve the moment you sit in the boat, so the kayak you thought was a little tippy the first time you sat in it could feel like a lifeless plank in a week's time. Don't delude yourself into thinking that width brings stability. Many boats have been bought with flat bottoms and wide beams with the mistaken idea that this type of stability is seaworthy. In a flat sea, the kayak does sit flat on the water, but because the hull shape follows the wave slope (Figure 1.4 A), it is unsuitable for anything but flat, calm water.

The other cross-sectional hull shapes you will meet up with are the chine or V-shaped hull, the round hull, and the semi-elliptical hull. The chine hull (Figure 1.2) is the traditional shape of many Greenland Eskimo kayaks; as long as the amount of rocker is not too excessive, these hulls can have good directional stability. Chine boats are not as fast as those with round bilges, but as long as the bottom V is not too acute, these boats can be extremely stable and comfortable. The multi-chine, round hull is the traditional shape of Aleutian Island kayaks. It is a faster hull than the Greenland kayaks, and the rounded hull gives a softer ride in beam seas. The true round hull is certainly the fastest through the water, which is why racing kayaks have this kind of hull shape. Unfortunately, they are also frighteningly unstable, so if you fancy racing (see Chapter 6), mastering this instability could become a lifelong pursuit.

Being very practically minded, Derek always based his hull designs on a semi-elliptical cross section. He found that this compromise between speed and stability gave him a feeling of security in rough water and a smooth, fast ride.

Once you find a boat that has comfortable seating and the stability you are looking for, there is one other important test you need to perform: Can you easily do capsize recoveries with that kayak? A good paddling boat is not going to help you if you cannot climb back in after a wet exit because the deck is too high or the cockpit is too narrow. There is only one way to tell, and that is to get wet and practice with full paddling attire.

The Perfect Kayak

You will be pleased to know, dear reader, that we all want the same type of kayak. It must be light enough to lift up onto the top of a vehicle (see Figure 13.2, Chapter 13), yet strong enough to withstand the battering of rough usage. It must be stable enough to stand up in and narrow enough to be fast. It must run straight regardless of the strength and direction of the wind, but it must turn without effort. Hatches must be large enough to pack the kitchen sink in and be

completely watertight no matter what shape they may be . . . and the list goes on.

Seriously, if there were a perfect kayak, we would all be paddling it. Since we all come in different shapes, sizes, and ability, how can one kayak fit all of us? In addition, we want our kayaks for different reasons. As I mentioned before, before you go shopping for your first kayak, you need to make a list of your priorities and know the type of water in which you will be using it. The following points will help make an informed decision.

Stability

Find a kayak that gives you the primary stability and the secondary stability you desire. Your stability may change when a kayak is fully loaded for a long trip, usually for the better. That is why some folks add ballast when paddling an empty kayak (Figure 1.20).

As you get more comfortable in your kayak and increase your experience, a kayak you originally thought was unstable may now be the exact boat you are looking for. The good news is you get to buy another kayak. Like any other sport, increased experience means needs change. Don't fret; you can usually sell a well-kept used kayak for a reasonable price.

Cockpit and Seat

Cockpit size is another preoccupation of the novice. I remember my own thoughts: "That hole is too small! A dwarf couldn't get *into* it . . . let alone get *out of* it!" Luckily, they were all groundless fears. With a little experience you will find that *staying in* is the difficult part.

After hearing from numerous former paddlers, the two main reasons those folks stopped paddling were: "I was not comfortable in my seat" and "The kayak was too heavy for moving." Since you are sitting the entire time you are in your kayak, the comfort of the seat and the fit in the cockpit are critical. Before purchasing a kayak, spend a lot of time sitting in it to see how it affects your body. If you feel tingling in your legs, it is not a good seat for you.

When you try the seat in a kayak, always start by sitting on the rear deck. Lift your legs into the cockpit, straighten your legs, and then slide forward. Getting out is the same movement in reverse. The back of your seat rest should not be too high, nor should you be able to dislodge it if it happens to be located in a preformed slot. Semirigid back straps or back bands are best. These should be slung to give your back plenty of support, but they should also be flexible enough to allow you to lean back onto the rear deck. If you cannot lean back onto the rear deck, a number of advanced techniques will be closed to you.

Sitting on the seat with your back comfortably supported and your feet resting on the foot braces, you should be able to hook your knees under the cockpit coaming or under specially made knee-grips that protrude inward from the side of the coaming. You should feel snug and comfortable. It is said, "You don't sit in a kayak, you wear it." You want to feel support in the small of your back. There should be enough support to keep you in proper paddling posture, which is upright with a slight forward lean.

Workmanship is important. Is the cockpit smooth and well finished? You should feel around the underside of the coaming to make sure that there are no jagged edges. Take special notice of the area where the topside of the seat meets the underside of the coaming.

Foot Braces

During the forward paddling stroke, it is essential that you are able to exert pressure on some kind of foot brace. Almost all modern foot braces are sliding, adjustable supports that have a notched rack that can be locked into any number of positions to fit the length of your legs. When you are sitting comfortably in the kayak with the balls of your feet on the foot braces, your heels should be pointing inward towards the center of the hull. Without moving the ball of your foot, you should be able to hook your thighs under the shaped supports that are situated on either side under the cockpit coaming. You should also be able to straighten your leg out so that your calf is almost touching the bottom of the hull.

Solid, non-giving foot braces allow a better transfer of energy to your kayak. Spongy foot braces (found in older rudder systems) are not as efficient. That is why some paddlers disliked the older rudder systems. There are now rudder systems with solid foot braces that have eliminated that concern.

Cockpit Coaming

The coaming is the raised flange between 1 and 2 inches wide around the top of the cockpit (Figure 1.1). This is what the spray skirt fits over in order to keep out the water. Run your fingers carefully around its rim. If it is very thin and sharp, it could damage your expensive new spray skirt (as well as your fingers). In cross-section, the best coamings are slightly convex (raised up). This allows the material of the spray skirt to press firmly against the surface of the coaming, giving you a more watertight seal.

Rocker

When you look at a boat from the side, the rocker is the curve of the keel from the bow to the stern. This rockering tends to govern directional stability, making the kayak easier to turn. The amount of rockering in sea kayaks has to be limited, as it causes stern drag and hence a reduction in forward speed.

The shape and degree of rocker is important. For instance, you may see kayaks where the gentle curve of the bow starts somewhere near amidships, but the rocker at the rear of the boat is hardly discernable and may even be formed into the shape of a continuous skeg or fin. This means that in any kind of a crosswind, the rear of the boat will lock itself into the water while the front end will blow uncontrollably downwind (sometimes called lee-cocking). In other words, the kayak cannot be turned to face into a strong side wind even with the use of a rudder. This is probably one of the most dangerous faults a hull can have, especially if the winds are offshore. The good news is that most kayaks with well-balanced rocker will tend to "weathercock" or blow slightly into the wind, but this can be easily corrected by the use of a skeg. Kayaks that "lee-cock" are bad news because they are almost impossible to correct, either with a skeg or even with a rudder.

Rudder versus Skeg

You will have to decide if you want a kayak with a rudder or a skeg. It can happen that the best-fitting kayak for you doesn't let you choose. Since a rudder and skeg are primarily there to keep you on course when moving, it shouldn't make much of a difference. However, if you prefer to do your steering with your feet, a kayak with a rudder needs to be your pick.

I own both types of kayak. When I am shooting video or taking pictures, it is nice to be able to steer with my feet to keep the image in my viewfinder rather than contorting my body. The other advantage I find helpful is the extra storage space in the back hatch since there is no skeg box. As I am 6 feet 7 inches, my clothes take up more space, so extra room is a concern for me. I know Derek is rolling over in his grave as I write this, because he hated rudders. He thought they were dangerous and detracted from the design lines of the kayak. Both skegs and rudders work well. They both have pros and cons.

Here are two opinions from experienced long-distance paddlers: Paul Caffyn, who circumnavigated Australia (over 9,000 miles, 360 days), and Sean Morley, who circumnavigated the UK and Ireland (4,500 miles, 183 days).

Paul averaged 34.3 miles per day from Brisbane to Cape York (approximately 1,700 miles) using a skeg. He averaged 39.2 miles a day from Melbourne to Sydney (approximately 800 miles) using his rudder.

Sean also experienced more efficiency over distance with a rudder. However, he also says, "A boat designed to have a skeg is often more maneuverable and playful than a kayak that is designed to be used with a rudder. And since the majority of us use our kayaks not just for expeditions but for regular play in rock gardens, tide races, coastal touring, etc., it is perhaps better to have a personal kayak that has a skeg." He goes on to say, "I would advocate a ruddered kayak for expeditions and a skegged kayak for regular paddling." You can read the full article at www.expeditionkayak.com/resources/skegs-vs-rudders.

Fixed Ballast

Naturally, you don't want a boat that feels too "tippy," nor do you want to buy a boat that will not grow with you as your skill level increases. Since your skill will increase, how do you decide what is too tippy?

There are often times when we could all do with that little extra stability. Some expedition kayaks, when completely empty, can be very unwieldy in strong winds. Some paddlers may feel they are too light for their kayak; others may have bought a kayak that now feels a little unstable. Potential paddlers may look longingly at the beautiful lines of a particular kayak, only to be informed by friends that it's unstable. Adding ballast could address these issues.

Aspects to consider when adding ballast:

- Some kind of ballast that is so fixed that it could not slide about
- Something portable
- Something that will not affect the handling of the boat
- Something to provide the type of stability found in those little round-bottomed toys that are weighted so that when they are pushed over, they immediately rock back into the upright position again

How much weight you need is up to you and the stability you desire. If you attempt to make your own system, be warned that moving ballast is dangerous.

Derek designed a fixed ballast system that is situated behind the seat (Figure 1.20). As a result of his drawing of the design, Carl Vopal developed an excellent (commercially available) fixed ballast system that met and exceeded Derek's recommendations.

Here are Derek's comments after using his fixed ballast system:

> When paddling the kayak I found the effect of all this quite remarkable. Although I could still lean my kayak right over onto its side in order to perform the various strokes, the weight, which was fixed dead center, was constantly trying to bring the kayak upright again. The further I leant the kayak over, the more it tried to pull me back again.
>
> If you are transporting your kayak to the water alone, you might be wise to carry your boat and the ballast separately.
>
> For those who have a suspect Eskimo roll, the fixed ballast is a godsend. The Eskimos often needed ballast in their empty, large-volume, load-carrying kayaks. For this purpose they used smooth, rounded stones. This worked well most of the time, but the kayak could not be rolled, and the paddler could not lean over too far because the rocks were not fixed in place.

If you want to add some extra stability to your empty kayak, I recommend considering the Paddling Partner by Balance Solutions.

Figure 1.20 *Derek's early fixed ballast design*

General Shape

There are some points worth considering regarding general shape. As mentioned previously, you should be able to lie back onto the rear deck even if this means raising your posterior off the seat. Because of this, you are looking for a boat with the rear deck lower than the foredeck. However, the height of the front deck should not be so high that it prevents you from placing your paddle at a low angle to the water. It is for this reason that I advise against very high-peaked foredecks. The sales pitch is that it helps to shed water; in reality, oncoming water never gets that far up the deck unless you're in surf.

This brings us to the question of bow shapes. Rising bows and V-shaped hulls slice through the water when running through large waves or short, steep seas. Bows that in cross-section widen out in a concave sweep as they rise upwards towards the deck tend to look graceful. However, in a boat as small as a kayak, as a flared bow plunges downwards, it will throw water upwards and outwards. This water then hits you in the face at around 3 miles per hour. Fine, narrow, upswept bows, on the other hand, allow the front of the boat to plunge cleanly into an oncoming wave and then slice upwards and out again, with a minimum amount of water thrown into the face of the paddler.

Length

Most sea kayaks are between 16 and 19 feet long. The length of a kayak has a huge effect on its tracking ability, maneuverability, stability, and speed. Long kayaks take less effort to paddle than those that are short and stubby because the flow of water past the hull, known as laminar flow, is offered less resistance. This allows long boats to glide farther with each stroke, and they are also able to bridge the smaller wave troughs, thus giving you a smoother, faster, drier ride. Shorter boats—i.e., those less than 16 feet long—are easier to turn but they are slower and will cause you to expend more energy, especially in wind tossed waves.

Weight

Sea kayaks, depending on their dimensions, usually weigh in at around 50 to 55 pounds. Since weight was a concern for many of those who stopped paddling, think about your ability to move, carry, and load your kayak onto your vehicle. Kayak wheels can help a lot, but there is a time when you will be holding the weight of the kayak, by yourself if you paddle alone. As a side note, a good set of kayak racks can make loading your kayak on your vehicle less stressful. Thule's Hullavators are expensive but can save your back.

Whenever possible, get help when moving your kayak. Once you strain your back, you will not want to be sitting in your kayak and paddling.

Even though lighter-weight materials cost more when building a kayak, the extra cost is well worth it when it comes to a healthy back. If you factor in the cost of physical therapy, Kevlar kayaks become cost-effective.

If you have a heavy boat or a fully loaded one, it will take more energy to get it up to speed. Once you are moving, you will not feel it. That extra weight is helpful when punching through waves. It will also take more energy to stop the boat quickly.

Storage Capacity

If you intend to undertake lots of long-duration camping trips and plan to carry large quantities of equipment, or if you are, shall we say, a large-volume person, you should choose a large-volume kayak for your needs. For most paddlers, however, a medium-volume kayak will carry enough equipment for two-week trips and can also be used as a "day boat."

Considering the valuable equipment you are going to pack, such as your sleeping bag, look inside the hatches. See if your waterproof bags will be in danger from any jagged edges of unsmoothed fiberglass, or the screws that hold the hatch rim, or the blank end of long pop rivets. Check to see that the inside of your waterproof compartment is smooth all over.

Color

Some people may think pastel shades are sweet. It's also fashionable to be color coordinated and have all your equipment in tune with your dark blue or purple life jacket. If, however, you find yourself in a busy shipping lane, you may wish that even your nose was Day-Glo red so that you could put it on a stick and wave it. For safety's sake, and so that you can be easily spotted in time of trouble, make sure that either the deck of your kayak or at least some large piece of your equipment, like your life jacket or your paddle, is brightly colored or incorporates fluorescent colors as part of its design.

Loose Ends

Try to choose a kayak with recessed deck fittings. These have no projections on the inside and do not shred human skin on the outside.

End-toggles should be comfortable to hold. You should *not* be able to put your fingers through rope loops. These could act as a tourniquet while you are trying to tow your boat to shore.

They are not as common in recent years, but if you want a deck-mounted pump, you will have a limited choice in kayaks. Electric pumps are added on after you purchase your kayak if you want to go that route. The vast majority of paddlers use the hand pumps.

All else aside, you want to enjoy your kayak. You want to feel good when you sit in it. Make it your own. Since it is your kayak, feel free to augment it to fit your particular needs and desires. Remember, if you own a kayak, you are the captain of that vessel. As I say in my symposium lectures, "I own eleven kayaks, so I am the admiral of my fleet and I have my wife's permission to say so."

There are ID labels you can put in your kayak in case you lose it. Your name and phone number should be in all boats, usually in the cockpit.

Once you choose your kayak, get out there and enjoy the adventures.

Paddles

Your paddle is your propeller, and your body is the engine. Changing paddles can change your speed and distance. Paddles come in many blade shapes, shaft lengths, construction materials, and prices. As with kayaks, if there were the perfect paddle, we would all be using it. Your goal is to find the paddle that gives you the performance you desire when you need it.

Photo 1.8 will be referenced as I review different types of paddles. The term **Euro paddle** is used for modern-day sea kayaking paddles (Photo 1.8 B, C, D, E, F). A **traditional paddle** (Photo 1.8 A, G), a native paddle design, is another category. A **wing paddle** (Photo 1.8 H) is in the racing category.

Greenland paddles (sticks) are usually carved out of one piece of wood (Photo 1.8 A). The ends are wider than the shaft, which is usually carved with some indexing. There are some gorgeous paddles made from different-colored woods that were laminated together. When I am not using my Tuktu paddle, made by Chris Raab, I hang it in my den as a showpiece.

The length is sized to the person. When you stand straight with arm extended, your fingertips just go over the top of the paddle. The width is about 3.5 inches, which is the size of the average grip. Several Greenland techniques utilize extended paddle maneuvers, so being able to grip the width of the blade is necessary.

Many of my maturing paddling friends have adopted the Greenland paddle for their touring paddle because the flex in the paddle and the narrow blade reduce stress on the body.

The **Toksook paddle** needs to be mentioned because this is Derek's book and he designed it

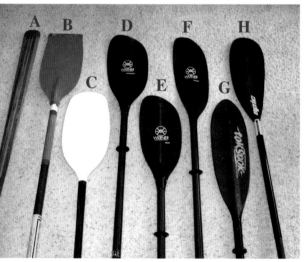

Photo 1.8 *A: Greenland blade. B: old metal-tipped blade. C: whitewater blade. D: wide asymmetrical blade. E: medium asymmetrical blade. F: narrow asymmetrical blade. G: Toksook blade. H: wing blade.* WAYNE HORODOWICH

(Photo 1.8 G). After trying all the paddles available, he couldn't find one that gave him the features he wanted in a paddle. This paddle falls into a special category. It is based on a traditional native paddle used in Alaska and is a willow leaf design used by numerous Alaskan kayak hunters (Kotzebue, Nootak, Nunivak Island, etc.; see Photo 14.12, Chapter 14).

The modern Toksook (pronounced took-sook) is made of graphite or carbon fiber. It is symmetrical with a double spine. The original design had a metal tip, which has been changed to a carbon tip. Derek wanted a strong tip when pushing off of rocks. The blade is about 5 centimeters longer than the regular Euro blade, which adds 10 centimeters to the length of the paddle given the same shaft length of a Euro paddle. The blade has a hollow interior, which is filled with a light buoyant foam, making the blade convex on both sides. This makes the blade a thick one, which makes it one of the most buoyant blades available.

Due to all the features of this paddle, it is one of the heaviest paddles on the market. The flotation and the spines on the blade make it the most forgiving and supportive paddle I have ever used, especially when bracing or sculling.

The Toksook is my primary paddle. I have it feathered at 90 degrees because I utilize extended paddle stokes regularly. As a side note, I have never had any wrist problems. The only time I do not use this paddle is when I race. Then I use either a wing paddle or a large-bladed Euro paddle.

Paddle Features

A paddle is made up of the blades connected to both ends of the paddle shaft. The throat is where the blades blend into the paddle shaft. The end of the blade is called the tip. The paddle shaft (loom) is the place where you grip your paddle during the majority of your strokes and can vary in length.

The materials, along with the design, used to build a paddle determine the weight and strength of the paddle, aside from the cost.

The angle of one blade with respect to the other is the paddle's feather angle. The angle can range from 0 to 90 degrees.

Paddle Blades

The blade provides the resistance (due to its surface area) that propels the kayak. Blades can range from long to short and from wide to narrow. They can be thin or thick, symmetrical or asymmetrical.

Wider blades provide more resistance, which gives you more power. It also means more stress on your body (Photo 1.8 D).

Narrow blades provide less resistance and less stress on the body (Photo 1.8 F).

Average-size blades are Goldilocks' choice. Not too much power and not too much stress on the body (Photo 1.8 E).

Many kayaking guides carry a few paddles with extra-narrow blades in case their clients complain about soreness or strains. If you choose a wide blade, understand that you will probably need to work up to it.

Modern-day paddles started out with **symmetrical blades**, which are still common in whitewater paddles and traditional paddles (Photo 1.8 A, C, G). If you do not paddle this blade shape completely vertical, the corner of the blade enters the water first, which can cause uneven torque on the paddle. It will be imperceptible to you, but it is less efficient, especially for long-distance touring.

Asymmetrical blades are designed to be more efficient when entering the water (Photo 1.8 D, E, F). Depending on your stroke style, your paddle blade enters the water at an angle. The shape of your asymmetrical blade should match your stroke style. The most efficiency occurs when your blade enters the water with the end of the paddle parallel to the water's surface. The off-set angle at the end of your blade should match the stroke style. High angle strokes need less off-set and lower angle strokes need more offset at the end of the blade.

As you settle into your all-day touring stroke, which may take a few hundred miles of paddling, you will be able to decide what really works for you with respect to paddle design. You cannot go wrong with an average-size blade with a touring angle on the blade. You will be purchasing many paddles during your kayaking career. After selling off some paddles, I am down to around fifteen paddles in my quiver.

Thin blades are the ones commonly found on the market (Photo 1.9). Thinner blades usually weigh less. Thin blades can slice through the water very quickly when on edge, which could surprise the unsuspecting paddler, resulting in a capsize. I find thin blades unforgiving.

Photo 1.9 *Thin blade*
WAYNE HORODOWICH

Photo 1.10 *Thick blade*
WAYNE HORODOWICH

Thick blades are a bit more forgiving when on edge (Photo 1.10). If, in addition, you have a spine down the center of your blade (on one face or both faces), that spine slows down the speed of the slice. I personally find this very reassuring in rough-water maneuvering.

Curved and spoon-faced blades create a specific power face (concave face) for forward strokes and a back face (convex face) for reverse strokes (Photo 1.11). This bend of the blade gets more purchase in the water than a flat blade. When you cup your hand as you do when you swim, the bend from the wrist to your fingertips is referred to as "curve." The bend in the hand from side to side is "spoon."

Flat blades may have an advertised power face, but it really doesn't make a difference in performance if you rotated the blades. However, you may feel the difference in your grips. Flat blades have a tendency to flutter (wobble) during the stroke.

Dihedral blades have a split power face when you look at the blade from the tip. The raised portion in the middle of the face, like a little spine, allows water to shed off the blade to either side more evenly. Paddle blades with pronounced spines in the middle do the same thing. This design is supposed to reduce flutter during your stroke.

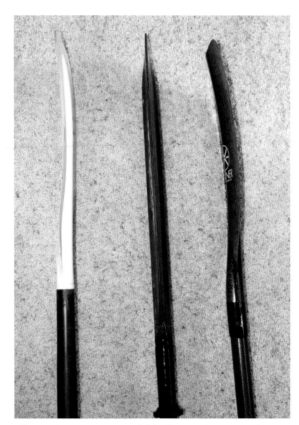

Photo 1.11 *Two curved blades with a straight blade between them* WAYNE HORODOWICH

Wing blades are primarily used for racing due to the efficiency of the blade (Figure 6.1, Chapter 6, and Photo 1.8 H). Since the blade is cupped, kayakers need to adapt how they perform the normal strokes needed when touring, especially bracing and sculling strokes. (See Chapter 6 for more details on racing and the wing paddle.)

Paddle Shaft

The paddle shaft is the section between the two blades. The neck or throat is where the blade blends into the shaft. Paddle shafts were originally one piece before manufacturers developed strong joints that were reliable, allowing a paddle to come apart.

Shaft shape can tell you where and how to grip your paddle. It is important for you to know if your blade is in the correct position for entering the water just by feeling the paddle shaft. The shape of the shaft is altered for this purpose. The offset shape is referred to as an **indexed grip**.

Modern paddle shafts started out round. Raised handgrips were added to the shaft under shrink-wrap. Over time, manufacturers began squeezing aluminum shafts to make them oval, so you could find the index. The vast majority of composite shafts are built with an oval shaft. My only objection to the oval shafts comes on cold days where your hands get so cold you cannot feel the index easily. I have raised grips added to my paddle for just that reason.

Straight-shaft paddles mean just that. The paddle shaft is straight and it has an oval index or a raised one. You can easily slide your hands along the paddle shaft if you want to paddle with an offset grip (Photo 1.12).

Bent-shaft paddles have two bends in the shaft designed specifically for hand placement (Photo 1.12). Their goal is to reduce your wrist flexion during the catch phase of your forward stroke when your wrist flexes the most, with the hopes of reducing or eliminating overuse injuries (specifically, carpal tunnel syndrome). The one downside of bent-shaft paddles is the limitation the bends cause if you like to paddle with your hands offset. They also don't allow you to adjust the width of your grip, which will be discussed in Chapter 3. I have found some paddlers fanatic about their bent-shaft paddles, while others dislike them. The vast majority of the paddling world still use straight-shaft paddles. It is a personal choice. Try it to see if it works for you.

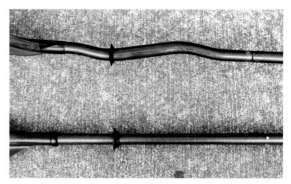

Photo 1.12 *Straight shaft and bent shaft*
WAYNE HORODOWICH

Shaft joints allow us to take our paddles apart, adjust shaft length, and adjust feather angle. I have seen two-, three-, and four-piece paddles. The most common are the two-piece paddles. Taking a paddle apart makes for easier storage in your car and more importantly allows you to carry a spare paddle on the deck of your kayak. There are still one-piece Euro paddles being used, but they are not very common.

The locking mechanism is either a button system, a locking collar, or a stainless steel bolt system. If you like to travel with your paddle and keep it in your suitcase, I recommend getting a four-piece one. With current airline restrictions and how baggage is handled, traveling with a two-piece paddle is difficult, if allowed at all. Also, will it be broken in the cargo hold? Keep in mind, each joint adds weight to the paddle, and joints are common breakage areas.

Shaft length, which translates to paddle length, is determined by a few factors. Your reach, the width of your kayak, how high you sit above the water in your seat, and your preferred stroke angle need to be considered when choosing a paddle length. When you take your preferred stroke and have the blade totally submerged, your hands should not hit the side deck of the kayak. If you move into a wider kayak, such as a tandem, you may need a longer paddle. High-angle strokes could use a shorter paddle. Low-angle stroke need a longer paddle. The differences of stroke style will be discussed in Chapter 3.

From a physics perspective, the shorter the paddle length, the more revolutions you can perform in a fixed period of time through the water. However, you do want the entire blade submerged. Your paddle length selection needs to be a combination of efficiency, comfort, and what your body can sustain over time.

Paddle Weight

The weight of a paddle is a major consideration for most kayakers. The heavier the paddle, the more you have to lift for every stroke. At 1,000 strokes to the mile, that weight adds up. What is often overlooked when considering the weight of the paddle is the paddler's stroke style. The higher your stroke angle (more vertical paddle shaft), the more you have to lift your arms for each stroke. Your arms are significantly heavier than any paddle on the market. This concern will be discussed in greater detail in Chapter 3.

If you need a very strong paddle, you will probably have a heavier one. If you want to race, you will be looking for the lightest one you can find. Regardless of the weight, your paddle needs to have the features that provide the performance you desire.

Paddle Materials

Carbon fiber and graphite are light yet strong materials, but you pay for the privilege. Fiberglass is strong and slightly heavier, but more reasonably priced. Aluminum paddle shafts with plastic blades will be heavier, but the price point will be the lowest. Wood paddles usually weigh the same as the fiberglass ones. The price of wood paddles varies because some are works of art that you would rather display over the mantle instead of actually using. However, the feel of wood is so nice.

Regardless of the materials used, all paddles will flex to some degree. Every time a paddle flexes, you are losing a little bit of energy that is not being transferred to moving your kayak. Stiffer paddles are more efficient but increase stress on the body, usually your joints. More flexion is less efficient but kinder to your joints. I know a number of paddlers who have gone to wood paddles as they aged because of the flexion, which was easier on their joints. Others went to narrower blades as they got older.

When I train for a race, I start with my Greenland paddle because it puts the least stress on my joints while increasing my cadence. Then I move to my wide-blade Euro paddle. The last part of the training is with my wing paddle. I know from experience that if I jump into training with my wing paddle, I feel it in my joints because the sudden increase in cadence with a stiff paddle, which does not back slip, means my body is getting the full impact of the stroke.

Feathering

The relation of one blade to the other is known as the "feather angle." If the blades are aligned the same, it is called unfeathered or a 0-degree feather. If they are at right angles to each other, it is a 90-degree feather, which is the greatest offset. There is no set standard among paddlers, because everyone has their preferred feather angle from 0 to 90 degrees.

Since native paddlers simply carved their paddles from driftwood, they were symmetrical and unfeathered (Photo 1.8 A). Modern-day paddlers started feathering blades for efficiency when racing. When I started paddling, 90-degree paddles were the norm because the nonworking blade presented no resistance to the air as you paddled forward.

When overuse wrist injuries began to occur, they were blamed on the 90-degree feather angle. Manufacturers began lowering the feather angles on their paddles, and this became a retail dilemma due to the stocking of differently angled paddles. Finally reliable adjustable shaft joints were developed to allow paddlers to choose their particular feather angle.

The rush to blame the extreme feather angle for overuse injuries was unjustified. The leading cause of overuse wrist injuries is too tight of a grip on the paddle shaft during the stroke cycle. The side-to-side flexion of the wrist is the action that needs to be reduced, which the bent-shaft paddle is trying to accomplish. If one paddles correctly, with a loose grip, they can choose any feather angle that makes sense to them and provides the options they need for the strokes they use.

If there were a perfect feather angle, all of the racers would be using that angle. When I canvas racers, their feather angles are all over the map. It is a personal choice.

I personally believe that 0 degree or 90 degrees are the only two angles that make sense for sea kayaking because of extended paddle strokes. If I am holding one end of the paddle, I know exactly what my other blade is doing at those two angles. Any other degree setting can be confusing when you are switching extended strokes from one side to the other. If you depend on the extended paddle roll, it really gets confusing when upside down with water up your nose.

If you do not use extended paddle strokes, your feather angle is just a personal choice. You should have a good reason for your choices. "That is what my instructor [or the store owner] told me" is not good enough. Find out why.

If the feather angle is the reason for overuse wrist injuries, why do paddlers still get them throughout the entire range of angles, even unfeathered?

Left- or Right-Hand Control

When paddling you will have one hand, usually your dominant hand, maintaining the overall control of your paddle indexing. If your paddle is feathered, it will either be a right-hand or left-hand controlled paddle.

To determine whether your feathered paddle is right- or left-hand controlled, stand with the driving face of the lower blade facing your feet (Figure 1.21). Now look at the upper blade. If the power face is on the right, it is a right-hand

Figure 1.21 *Left-hand or right-hand control*

control for right-handed paddlers. If the power face is looking the opposite way, it is a left-hand control for left-handed paddlers. If both power faces are facing the same direction, your paddle is unfeathered. You will decide which hand you wish to be the control hand.

Choosing Your Paddle

After reading about all the different features you can find in a paddle, how the heck can you choose? Derek would say, "Don't choose, it's too confusing. Take up cycling!"

It can be overwhelming. As a novice you have no idea how your body will react to the different blades. You do not know what stroke style you prefer. If you do not have a kayak, you do not know the length you will need until you are sitting in the boat on the water.

A seasoned kayaker can make an informed decision. Therefore, when you begin, getting an average-performance paddle will be your best choice. An average-width Euro blade, asymmetrical, with an adjustable feather joint gives you a good base from which to begin. As you gain experience, it is wise to try as many paddles as you can to see which features suit you best.

In general, the preferred paddle length at the time of this writing is in the 210-to-230-centimeter range, with 220 centimeters being a safe choice for most kayaks. You need to try your paddle in your boat to know for sure. When you grow into your second paddle, you can always use your first paddle as your spare. Having a quiver of paddles is common among kayakers. Do your spouse a favor by not making him or her guess what you need for your birthday or the commercial holidays. "I could always use another paddle, my dear."

At the beginning of this section on paddles, I compared a paddle to a propeller. If you have the same engine and change the propeller, you will change your speed. Following are my average training speeds using the same kayak over a fixed distance of 6 miles (four laps around the lake). During a month of timed trials (five-plus per week), I switched between four paddles during different laps. I rotated the paddle usage order each day. The recorded results were pretty consistent. My Greenland paddle averaged 5.6 to 5.7 mph. My Toksook and big Euro blade paddle averaged 5.8 to 5.9 mph. My wing paddle averaged 6.0 to 6.1 mph.

Clothing

Kayaking is a wet sport. Let's face it: You are surrounded by water. Sometimes you are in or under the water. There is rain, waves, and spray. Therefore, staying dry and maintaining your body temperature are your primary goals. I ran UCSB's Adventure Programs for twenty-five years. My experience has taught me that dressing properly for the outdoors is one's key to survival. We always told our participants, "There is no such thing as bad weather, only inappropriate clothing."

The number one cause of death in sea kayaking is drowning precipitated by exposure. You can lose body heat ten times faster in water than in air of the same temperature.

When a paddler capsizes in cold water without thermal protection, they first experience "cold shock." The symptoms are hyperventilation, disorientation, dizziness, and loss of motor control. After the initial shock, if you didn't drown from the uncontrolled gasps, you will still be losing body heat rapidly. You may have about 10 minutes of function. In one hour or less, you will likely be unconscious due to hypothermia. Once unconscious, you will probably drown if your life jacket doesn't keep you face up.

If this scares you into taking "dressing for immersion" seriously, then another life may have been saved. We kayak for fun. We want to be kayaking for many years. If you dress properly, you will have many fine adventures in your kayak.

Your first goal in dressing for immersion is to eliminate or reduce the cold shock, and then to prevent or slow down the onset of hypothermia. The time you can spend in cold water will depend on the clothing you are wearing.

Eskimos had no trouble keeping warm in their kayaks. Keeping cool was their big problem. You will soon discover that paddling a kayak, even in cold weather, can be a warm business. Your clothing should therefore be comfortable and should keep you warm and dry. If the worst happens and you do get wet, your clothing should still keep you warm.

Your Body

Protecting the area from your elbows to your knees, which I will refer to as your trunk, maintains your core temperature. The rest of your arms and legs are important too, but keeping the trunk protected is how we maintain our core temperature.

Dry Suit

Dry suits are designed to keep you dry and warm by providing a thin outer waterproof fabric. They should fit loosely over the arms and body and have thin latex seals at the neck, wrist, and ankles. Many suits now come with waterproof socks at the end of the legs, eliminating the need for an ankle gasket. The suits can be bought as one- or two-piece. Dry suits made of waterproof

"breathable" fabrics such as Gore-Tex are worth the cost.

The thermal protection provided by a dry suit comes in two ways. Keeping air inside and water out means you are not losing heat quickly, which eliminates cold shock. The actual "keeping warm" comes from the clothing you wear under the dry suit. If you are nude under the suit, you will still get hypothermic over time in cold water.

My daddy always told me when we went fishing, "You can always take it off, but you can never put it on." Meaning if you don't bring it with you, you can't use it.

Developing the perfect layering system is learned with experience. The water and air temperature will be factors (water temperature being more critical) aside from your natural body insulation and metabolism.

Your undergarments should be made from the new synthetic fibers or wool. These materials keep you warm if wet (due to perspiration or a leak) and they wick moisture to the outer layer so the Gore-Tex can do its job. Cotton feels good but "cotton kills" because it holds moisture next to your body. You lose more body heat trying to warm that wet cotton T-shirt. You should layer your undergarments so you can peel some off if you get too hot.

Instead of an entire dry suit, there are also "dry tops" for paddlers. These are typically combined with a wetsuit. Again, whether you get a dry suit or top, I highly recommend a breathable waterproof fabric such as Gore-Tex.

Wetsuit

Wetsuits are designed to reduce the speed at which you lose your body heat. A wetsuit is made of neoprene (closed-cell foam). It does not keep you warm, even though it feels that way at the beginning. A proper-fitting wetsuit needs to be form-fitting and close to the skin. It allows a thin layer of water in through openings at the neck, wrists, ankles, and zipper. You get an initial chill when you first capsize and the water comes in, but your body quickly heats that thin layer of water and then you feel warm. The thicker the suit, the more insulation it provides from the outside cold. Even though you feel warm, you are still losing body heat because you are constantly heating that water layer. Wetsuits are significantly less expensive than dry suits. A wetsuit also minimizes cold shock.

A full-body wetsuit will be the most efficient, but paddlers usually find them too restrictive on the arms because you end up fighting the fabric as you paddle. The paddlers who use wetsuits typically wear a pair of sleeveless Farmer Johns or Janes and synthetic layers for the rest of their protection. They finish it off with a waterproof jacket (paddle jacket) of coated nylon. Loose-fitting wetsuits defeat the purpose because they allow too much water to move in and out of your suit, which means you lose body heat more quickly.

My favorite wetsuit is my "shorty," which covers my body from thighs to upper arms. This is that critical area I mentioned. I love this suit when I am playing in the surf. Adding a long-sleeve or short-sleeve paddle jacket depends on the air temperature.

Tropical Wear

If you are paddling in tropical areas, hypothermia is not your greatest concern. Earlier when I mentioned maintaining core temperature, it also means not getting overheated. When I paddle along the Nā Pali Coast of Kaua'i, I wear a white silk shirt and sometimes silk leggings, which protect me from the UV rays. I also keep them wet if it is a hot day. The wet clothes keep me cool.

As a warning, long exposure to tropical waters can cause hypothermia if exposure is too long.

Your Head

You will need appropriate headgear. In cold weather you can lose more than half of your body heat through the top of your head. That is one of the reasons they say, "If your feet are cold, put on a hat."

If you are planning for repeated immersions in cold water (such as surfing), a neoprene hood can be worn under your helmet. In extremely cold weather, winter hats are recommended.

Numerous rain hats are available to the paddler, some even made out of Gore-Tex. Those same hats can also be used for sun protection. The traditional Sou'wester is still tops for torrential rain and can also be worn back-to-front if you feel the need for the large brim.

Hats with big brims are ideal for deflecting water when you are paddling head on into waves. Merely bend your head so the oncoming water is deflected away from your face. The wooden hats worn by the Aleuts when paddling were the classic solution to this face-stinging problem (see Photo 14.12, Chapter 14).

If you cherish your hat, you can attach it to your PFD with a short cord (with alligator clips) or use chinstraps. Most of the wide-brimmed hats come with chinstraps to keep them from flying off on windy days.

For surf, rock gardens, caves, tidal streams, and any other area that is harder than your head, you should wear a helmet designed for kayaking. In rough seas, a capsize recovery can cause significant head trauma if the kayak smashes the swimmer on the head. I have a few kayaking friends that paddle with a helmet all the time, just in case.

Your Feet

Your footwear needs to do double duty—thermal protection and injury protection to be exact. Aside from barnacles, today's shorelines can be littered with all kinds of debris. These sharp objects can cause serious damage, which could easily get infected. Paddling barefoot is a no-no.

Neoprene boots are the favorite choice for most paddlers. Some prefer neoprene socks with an outside water shoe that allows hiking. Tall rubber boots are favored by some Pacific Northwest paddlers because of the barnacle-covered shorelines. Paddlers get out of their kayaks in the shallows so they don't scrape their hulls on the barnacles, and the height of the boot is enough to keep their feet dry. I prefer neoprene boots that are mid-calf high and have a very sturdy sole for those types of shorelines.

In the tropics I use lightweight water shoes that cover the tops of my feet. Derek once burned the tops of his feet because he didn't use sunscreen with his sandals. Using a sit-on-top boat was new to him. His career was in a closed-cockpit boat in England, so sunburn to the tops of his feet was never even a thought. His feet swelled up and he had trouble walking for three days.

Your Hands

If your arms and body are warm, your hands will usually arrive at the same temperature after a short period of paddling. However, there are a number of ways in which you can prevent your digits from dropping off with the cold.

Try to keep your hands dry. Wet hands soon freeze in cold winds, but drip-rings on the paddle shaft will prevent water from dribbling down. Even wet hands can be kept warm by open-palm mitts made of neoprene. These are good because they still allow you to retain the "feel" of the shaft against your palm. In a cold wind I prefer loose-fitting pogies. In these your hands are cocooned inside a type of mitten that fits around the paddle shaft. You merely slide your hand inside and grip the shaft without any hindrance. I do not recommend pogies that fit tightly around the wrist; they will keep you no warmer, and there is always a problem in getting your hands in and out quickly.

There are also numerous styles of paddling gloves. Neoprene ones try to keep your hands warm. Fingered gloves provide warmth, but mittens and pogies seem to work better. Gloves are also used for UV protection or abrasion protection if you are around sharp rocks or in sea caves with barnacle-covered walls. I shredded my palms on the wall of my first sea cave. After that, I wore heavy rubberized gardening gloves when I played in the caves.

The only downside of full gloves is not being able to feel the indexing on your paddle shaft. That is why I prefer pogies to keep my hands warm.

Testing Your Clothes

The best way to see if your choice of clothing is appropriate for the conditions is to get in the water and test it. Have a partner close by on shore in case you need help. Let's say you typically paddle a half mile from the shoreline. Get into the water fully dressed, which means wearing what you will be wearing in your kayak (immersion clothing, spray skirt, and PFD). Swim at least a half mile, close to the shore, to simulate losing your kayak. If you want to do the paddle swim (discussed in Chapter 2), it is a good time to practice that too. After the swim, walk ashore and check to see if your clothing is performing as expected.

I also tell my students to do a full immersion at different times during their day trips. It lets you know if your clothing is appropriate for the immersion and still functions well for the rest of the trip. This is best done in a group situation. Of course, you will adjust your clothing, as needed, after your tests.

Dressing Game

One of the many articles I have written for my University of Sea Kayaking (USK) website is titled "The Dressing Game." I play the game every time I get on the water. Before I go, I check the forecast for the day. I know my float plan. I ask myself, "If I were to capsize in these waters, how long will I be in the water (the speed of my capsize recovery), and if I lost my kayak, how long will it take me to get to shore?" I dress accordingly. I always dress for my anticipated immersion time.

The difficult combination for the paddler is the hot, sunny day with cold water. In such a case, I dress for the water and take steps during the day to keep from overheating. The easiest way to do this is to use your hand pump and soak yourself as needed. Keeping a cotton cap wet on your head is a great regulator.

As you play this dressing game, you will be layering your clothes in different ways depending on the weather and water conditions. It is amazing how good a paddle jacket feels on a windy wet day. It keeps the wind and rain off of you and helps hold the heat in.

I keep a large plastic trash bag in my emergency kit in case someone is wet and cold and he

or she does not have a paddle jacket. Cut holes for the head and arms, and you have an emergency jacket.

Regardless of the clothing you choose, make sure you clean and dry it before storing it away. Salt water is not friendly to clothing or equipment. Well-maintained gear will last a long time.

Remember, your goal in the dressing game is to win, which means you can survive the elements to paddle another day.

It is perhaps of interest to mention that the Eskimos did not wear wetsuits, but then they didn't wear lifejackets either. The majority could not swim because there was nowhere for them to learn! They depended on their clothing and skill to survive in those harsh elements. Paddling was not a sport—it was a way of life and survival. They took it very seriously.

Standard Safety Equipment

PFD (Personal Flotation Device)

The thing to remember about a PFD (Photo 1.13) is that it will not turn and hold the body in the lean-back survival position, but rather hold it in an upright position, allowing the head to fall forward if it wants. A true lifejacket is designed to keep your head and face out of the water if you are unconscious. That being said, modern-day paddlers, if they wear a flotation device, will wear a PFD.

The primary purpose of a PFD is keeping your head above water, while you are conscious. Therefore, the fit is critical. It should be snug, but not restrictive. It needs to be adjustable for the different layers of clothing you will be wearing. When floating in the water, it should not ride up over your face. A secure waist strap, under the rib cage, will keep the PFD from riding up. You

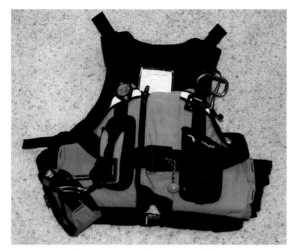

Photo 1.13 *My PFD has a quick-release cowtail with a mini towline attached to a carabiner. In my pockets I have my knife, whistle, stirrup, lip screen, and VHF radio. I also have nose clips attached by a lanyard that tucks on the inside after the PFD is zipped up. I have a water pouch on my back with a tube to the front for easy hydration. I also have a waterproof watch clipped on one shoulder strap and a carabiner on the other so I can attach my spray skirt loop to keep it out of the way.* WAYNE HORODOWICH

Figure 1.22 *Beware of badly fitting PFDs.*

should not fall out of it if you lift both arms, as in Figure 1.22. A proper-fitting PFD should not hinder your paddling motion.

We now require pockets to carry all the small items that have to be kept close at hand. It is obvious, therefore, that lots of pockets of varying sizes are desirable, and indeed many manufacturers supply extra pockets that can be added to the original garment. Knives can also be carried in pockets, although most PFDs now have some kind of external fastener fitted on the front of the vest, which can hold the sheath of a quick-release knife. A large rear pocket can be used to carry just about anything.

Additional features that I look for in my PFD are reflective patches, a quick-release belt with cowtail (used for towing), zip and buckle pockets, and easy adjustability. Since dehydration is common among paddlers, having my hydration system in the large back pocket is a necessity. The tube feeds out to the front of my PFD so water is easily available.

Now that we have lots of pockets in PFDs, there are some safety issues worth mentioning. If you are into kayak fishing, don't fill the pockets with too much lead shot because you will become the sinker. The other concern is that protruding objects (VHF antennas or knives) could snag on deck lines when you're trying to reenter the kayak while climbing on the back deck.

You should have a whistle attached somewhere on your PFD, but not on the zipper. It could pull your zipper open if it gets snagged.

Since your PFD is there to possibly save your life, keeping it in good condition is in your best interest. Store it clean (freshwater rinse) and dry. Keep it out of the UV when not in use. Do not use it as a seat. The only exception is if you are in a lightning storm and you need to insulate yourself from the ground. Stand on it and crouch down.

Whether or not you are required by law to wear a flotation device should not even be a consideration. If you are on the water, in your kayak, you are wearing a PFD. This is not only for your own sake, but also for your family and rescue personal who have to go looking for you. This is terrible to say, but in the event you do drown, you will still be floating to be found. It reduces the time spent by rescue personnel risking their lives, and it brings closure to your family.

Here, in his own words, is why Derek felt so strongly about wearing a PFD:

I was carried from the sea one cold Sunday in December 1966 while training a group of lifeguards in surf techniques. I "drowned" into unconsciousness over a period of about 15 minutes out in the surf. Exhausted, breathless, and confused, I was prevented from turning my head to one side to vomit by the same lifejacket that kept bringing me to the surface in the huge tumbling storm waves. By the time I used my failing energy to twist sideways, clear my blocked throat, and suck another breath, the next wave sent me choking underneath. I must have blacked out several times until I awoke, after resuscitation, standing against a wet wall, I thought. It was no wall, but the sand by the water's edge where I had been dragged after being taken from the water.

Paddle Float

A paddle float is a flotation device that you can attach to the end of your paddle, over the blade, which turns your paddle into an outrigger if held perpendicular to your kayak (Figure 2.19, Chapter 2). These floats can be inflatable or solid foam. The design and features of paddle floats have improved over the years. As with all pieces of equipment, there are pros and cons to different features.

Inflatable floats take up less deck storage space when not in use. Since it is inflatable one could puncture it, which makes it useless. Inflatable floats usually provide more buoyancy than the commercial foam floats.

The features I look for in inflatable floats are dual chambers (rare for both chambers to get damaged), valves that inflate and deflate quickly, one-hand operation on the valves, and a security strap to hold the float to the paddle shaft. Having reflective tape on the float is a great idea.

Foam floats are ready to use without the need to inflate them, which reduces your immersion time. They do take up space on the deck of your kayak. Again, they are less buoyant than the inflatable floats. I have heard large paddlers say they don't give them enough support.

Regardless of which float you choose, never leave home without it. The paddle float and pump are absolute essentials for every paddler. As you will read in the next chapter, if you cannot roll a kayak, the most reliable solo recovery requires a paddle float. Those in tandem kayaks should carry a separate pump and float for each paddler.

Sea Wings, or Sponsons

These are two cigar-shaped floatation bags that are secured, via straps and buckles, to the outside of your cockpit, thus increasing the beam of your kayak (Photo 2.19, Chapter 2). They give support in both directions, unlike the paddle float, which only provides stability in one direction. These floats are orally inflated. Even though they are a good product with many positive features, they never caught on in the paddling community.

Hand Pump

Pumps were discussed earlier in this chapter. Again, even if you have a deck-mounted or an electric pump, you should also carry a simple hand pump with a float collar on it. Most sea kayakers today just use these portable hand pumps. Pumps are mentioned again because they are a part of standard sea kayaking equipment.

Stirrup

A kayak stirrup is a sling that provides a step into the cockpit, just like the saddle stirrup used by a rider when mounting a horse. Some people simply do not have the necessary strength in their upper body or arms to haul themselves back into the cockpit from a swimming position at water level. If the swimmer has this difficulty, the stirrup reentry should solve the problem. Photo 1.14 is an example of an adjustable stirrup that folds nicely when not in use, so it can be stored in a PFD pocket for easy access when needed.

Photo 1.14
Adjustable stirrup
WAYNE HORODOWICH

Whistle

Every PFD should have a whistle attached. Mine is attached with a short string and kept in my pocket. Since a whistle will carry a lot farther than your voice, it is a great safety device for such a little cost. A plastic whistle without the little pea inside is recommended. A favorite of paddlers is the Fox 40. Some paddlers are passionate about their whistles. Do your own tests.

A word of caution is needed here: Just because you have a whistle do not believe everyone will hear you. Once on the return leg from a buoy off Martha's Vineyard, my group split, as many groups do. Those in the lead were about 200 to 300 yards ahead. We had a headwind, and I wanted to show the group the limitations of whistles. Those of us in the rear blew our whistles to get their attention. None of the paddlers in the front group turned around. During our debriefing, there was a lot of discussion about whistles, staying together, and always keeping the entire group in visual distance.

Knife

A knife on the outside of a PFD is the norm, especially for whitewater boaters. The history of the knife attached to a PFD goes back to whitewater raft guides. They needed it, immediately ready, in case participants got tangled in ropes or straps in fast-moving water. I also admit it looks cool to have a knife displayed on your PFD. It makes you feel like you are in Special Forces.

However, in sea kayaking I can say with 100 percent conviction that a knife on the PFD causes more problems than it helps. I cannot count the number of times I have seen a PFD-mounted knife inhibit a paddler when they tried to climb onto their kayak after capsizing, but I have yet to hear a story from a sea kayaker where they needed their knife so accessible.

The need for a combat-ready knife is rare in sea kayaking, but a folding knife in a PFD pocket is perfect for sea kayakers. I also have an elastic loop at the end so it can slide over my hand and stay on my wrist if it slipped out of my hands. Since salt corrodes, clean your knife regularly.

Nose Clips

When you flip over in your kayak, water can go up your nose. You can keep water from entering if you learn to slowly exhale from your nose. Unless you plan to wear your nose clips all the time, they cannot help you if you capsize. They are comforting when you practice rolls or certain wet reentry recoveries. However, if your roll depends on wearing nose clips, it is not a reliable roll.

The best purpose for nose clips is for any planned immersion because of the general absence of water quality in most paddling locations. There are a few capsize recovery techniques that have the paddler intentionally going underwater. That is when I use my nose clips. It keeps bad water out and increases breath-holding time. My nose clips are attached to my PFD, tucked away but easily accessible.

Sunglasses and Sunscreen

Paddling directly into the sun not only affects your view ahead, it can also give you a severe headache and long-term eye damage. Even if not directly facing the sun, the reflective quality of water makes the day even brighter. Get good sunglasses and keep them on a lanyard so they don't get lost if you capsize. There are even some good floating ones on the market.

Native paddlers used a solid, filled-in type of eye shield with thin slits cut out for each eye, allowing only a limited amount of sunlight to enter.

The use of strong sunscreen is highly recommended. Skin cancer is real, and sun exposure is greater on the open water. Don't forget the tops of your hands and your feet if they are exposed. Manufacturers recommend keeping sunscreen off of the latex gaskets on dry suits.

Watch

Having a reliable waterproof watch is important for many reasons. Knowing your pace, timing the tides and currents, checking your itinerary, monitoring your heart rate (for training and first aid), and using it as an alarm when needed are just a few of the reasons you should have one. If you are a trip guide or an instructor, it is an invaluable tool.

Personal Tow Belt

There are many reasons for carrying a tow belt (Photo 1.15). How and when to use them will be discussed in Chapters 12 (Rescue Procedures) and 13 (Touring and Trips). Following are the features one should look for when purchasing a personal tow belt.

The most important feature is a quick-release buckle, which allows you to easily disconnect yourself from being dragged. This feature also allows you to pass the tow belt to another paddler if you get tired of towing. Many release buckles have a small ball attached to the buckle for easier access.

A clip that is not notched allows easier disconnects after it is attached to another kayak. Stainless steel clips are less likely to corrode, but rinse them after each use. Having a small float near the clip is useful.

Photo 1.15 *Quick-release tow belt*
WAYNE HORODOWICH

A small section of shock cord integrated into the towline reduces the jerking action on your body when you are towing someone.

Having at least 50 feet of (sturdy) floating line is good if you are towing in large following seas. Too short of a towline can cause the kayak behind you to surf into your kidneys. In some very large swells in Hawaii, I had to connect two towlines to keep this from happening.

The line needs to be easily accessible and easy to re-stow, especially in rough-water conditions, where you are more likely to need to tow another due to the wind.

The vast majority of tow belts I presently see on the market have most of these features. My favorite is the Dynamic Tow Line from North Water. It has all of the features I look for in a tow belt.

Compass

If you are paddling familiar waters along the shoreline, you probably will never need a compass, right? I wish I could agree with you, but I have been in such thick fog that everything beyond 10 feet from the end of my kayak was white. The scary part was that the fog enhanced the sound of the fishing boats around me, so it sounded like they were going to run me over.

Fog does not suddenly appear, nor does nightfall. You do have a little bit of time to take a reading (heading) before you are engulfed in gray or black. That is why you want to carry at least one compass with you when you head out on the water. I carry two, one deck-mounted and the other a handheld orienteering compass (Photo 1.16).

In the case I mentioned above, you would use your compass to take your heading to your destination while you can see it, then follow the compass to that destination. Of course, you need to know how to use the compass in order to do this.

The advantage of a deck-mounted compass is that you can see it as you look forward, which makes it more efficient and reduces the chance of getting seasick from looking down at a handheld compass. I always have a handheld compass in my "essentials" dry bag, which stays behind my seat.

Your compasses need to be waterproof. A deck-mounted one needs to be easily seen and have luminous markings that will glow after shining a flashlight on it for night paddling.

Additional Recommended Items

Dry Bags and Containers

As I mentioned earlier, waterproof and watertight are concepts when sea kayaking. Dry bags and watertight containers are designed to keep the contents dry. Ninety-nine percent of the time they do a good job, but sometimes water seems to find its way in—not flooding in, just a little seepage.

Since we carry all kinds of equipment with us, especially when camping, we need a variety of dry bags to meet our needs. Since kayak hatches are small and the compartments are long and narrow, several smaller bags make storing the bags easier. You can also make better use of the space with a few smaller bags compared to one big one.

The key to any of these bags or containers is sealing them properly. Take your time to seal them well. Make sure you clean sand from all seams needed for sealing. There are two givens in sea kayaking: water and sand.

When I day paddle, I have a few different dry bags for specific necessities. These are my bailout bag, first-aid kit bag, repair kit bag, essentials bag, and a bag for lunch or snacks. Camping adds bags for the following: sleeping bag, sleeping pad, tent, clothing, chart case, food, books, tarps, cooking kit, hammock, and miscellanies.

Bailout Bag

This bag contains the items you would want to have with you if you found yourself in the water and the kayak was blown away from you. You grab it as you are wet exiting or just before. Think about what you would want to have with you

Photo 1.16 *Deck compass and handheld orienteering compass* WAYNE HORODOWICH

Some deck-mounted compasses are attached (almost permanently) in a deck fitting. Mine is attached with a bungee cord to my deck lines; this way I can remove it when carrying and storing my kayak.

Even though this book has a chapter on navigation (Chapter 11), how to use a compass and a chart are skills you need to learn if you want to expand your adventures.

if you were floating alone in the water, hoping you will get rescued. My signaling devices would be at the top of my list. I also include a snack bar. I have a water pouch attached to my PFD so there is no water in my bailout bag. There are also matches and a space blanket included if I do make it to shore.

First-Aid Kit Bag

Any outdoor pursuit has the potential for injury, and these can range from minor to severe. I am not going to tell you what to put into your first-aid kit. There are excellent kits sold in outdoor equipment stores that will have basic needs covered. As your experience increases, you will add and subtract items from your kit. I also implore you to take a Wilderness First Responder course if you venture far from immediate help. Then you will make your own kit.

You and your basic kit need to be able to deal with cuts, scrapes, burns, punctures, infections, bites, allergies, nausea, sprains, blisters, dislocations, and breaks. You shold also learn CPR.

Repair Kit Bag

The minimum repair kit has been said to be a roll of wide, waterproof, self-adhesive tape for patching the kayak. However, it is foolhardy to go to sea with the minimum amount of equipment: Consider some of the things you may have to do either for yourself or for some other unfortunate paddler. Aside from a hole in your kayak, you may need to fix a spray skirt, hole in a float bag, broken paddle, broken rudder or skeg, stove malfunction, broken seat, broken zippers, and torn booties, to name a few.

My kit contains tape, a Leatherman (utility knife with pliers and wire cutters), bailing wire, cord/rope, waterproof matches, hose clamps,

and a patch kit. This has suited me well for thirty years of leading trips. Other items get added for different trips to varied locations.

Essentials Bag

I keep this bag behind my cockpit. It is filled with items I have needed during my time teaching and guiding. It includes a snack bar, wind meter, compass, extra whistle, headlamp, Swiss Army knife, space blanket, large trash bag, extra nose clips and sunglasses straps, money, rescue mirror, glow sticks, bandana, water purifier pen, and two Smurf kayakers as teaching tools.

Liquid and Food

By the time your brain tells you that you are thirsty, you are already dehydrated. One of the main reasons paddlers get dehydrated is difficult access to their water supply. That is why a water bladder stored in your PFD is so useful: The water hose is kept right near your mouth for easy access. Drink regularly because most kayak clothing causes the paddler to sweat inside aside from exertion.

In addition to water, food is important during the day. You want to fuel that engine. Since diet is such a personal choice, all I can say is you need to eat if you want energy for paddling.

As for comfort food, a nonbreakable thermos of hot chocolate and a PB&J sandwich is unbeatable, especially on a cold, rainy day.

Kayak Wheels

Folding kayak wheels are worth their weight in gold. I know my four herniated discs were partially a result of carrying kayaks. Now I use my wheels whenever possible.

During my last solo trip out of Telegraph Cove on Vancouver Island, BC, I loaded my

PEE AT SEA

What goes in must come out. Sooner or later you are going to have to pee at sea. For either sex, the clothing you are wearing will be your biggest restriction. After gaining access, it is easier for a male than a female because males have a hose. Not to fear, ladies—the FUD has solved that problem.

Photo 1.17 *FUD* WAYNE HORODOWICH

The FUD (female urinary device) is anatomically friendly to females. Put it in place and you will be able to write your name in the snow, just like the guys. Seriously, it does work with some practice. Sitting on your back deck is required; therefore, your partner is stabilizing your kayak. There are numerous FUD models out there. Most of the female paddlers that I know prefer the Freshette (Photo 1.17).

As for solid waste elimination at sea, I had to deal with this only one time on a long crossing. Rafting the kayaks together and hanging my buns over the paddles, spanning both kayaks, I took care of business. The water surging up between the boats provided a very cold bidet. Normally, solid waste relief occurs when we are on shore.

Whether male or female, dispose of your urine or solid waste in an environmentally sound manner.

---

kayak next to my van and then rolled it down to the boat ramp and gently slid it into the water. I repeated the process on my return. The fully loaded kayak probably weighed about 120 pounds (it was a weeklong trip). When I got to my camping areas, I used small driftwood logs, spaced over the barnacle-covered rocks, to slide my boat up to the high-tide line (Photo 13.2, Chapter 13). I repeated the process when leaving.

Rinse and maintain your kayak wheels if they are used around salt water.

Communication and Signaling

There are numerous ways to communicate with your paddling partners and to the rest of the world. Right now I want to focus on contacting the outside world. Mostly due to good planning and I am sure a little luck, I have never had to call for a rescue. My regular contact with the outside world was listening to NOAA weather forecasts and whale sightings. However, if an emergency arises and you need to contact help, let's review your options. I already mentioned carrying a whistle, headlamp, rescue mirror, and glow sticks in my different kits.

VHF Radios

When the first edition of this book went into print, those who ventured onto Britain's coastal waters did so warm in the knowledge that there were manned coastguard stations placed at regular intervals around the shores. Because of this, any parachute flare directed heavenwards had a good chance of being seen firsthand by some sharp-eyed coastguard. Unhappily, this is no longer the case. Visual watch has given way to a different system. Monitoring is now done on VHF radio distress frequencies; i.e., channel 16 (Figure 1.23).

In those early days when sea kayaking was really beginning to develop, many considered it a heresy to carry a VHF radio in a sea kayak. Even now there are those who would argue that this equipment detracts from the sense of freedom and self-sufficiency that is the essence of the sport.

The size and reliability of VHF radios for kayakers have come a long way since Derek wrote that first book. To venture far from shore without one is not prudent. The sea is very dynamic. When Mother Nature and King Neptune get into a tiff, you will wish you had a radio.

There are numerous models from which to choose. Size, range, and waterproofness are your biggest concerns. As I said, I use mine most of the time for the latest marine weather forecast. Get a radio and learn how to properly use it. I will add, with the aid of a GPS unit (discussed later), you will be able to give the rescue vessel your exact location.

Figure 1.23 *VHF radio*

Cellphones

Now that cellphone towers are finding their way into many remote areas, the use of a cellphone for emergencies is not unreasonable depending on where you paddle. Your biggest concern is keeping it waterproof, which is not difficult given the many waterproof cases on the market.

Many years ago I heard of a windsurfer outside of the Golden Gate calling in for a rescue after his boom had broken. He thought he was heading to Japan. The 911 dispatcher eventually patched him into the coast guard rescue helicopter and he directed the chopper to him as he saw them approaching. His cellphone was in a ziplock baggie in his fanny pack.

Flares

After the VHF radio, your next line of defense is a flare. Flares are visual signals, so they work only if someone happens to be looking where you set them off. Therefore, the brighter the flare and the longer they are aloft, the better. Needless to say, all flares are more easily seen at night. However, most of us are out during the day. After seriously testing flares for my *Rescue Procedures* video, I have a definite opinion as what I want with me with the hopes of being seen.

When we shot off the flares 1 mile offshore, on an overcast day, here is what we learned: Pencil flares were not seen; one of the three misfired. The ones from the flare guns were barely visible, but very easy to use and reload. The $40 parachute flares were great. The handheld smoke flares were also great. Orange smokes shows better when there are whitecaps.

During the demonstration there were folks walking along the beach, and they never saw any of the flares because they weren't looking out to sea. The local Harbor Patrol only received two calls during the full hour of testing the flares.

Given the locations I paddle, I take the flare gun for use if I see boat traffic or I am near shore. In addition, I have three handheld smoke flares, each lasting at least a minute, which helps their being seen. I am not inclined to carry parachute flares due to the cost.

All flares have expiration dates. Follow local regulations regarding proper disposal, and don't just set them off. That is when they will be seen and rescue personal may risk their lives looking for a victim that is not there.

Strobe Lights and Lasers
If you need to be spotted at night, a strobe light is an excellent option. The strobe is a great visual signal, but only if they are looking for you. There are also some laser lights that send a beam high into the sky.

Radar Reflectors
Speaking of being seen, if you intend to do a lot of paddling in busy shipping lanes, a radar reflector mounted on your rear deck may be a good idea (see Photo 13.1, Chapter 13). Since kayaks are so close to the water, a reflector might not be picked up by radar, but it can't hurt.

Emergency Position-Indicating Radio Beacon (EPIRB) and Personal Locator Beacon (PLB)
Your last line of defense is the radio beacon (Figure 1.24). When you feel that all is lost and the shadow of the Grim Reaper falls across your foredeck (or upturned hull!), all you need to do is to pull the pin on your little box. The radio beacon housed therein will immediately start to transmit your position via satellite. The satellite

Figure 1.24 *EPIRB*

can determine your position within 3 miles. GPS-enabled EPIRBs have positional accuracy of +/- 50 meters. EPIRBs are registered to a specific vessel, while PLBs are registered to a specific individual. Some EPIRBs are equipped with a strobe light for visual location.

Once that pin is pulled, you cannot recall the cavalry. These devices should be used only in life-threatening situations. They are recommended for remote expedition locations, such as Ed Gillette's solo kayak journey from Monterey, California, to Hawaii. Since they cost over $600, depending on the model and features, they are not standard equipment for the typical sea kayaker.

Global Positioning System (GPS)
With 60 miles of open sea behind him and 40 miles of haze in front, Derek declared with some feeling, "I wish I had a little magic box so that I could just press a button and we'd know exactly where we were!" That was in 1975.

Well, it had to happen and the little box has arrived. For those long, open crossings or trips along wilderness coastlines, there is now a small, handheld, battery-operated piece of electronics that will pinpoint your position on land or sea to within a few yards.

GPS works in conjunction with a number of satellites that circle around the earth. These satellites send out signals, which are picked up by your little receiver (Photo 1.18). As long as your GPS receives the signals, it can give you your longitude and latitude.

GPS units, like all electronics, get more sophisticated as time goes on. Your new model will probably be improved the next year. The greatest safety feature of the GPS is providing you your exact location if you need to call for help on your VHF radio or your cellphone. Unlike the EPIRB, which send location automatically to the rescue channels, you need to read and report the GPS info.

Newer GPS models have some wonderful features that are helpful when paddling. You can store and retrieve information while paddling, mark waypoints, calculate speed and distance paddled, see your actual course, and display your heading and many other useful items. Waterproof models are available.

Emergency communication equipment should be carried where it can be reached in a hurry. If you are concerned about the reliability of these electronic devices being waterproof, you can always put them in special waterproof bags made specifically for such devices. Remember, equipment only works if you maintain it.

It is up to you to choose which of these communication devices will best fit your needs given your float plan, experience, and paddling location. I personally believe you have the right to challenge yourself as you see fit. However, by

Photo 1.18
GPS unit
WAYNE HORODOWICH

doing so, I do not believe you have the automatic right to be rescued. Men and women put their lives at risk when they go out looking for someone in trouble. If you casually engage in high-risk activities in remote locations, believing help will get to you if you pull this pin, you shouldn't be there.

Any trip should be approached with sound judgment, which means you are well trained, well equipped, well planned, and capable of completing the trip in the worst possible weather. You should undertake your adventures with the knowledge that you are on your own (or in a group) and must deal with whatever comes along without any outside help. These rescue-signaling devices are meant for responsible users with the sound judgment I mentioned above.

CHAPTER 2
CAPSIZE RECOVERIES

Of all the skills to learn in sea kayaking, capsize recoveries are the most important. If you cannot get back into your kayak and back to shore, death due to exposure becomes very real. This is not meant to scare you. It is meant to warn you. While strokes are important, you don't die from paddling improperly. You may get overuse injuries, but they are not fatal. I feel so strongly about this that Volumes 1 and 2 in my sea kayaking Instructional Video Series are *Capsize Recoveries* and *Rescue Procedures*. *Essential Strokes* didn't come until Volume 6 because I prioritized the subjects with safety in mind.

When Derek wrote his first book on sea kayaking, the term *rescue* was used whenever you assisted another paddler if they capsized. Back then the term was appropriate because the risk of exposure to cold water was real due to poor immersion clothing. It was not only inadequate clothing that was a concern. In the 1960s the typical sea kayak did not have bulkheads, so a capsized kayak had a real possibility of completely flooding and sinking into the depths. Getting to a capsized paddler was vital.

Derek once told me a story about one of his capsizes in the surf. After he finally got to shore, he described the scene as he carried his kayak to the car. He said he was shaking and shivering because his immersion clothing consisted of a woolen jumpsuit. Anyone who has worn a wool sweater that is soaking wet knows what happens to the size of the garment. Derek said the legs on his jumpsuit dragged 6 feet behind him and the crotch was down about mid-calf as he slogged up the beach. He added he was walking like a penguin and the friction of the wet garment on the sand did not help.

Almost all of the current capsize recovery techniques used today were originally developed with different needs in mind. Many of the kayaks used when Derek wrote the first book were homemade. They did not have watertight hatches, bulkheads, deck lines, or end toggles. When a paddler capsized, the kayak had to be kept upside down because it kept the air trapped in the kayak. If you tried to turn the kayak upright, too much air could escape and the kayak could sink. Kayaking back then had much higher risks due to the equipment being used at the time.

Due to the improvements in equipment (kayaks and immersion clothing), a typical capsize does not have the urgency as in early days, unless there is an extenuating circumstance. With that in mind, I began using the phrase *capsize recovery* in my first instructional video in 1991 when discussing the techniques used in righting yourself and your kayak or when you assist another paddler towards that same goal. Since then there has been a shift in the use of the terms *rescue* and *capsize recovery*. As you will read later in the book, the term *rescue* is used when the safety and well-being of the paddler is at risk (see Chapter 12).

The best comparison I can make to illustrate the difference between the two is in the sport of skiing. When a skier falls down and is not injured or hanging off of a cliff, they just get up, brush off the snow, adjust their equipment, and continue skiing. The same is true for the sea kayaker. If they capsize they do the appropriate capsize recovery, shed the water, adjust their equipment, and continue paddling. However, if the skier falls and gets injured and they need the help of the ski patrol because they cannot continue, then it is a rescue. The same goes for the paddler. If a paddler cannot get back into their kayak and/or they are injured, it becomes a rescue.

Capsizing

In kayaking it's not *if* you capsize, it's *when* you capsize. Capsizing is part of kayaking, especially when you are learning the sport. An attitude I have regularly seen among paddlers is the "I do not want to capsize" attitude. When you are in a boat and sitting out of the water, it is natural to feel you are up here "high and dry" and you do not want to be there "under and wet." While this feeling makes perfect sense, it also leads to apprehension, which can cause you to tense your body. Any instructor will tell you the more you tense up your body, the more likely you are to capsize. The more relaxed you are and allow the kayak to move with the motion of the water, the greater chance you have for staying upright.

I try to teach my students that a capsize is no big deal because the more comfortable a paddler is with their capsize recovery techniques, the more relaxed they will be in their kayak. In fact, I tell my students, "Kayaking is a wet sport." This is completely opposite of what Derek told his students, which is, "Kayaking is a dry sport." Derek and I finally came to realize that we both had the same goal in mind, which was having the student upright and relaxed in their kayak regardless of the conditions. We just approached the challenge differently.

Derek's "dry sport" reference was what he wanted for his students: Develop your skills so you never capsize. I believe looking forward to a capsize or believing capsizing is fun (wet sport) will develop the paddler's skills through relaxation and greater confidence. Kayaking will then end up being a dry sport. A different approach with the same goal.

Capsize Recovery Goals

You should always have a reason for what you are doing. It is wise to have a prioritized list of steps to follow that will get you to your goals. My capsize recovery goals are:

1. Minimize my exposure to the elements by dressing for immersion and/or by getting out of the water as quickly as possible.

2. Finish upright with a seaworthy kayak. This means water out of my kayak, spray skirt attached to the coaming, and all gear re-stowed.

3. I am seaworthy, which means I am ready to continue paddling, physically and mentally. This may require a rest period, a change of garments, or a snack to fuel the internal engine.

4. Stay upright if I am helping another kayaker recover from a capsize. Aside from maintaining my balance, I need to approach the victim quickly, but cautiously. A panicked victim can be dangerous.

As we review the numerous capsize recovery techniques, we will be referring to these goals.

Components of a Capsize Recovery

Standard capsize recovery techniques are taught in basic sea kayaking classes. Although I will present them here, I prefer to first discuss the components one needs to do all of the possible techniques. If you learn how to perform the following components, you will be able put them together to best meet your needs given the conditions, your equipment, and your abilities.

If you stay in your kayak after a capsize, you need to find a way to get upright. If you cannot, you will need to exit your kayak. Once a paddler exits their kayak, they need to get back in the kayak and get the water out. These components address the many ways to accomplish that.

Emptying Water

Getting the water out is not necessary if you stay in your kayak after capsizing. If you do get out of your kayak, emptying water is not required but is strongly recommended. An experienced paddler can still paddle a kayak that is full of water; however, the stability of that flooded kayak is marginal at best, especially in choppy seas.

If you empty the water, not only will you be more stable, but you also will travel faster and have a greater chance of staying upright. Keep in mind, since you already capsized once in these conditions (when your kayak was not flooded), it is going to be more difficult to stay upright if you try paddling with a flooded boat.

The two main ways of getting water out of a kayak are either pumping it out or lifting one end while the kayak is upside down and letting the water drain out from the cockpit. There are hand pumps, deck-mounted pumps, and electric pumps, and all of these pumps will do the job. If you choose to pump, you must get back into your kayak first and then pump out the water.

If you plan to drain the water by lifting the kayak, the water needs to be out of the kayak before you reenter the cockpit. If you and your partner do not have a pump, draining by lifting will be your only option.

Most of the draining methods are named for the configuration of the kayaks while draining. It is a good idea to know a few different draining techniques even though you will most likely find a favorite that will work in most, if not all, conditions, locations, and circumstances.

Keep in mind that the paddler who wet-exited is most likely floating in the water (wearing their PFD, of course) and being exposed to the elements. Remember goal number one: Minimize exposure to the elements. The swimming paddler should be dressed appropriately for the water temperature and needs to get back into their kayak as quickly as possible.

If there are no bulkheads in the flooded kayak, the only way to get the water out of it is with a seesaw action over a base of support. Remember, at 8 pounds per gallon of water, a fully flooded sea kayak is extremely heavy.

More than one person may be required to help with the lifting. Remember, kayaks get even heavier if they are packed for an expedition. If you press down on the stern of the kayak, the bow will lift, which can be helpful. The swimmer can do that while you lift and guide the bow.

One must be careful when draining a kayak without bulkheads and/or float bags, because you can also drain the trapped air inside (letting it escape), which can cause a boat to sink if not done properly.

A sea kayak with fore and aft bulkheads is easily drained. In fact, a swimmer can sometimes lift the bow of his overturned kayak while he treads water, rests on his paddle float, or uses some other stable object to keep himself from going under in order to drain water. He can even go over to the stern and jump on the back to drain the water and roll it upright before it scoops water by the cockpit. Breaking the seal created between the cockpit and the water is the difficult part.

Reentering the Kayak

There are different ways to reenter your kayak. When you are ready to reenter, you can decide which of these reentry methods will work best for the conditions around you and the equipment you are using. Some kayaks allow easier access than others with these different methods. You should practice them all to find the ones that work best for you.

Side reentry is the one most commonly used. You slide onto the deck behind your cockpit

coaming by grabbing the coaming with one hand and the back deck with the other. When ready, kick your feet to the surface and press down with your hands, and try to launch yourself onto the back deck (Photo 2.1). Once on the back deck, you stay face down as you put the foot closest to the bow into the cockpit, and then move your body parallel to your kayak as you put your other foot into the cockpit. After both feet are in the cockpit, you slide down into the cockpit while rotating your body so you end up sitting upright in your seat. As you rotate, keep looking towards your support, which is either the person assisting you or your paddle float. The closer you keep your body to the deck (lower center of gravity), the less work there is for your partner and less chance of flipping over.

Between the kayaks reentry is done feet first while using both decks for support. The swimmer comes between his kayak and the assisting boat. He places his hands on the apex of both decks (his afterdeck and the other's foredeck). The head is thrown back level with the

Photo 2.1 *Side reentry* WAYNE HORODOWICH

Photo 2.2 *Between the kayaks reentry*
WAYNE HORODOWICH

water, the legs are hooked into the cockpit, and entry is accomplished by pressing down with the arms to help get his behind over the cockpit coaming (Photo 2.2). He then slides into the cockpit. If the seas are extremely rough, you will need to decide if you want to be between the kayaks, which are being banged together. This should not be attempted in a surf zone.

Leg hook reentry, aka the knee hook, is when you hook your leg over the cockpit coaming and essentially wedge and roll your body up into the cockpit. As you face your cockpit, hook the leg that is nearest the bow over the cockpit coaming (Photo 2.3). This is not recommended for kayaks with high freeboards. When ready, reach across the coaming with the same hand as the hooked leg. By using the hooked leg and pulling with your arm, you should be able to lift yourself out of the water and roll into your cockpit. As you rotate up, slide your other leg into the cockpit.

Cowboy reentry has you sliding up along the rear deck while straddling the kayak. (It is difficult to do if you have a rudder.) Some paddlers find it easier to climb onto the back deck because the stern of the kayak is often easier to submerge, which allows you to throw a leg over the boat. With your legs straddling the kayak, you work your way towards the front of your cockpit (Photo 2.4). Trying to straddle a wide boat with short legs is extremely difficult. When you are far enough forward (depends on cockpit size and butt size), you quickly sit back into your seat by bringing your knees up towards your chest. Once

Photo 2.3 *Leg hook reentry* WAYNE HORODOWICH

Photo 2.4 *Cowboy reentry* WAYNE HORODOWICH

in the seat, you can bring your legs in. This is the primary reentry method employed during the "scramble" recovery discussed later. To keep your spray skirt from getting caught underneath your body while you move towards the cockpit, hold the grab loop of the skirt in your teeth to get it out of the way. I personally have a carabiner on my PFD, which allows me to clip my spray skirt loop so the skirt stays out of the way and keeps my dentures from taking a swim.

Stirrup reentry utilizes a sling, which provides a step for those people who simply do not have the necessary strength in their upper body or arms to haul themselves back into the cockpit when they are in the water.

There are many ways to use a stirrup. The most reliable and quickest method has the assisting paddler stabilizing the kayak and then looping the stirrup around the cockpit coaming. The remainder of the stirrup goes down in the water near the swimmer by the side of the cockpit. (Using a quickly adjustable stirrup allows easy adjustment for different leg lengths.) The swimmer faces the cockpit and puts the foot nearer

the stern of their kayak into the stirrup. While grabbing the front and rear of the coaming, the swimmer steps down with their foot and pulls with their arms to stand up and then fall face down onto the back deck (Photo 2.5). The foot nearest the bow is free to slip into the cockpit. The stirrup is then kicked away from the foot before the leg is brought into the cockpit. As in the side reentry method, you slide down and

Photo 2.5 *Stirrup reentry* WAYNE HORODOWICH

rotate (looking at your support) until you are sitting upright in your seat. Then remove the stirrup from the coaming and re-stow it for future use.

I have included two other examples, Figure 2.1 and Figure 2.2, of how stirrups had been used in years past. These are methods Derek developed along with his own homemade stirrups. While these do work, they take time to set up and the stress on the paddles is not recommended for

Figure 2.1 *Stirrup anchors no longer used*

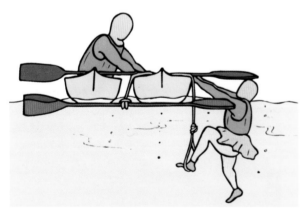

Figure 2.2 *Stirrup-assisted reentry, which is no longer used*

today's lightweight paddles. In addition, looping the stirrup around your torso can be dangerous.

Wet reentry has you getting back into your cockpit while the boat is still upside down. It is the least physical of all reentries, but you do have to hold your breath. This is a perfect time for using nose clips.

You start by the cockpit, facing the bow of your kayak. While resting back on your PFD, slide the leg closest to the kayak into the overturned kayak. (As a side note, this is a great hands-free way to keep hold of your kayak. I use this technique often when I am using both hands to put my paddle float on my paddle. This is when I put on my nose clips.) Now slide your second leg into the cockpit and then slide your body farther into the cockpit. Your head is still above water. When ready, take a normal breath, lift the cockpit with your inside hand on the coaming, and reach your outside hand under the water to grab the opposite side of the coaming (Photo 2.6). As you do this, you are rotating your body so you can sit in your seat. You need to pull yourself into the seat and then place your feet on the correct foot pedals and your knees under the coaming. Your goal is to be sitting in your seat as securely as when your kayak is upright. This should not take more than 10 seconds after your head goes under the water. (With practice, you will be able to do it in 5 seconds.) You then reach for some outside support to roll your kayak upright before you pump out the water.

Since you are weightless in the water, this really takes a lot less energy than climbing out of the water onto the deck of your kayak. Some energy is used for pumping, but not too much if you have bulkheads in your kayak. If another boater is assisting, you will have two pumps

Photo 2.6 *Wet reentry* WAYNE HORODOWICH

working. If a third boater wants to come on the free side, they too can join the pump party. Since you were in the water, pumping can help warm you if you are chilled.

As we review the different capsize recovery methods, keep in mind you may be able to use one of the other reentry techniques mentioned above instead of the one being shown.

Wet Exit

The wet exit is typically one of the first skills on the instructor's agenda. He or she wants students to feel confident they can exit the kayak and come to the surface. The instructor also wants to see that students don't panic and shares the same sigh of relief when their head comes to the surface. Some students have a fear of entrapment before trying their first wet exit. Once a kayak is completely over, it takes energy to stay in the cockpit. Students often remark, "I just fell out of my kayak."

It is my belief, however, that by teaching the wet exit first, instructors are inadvertently instilling a subliminal message that a capsize automatically means getting out of your kayak. As we will see later, there are other alternatives. The wet exit need not be the first option after you find yourself upside down in your kayak.

Preparing for Your First Wet Exit

For your first attempt, choose a piece of calm, sheltered water and enlist a friend for moral support, unless you are lucky enough to practice this in a swimming pool (which is highly recommended). You should always wear some kind of flotation device when kayaking. You should not be eating. Remember, *chewing gum and water sports do not mix!* To prevent water from getting up your nose, you may want to try your first exit wearing a nose clip. Without a nose clip, you will soon discover that slowly breathing out through your nose will prevent the water from going in. Eventually you need to feel comfortable without a nose clip unless you plan to wear one throughout your entire kayaking career.

The Exit

1. Make sure that the spray skirt release strap is on the outside.

2. Take a breath and capsize. Do not let go of the paddle.

3. Sit still until you are completely upside down.

4. Locate the release strap on your spray skirt. It doesn't matter whether or not you can open your eyes; most people find the strap by moving their free hand along the coaming until they find the loop.

5. Push the strap forward towards the bow and then lift upwards, bending your arm at the elbow so the lip of the skirt clears the coaming (Figure 2.3 A).

6. Lean forward. Place both hands behind you on either side of the boat (remember one hand still has hold of your paddle) (Figure 2.3 B).

7. Straighten your legs and push up and away in the direction of the arrow (Figure 2.3 C).

Once on the surface, grab the boat's cockpit coaming. If you did let go of your paddle, this is when you need to retrieve it, without letting go of your kayak. Go to the end of the kayak (closest to the paddle) and grab the toggle so you can more easily drag the kayak as you move towards your paddle. Remember, if you leave the boat, even for an instant, the wind may blow it away faster than you can swim after it.

If you cannot get to your paddle, it is better to stay with your kayak. Since it is recommended you carry a spare paddle, you can retrieve your

A

B

C

Figure 2.3 *The wet exit*

original paddle after you are back in the kayak using your spare paddle. Even if you only have one paddle (shame on you), it is still better to be with your kayak. If you have to choose between your kayak and your paddle, your kayak provides more options than your paddle.

It is natural for you to feel some slight lack of confidence prior to your first wet exit. By all means, do the first one without the spray skirt in place. In this case, bang three times on the upturned hull with your hands before allowing yourself to make the exit. Hanging upside down for these few added seconds will give you the confidence you need so that you will not panic when the time comes to remove the spray skirt. It will also be a signal to the person assisting you that you have not expired and are in fact in complete control of the situation. This is also the signal that you want an Eskimo recovery.

Remember, the first movement of your exit is like taking off a pair of trousers: You lean forward. (Nobody leans backwards when they remove their pants!) Do not practice this after a full meal.

Types of Capsize Recoveries

The two main categories for capsize recoveries are "assisted" and "solo." Within these two categories are the "stay in the kayak" and the "exit the kayak" (wet exit) options. Most of the time you will have a choice in the matter, but there are also times when King Neptune will decide for you. It is not uncommon to have your kayak ripped away from your body in a surf zone. I am a firm believer in learning as many methods as possible in case a unique situation arises and your "go-to" capsize recovery technique does not work in that situation.

Stay-in-Kayak Capsize Recoveries

Again, capsizing is part of the sport of kayaking. It is what happens after a capsize that is most important. Your first option should not be the wet exit. If you can recover from a capsize without getting out of your kayak, you will save time and minimize your exposure to the elements.

The roll is the first line of defense. The roll is a solo, stay-in-kayak recovery method. Of course, rolls can go wrong, paddles can break, and strange and weird things can happen to

technique on cold, windy days when the hands are numb. (See Chapter 5 for details on rolling.)

The next line of defense is the Eskimo recovery, which is an assisted, stay-in-kayak recovery method. There comes a time, however, in steep breaking seas following close on top of each other, that Eskimo recoveries, if indeed possible, should be attempted only with the greatest caution for fear of injury to arms, head, and boat. This is a great time to be wearing your helmet.

The Eskimo Bow Recovery

The Eskimo bow recovery is the easiest recovery method to teach as well as to do, and hence it is the most common. It is appropriately named because the native paddlers did not exit their boats after a capsize. This is one of four main ways the native paddlers assisted one another if the capsized boater could not roll up.

When you capsize, bang quickly and hard on the bottom of your kayak to attract attention, then slowly move the hands fore and aft in an arc (Figure 2.4 A), covering about a yard during the sweep. This gives you more chance of contacting the bow of the approaching kayak, which is presented to you, saving your assister unnecessary maneuvering and, of course, time. When you feel toggles or the round ending of the assisting kayak, pull yourself up, as in Figure 2.4 B. In the illustration, the patient is in such a position that he will now have to turn his left hand around to continue his upward push. It sometimes helps if the assister can paddle in towards the patient as he pulls himself upwards. The assister must lose no time in getting over to his patient, but the last yard must be careful and controlled. When practicing this in a pool, it is good to wear a helmet, just in case someone is overenthusiastic. This is a great backup to have when you practice your roll.

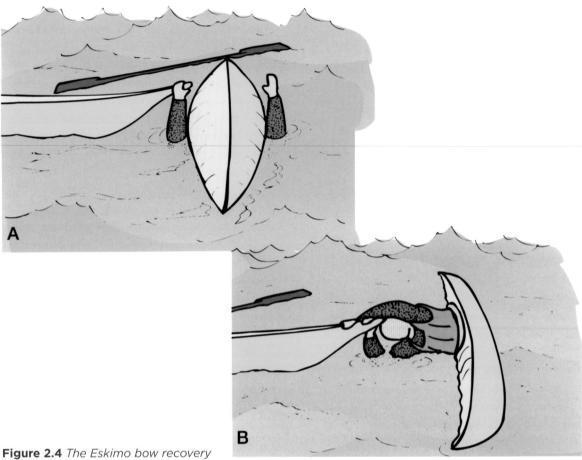

Figure 2.4 *The Eskimo bow recovery*

Have your partner nearby to offer you their bow if your roll isn't working that day.

The Eskimo Paddle Recovery

The paddle recovery is by far the more useful method because when you are paddling, you and your partner's kayak will most likely be in a parallel configuration. If someone capsizes in front of you, paddle fast towards his or her waving arms (Figure 2.5). If they capsize behind you, it is quicker to back paddle into position. As you come alongside the overturned boat, without slowing down, place your paddle over the hull of their kayak with your blade over your cockpit. Grab your paddle by the throat. Your outside hand will be holding your paddle in the proper position. Your inside hand (closest to the overturned kayak) is going to tightly grasp the nearest wrist of the upside-down paddler. Then, as your kayak loses momentum with the drag of the other, place their hand on your paddle shaft (Figure 2.6). Aim for their wrist so their hand is open to grasp the paddle shaft. You do not want them grabbing your hand.

Figure 2.5 *The Eskimo paddle recovery approach*

The placement of your paddle across your deck and the hull of the other kayak is the key to this technique. If your paddle is *not* spanning both kayaks, this technique cannot work and will likely lead to your being pulled over.

As the submerged paddler rolls up, he brings his other hand up to hold your paddle shaft so he can roll completely upright (Figure 2.7). The paddler in the illustration will have to change the grip with his right hand to finish off his push into the upright position. It is important that the assister place the nearest hand on the paddle loom; otherwise, the capsized paddler may well grab the loom on the wrong side. A hysterical little scene is then enacted as our hero tries to pull himself up on the wrong side, usually to no avail, while the rescuer tries as calmly as possible to inform the paddler, still underwater, of course, that he wants to be up on the other side. The paddler being aided must have sufficient control and air not to clutch in desperation the first thing his hand touches. Grasping the assister's wrist in a vice-like death clutch doesn't help anybody.

The joy of this recovery is that it can be done quickly. Even if the assister is approaching from a position at right angles to the upturned boat, he can always turn at the last minute and execute a paddle recovery rather than a bow recovery, thus minimizing the chance of putting a hole in the boat.

A word of advice to the capsized paddler: When you are upside down and waving your arms, you will not know if you are going to get the bow of a kayak in your waving hand or if your hand is going to be guided to a paddle shaft. Nor do you know which hand will be the target of

Figure 2.6 *Guiding the hand*

Figure 2.7 *Controlling the paddle*

the incoming helper. If you decide to wait for an Eskimo recovery, these are your two possibilities before wet exiting.

If your wrist is grabbed, wait until it is placed on the paddle shaft. If a bow is in your hands, react as mentioned above. Do not try to pull the helper or their kayak over. If you do run out of breath and decide to wet exit, remember there may be a kayak bow bearing down on you. Come to the surface with your hands protecting your head and face. If you do want to hang in the kayak longer, pushing down with both hands can give you enough lift to take a breath, but can also be very dangerous because a kayak may be coming right at you.

When you are upside down waiting for the assist, keep your paddle parallel to your kayak, at the cockpit, floating between the boat and your waving arm. When you right yourself, quickly look for your paddle. It should be right next to you.

Swimming While in Your Kayak

If you choose to stay in your kayak, there is another option if help cannot come to you. You can try to swim while still in your kayak towards help or to an object you can use to right yourself. Perhaps you went over as you were helping another boater. If your kayak is a few feet away, it may be easier and quicker to swim to that kayak and use it to right yourself (Photo 2.7). Maybe you lost your paddle and it is just out of reach. If you know how to roll, a short swim to the paddle may be doable. If you were to capsize near a dock or a rock, a swim with your kayak could be the quickest way to get upright. I had a friend who ended up capsizing here in the Pacific Northwest when his bow landed on a floating log. While trying to slide off, he went over. I was impressed

Photo 2.7 *Swimming while in your kayak*
WAYNE HORODOWICH

when he kept his composure and just hand-paddled over to that same log and used it for support to right himself.

The technique is relatively simple, just using a sidestroke (as in swimming) while keeping yourself in the cockpit. Of course, you will need to open your eyes to see where you are going. If you need to bring your head to the surface for a quick look or to get a breath, a push down with both hands could give you enough lift to do so. If you are going for the breath, be sure to exhale before you get to the surface, just as one does when swimming the crawl stroke. There will only be enough time to inhale when your head breaks the surface. How long and how far you can swim depends mostly on your breath control and state of mind (not to mention the water temperature).

Capsize Recoveries after a Wet Exit

If you decide to wet exit from your kayak after a capsize, you should maintain contact with your paddle and your kayak. As mentioned before, regardless of the recovery methods you use, two components are essential in any capsize recovery once you have wet-exited your kayak: emptying the water from the kayak and getting back into the kayak. The order and way you perform these components and/or the configuration of the kayaks is up to you.

Assisted Capsize Recoveries

Now that we have the components, it is time to put them together in different ways that have been tested and accepted by the paddling community. You are likely to hear of other variations that can also work. Not all methods work in all situations. It is important to master as many techniques as you can, because there may come a time when you will need to reach into that "bag of experience" due to a difficult situation. Here are a few of Derek's thoughts regarding some different rescue techniques:

Over the years, various methods of deep-water rescues involving emptying and reentering a capsized kayak have been devised, tried, and tested. Some have been rejected out of hand as being far too complicated, while others have failed in rough conditions.

One, called the "H," was popular for many years. The upturned kayak was lifted and emptied while being held at either end by the rescuers, their kayaks being parallel to each other and the boat to be emptied at right angles to them. In choppy or windy conditions, paddles went astray, the rescuers were unsupported, and the boats drifted together, putting the men in a very unstable position while they were still holding the kayak in the air.

I have not included this method, as its use is so limited and unreliable.

As Derek has chosen to eliminate certain rescues (capsize recoveries) from his many editions of his first book, I am doing the same for this edition. My goal is to include the ones that prove to be the most successful in the widest variety of conditions.

Before we review these different methods, it is important to remember that some of these techniques were developed when kayak design was in its infancy. Before reliable waterproof hatches, there were no bulkheads in sea kayaks. That meant a lot of water in the kayak, even when float bags were being used. It also meant the weight of the flooded kayak would take more than one person assisting. In addition, if the overturned kayak was turned upright too soon, more water would flood in, which could cause the kayak to sink into Poseidon's domain. Also, in order to drain the water out of a kayak without bulkheads, the kayak needs to be seesawed (back and forth) a few times to get all the water out from both ends. A kayak with bulkheads is more easily lifted at the bow and can usually be drained by just one assisting kayaker.

Now that we have fore and aft bulkheads in most sea kayaks, the methods used years ago may not be needed as often, if at all. I have tried to add appropriate historical reference when called for.

Stabilizing a Kayak

The greatest advantage to an assisted recovery is your partner can stabilize your kayak. It is nice to have a rock-solid platform when trying to climb onto the deck of your kayak. If your kayak is not stabilized, it is easily rolled over when trying to climb on.

The two main kayak configurations during stabilization are either bow to bow or bow to stern. Although bow to bow works, it can lead to difficulties. Since stabilizing is best done at the cockpit (gripping the coaming is the most secure method), the bow-to-bow configuration has the assisting paddler blocking the cockpit or ends up having the assister's back to the person climbing in. Therefore, I highly recommend using the bow-to-stern configuration (Photo 2.13). You don't block the cockpit, you can see and help the person climbing in, and when finished, you and the other paddler are face to face to discuss your next steps.

If you find yourself in the bow-to-bow position, you can easily get into the bow-to-stern position by sliding your kayak forward to the bow of the other kayak and pivoting around that bow and coming around on the other side without ever letting go of the other kayak. It can be done in about 10 seconds.

To stabilize a kayak, the assisting paddler grabs the front of the other cockpit coaming with both hands while resting their body over the front deck of the other kayak. Your body weight helps add to the stability. This can be done with or without paddles under your arms. The paddle(s) must span both kayaks (Photo 2.14). If you have short arms, the paddle bridge may not be your best option. When stabilizing a kayak you have to put your paddle and the swimmer's paddle somewhere. If you do not put the paddles under your arms, they need to go on paddle leashes or under your front deck bungee cords.

This bow-to-stern setup is a great way to take a break while on the water. You and your partner can actually take a quick rest by lying over each other's deck. It is also a great way to stabilize your partner when they want to shed or change clothes.

Reenter and Pump

By far this is the least complicated of all of the assisted recoveries after a wet exit. It also gets the swimmer out of the water quickly. As the assisting paddler approaches, the swimmer flips his kayak upright. After the kayak is stabilized, the swimmer reenters the cockpit via one of the many reentry options. Then one or both paddlers pump out the water. Of course, pumps are a necessity for this method. This is not recommended if the swamped kayak is without bulkheads. However, if the flooded kayak is too heavy to lift, then pumping, even if lengthy, may be your only option.

The "T" or "X" Capsize Recovery

If the capsized kayak has front and rear bulkheads, the "T" method is by far the fastest assisted capsize recovery technique out there if your goal is to drain the water before the paddler gets back into their boat. It is rare for this technique not to work, which is why it is the "go-to" method taught in sea kayaking classes for assisted capsize recoveries. I have included the "X" draining method in case you come across a kayak with only one or no bulkheads.

Responsibilities of the Assisting Paddler

1. Approach the bow of the capsized boat, keeping the overturned kayak between you and the swimmer until you establish through communication that they are not in panic mode. If they are, you do not want them getting hold of your kayak, thus compromising your stability. You can use their overturned kayak as a float and support, in case the panicked swimmer lunges for your kayak. You and the swimmer need to discuss which recovery and reentry method you will be using. (Photo 2.8)

Photo 2.8 *Approaching a capsized kayak* WAYNE HORODOWICH

2. Grab the bow of the overturned kayak ("T" position because your kayak is perpendicular to the flooded kayak). Put your paddle under your bungee cords or have it on a leash. Use both hands to rotate the kayak into an upright position so it can more easily slide onto your deck to drain the water. The swimmer could also help rotate the kayak if they are by the cockpit. (Photo 2.9)

Photo 2.9 *Righting an overturned kayak*
WAYNE HORODOWICH

Photo 2.10 *Bow slide* WAYNE HORODOWICH

3. Slide the bow onto your cockpit until the knife-edge of the flooded kayak causes the kayak to turn on its side. Help it turn so you can see the cockpit of the flooded kayak. (Photo 2.10)

4. Cradle the bow with both arms as you lift and rotate the kayak so the water drains out of the cockpit. You can see the water coming out. If the kayak has a bulkhead behind the seat, this is all the draining that needs to be done. Side note: If you firmly hold the flooded kayak, it is very difficult for you to capsize even if you are on rough seas because you are essentially holding a giant float. (Photo 2.11)

If the kayak does not have a rear bulkhead, you need to continue pulling the kayak across your cockpit until it is centered over your boat. (The "X" position is named for the formation of the two kayaks.) Turn it upside down and seesaw the kayak to get the water out of the forward and aft compartments. (Photo 2.12)

Photo 2.11 *Lift and drain* WAYNE HORODOWICH

Photo 2.12 *"X" draining method*
WAYNE HORODOWICH

5. Once the water is out (either "T" or "X"), turn the kayak upright without scooping water with the open cockpit. Slide the kayak back into the water and get it into a bow-to-stern configuration to stabilize the kayak. (Photo 2.13)

Photo 2.13 *Bow-to-stern cockpit stabilization*
WAYNE HORODOWICH

6. Take the swimmer's paddle. Stow it or use it to help stabilize the kayak. Get a strong hold of the front sides of the cockpit coaming so the swimmer can reenter the kayak. Tell the swimmer when you are ready for them to reenter using one of the reentry techniques previously mentioned. (Photo 2.14)

Photo 2.14 *Stabilizing a kayak with a paddle bridge* WAYNE HORODOWICH

7. Do not release the kayak until the paddler tells you they are ready to go. Just because they reattached their spray skirt does not mean they are ready. They need to be mentally seaworthy, as mentioned above and in Chapter 13. (Photo 2.15)

Photo 2.15 *Ready to let go* WAYNE HORODOWICH

Responsibilities of the Capsized Paddler

1. You have a choice to make: Will you passively stay by your cockpit until help arrives, or will you be proactive and get to your bow and tow your kayak and paddle towards another kayak if you are not alone? (Photo 2.16)

2. Communicate with the assisting paddler and tell them if you are OK and under control or are having difficulties. Lifting your arm over your head and touching your head with your fingers (making a circle with your arm) is a commonly recognized sign saying, "I'm OK."

Photo 2.16 *Swimming the boat and paddle to help* WAYNE HORODOWICH

3. Decide if you want to have the water drained or if you want to do a wet reentry or a reenter and pump. You need to communicate this to the paddler coming to your aid. You need to find out if they are able to perform the recovery method you prefer.

4. Keep contact with your paddle through the entire process and only give it up to the paddler assisting you when you are climbing out of the water back into your cockpit. You can always use your paddle as a paddle swim if you need to cover some distance. (Photo 2.20)

5. Always stay in contact with your kayak or the kayak of the assisting paddler. On a windy day the kayaks can get away from you quickly. The swimmer in the water is *not* moved much by the wind. Use the deck lines whenever possible.

6. If the assisting paddler can drain the water without your help, stay out of their way, but be sure they can see you. The bow of their kayak is a good location. If you are going to assist with the draining process, make sure you are communicating that to the assisting paddler. Remember, a kayak crashing down on your head can have serious consequences. That is why helmets are a good idea, especially in rough seas. (Photo 2.11)

7. Reenter the kayak when the assisting kayaker says they are ready for you. Once in your cockpit, adjust your clothing as needed and quickly get your spray skirt attached to keep water out.

8. When you are ready to paddle, tell the other paddler that they can let go of your kayak. Until then, do whatever it takes to get yourself ready to continue. Feel free to discuss concerns with the other paddler and elicit whatever help they can provide to help you get ready. (Photo 2.15)

The "HI" Capsize Recovery

This is one of those older techniques where two paddlers were needed because of the weight of the flooded kayak due to no bulkheads. I have kept this recovery in the book so you can see how Derek and his peers approached capsizes over forty years ago. Now that recreational kayaks are being produced without bulkheads, this old recovery technique may prove useful.

Derek believed the most successful method in really rough conditions is the "HI" (so called because of the position of the kayaks), also known as the Ipswich. There are two paddlers assisting the capsized paddler. During the draining the paddles are under control; the kayaks form a close raft giving stability, and the man in the water, besides being able to help considerably with the draining, need never lose contact with the assisting kayaks. The assisting paddlers position themselves at either side of the upturned bow about a yard apart, facing into the swell. The three paddles form a bridge across the boats, and the bow of the upturned boat is lifted high so that the cockpit clears the water (Figure 2.8).

The kayak is then fed backwards over the paddles and rested on its cockpit coaming, where

Figure 2.8 *Positioning the overturned kayak in a three-person "HI" recovery*

Figure 2.9 *Emptying the kayak*

Figure 2.10 *Feet-first method of reentry. The view is from the opposite direction in order to show the method of reentry more clearly.*

it can be seesawed by the upright paddlers. They are assisted by the man in the water, who supports himself on one of the bows while pushing upwards and then pulling down, all in time with the swell, thus emptying the kayak (Figure 2.9).

The boat is turned the right way up, put on to the water, pushed forward, then back under the paddles into the reentry raft position. To execute a between-the-kayaks reentry, the paddles can be kept across the boats or pushed out of the way. The positions of the arms of the supporters are also variable. They can be as in Figure 2.10 or they can be crossed over each other, one hand of each man grasping the opposite side of the cockpit coaming, thus making a stronger link. Practice will help the individual decide which is best.

When ready, the swimmer does a feet-first between-the-kayaks reentry. The upright paddlers keep supporting the raft until the spray cover is firmly secured and the paddler says, "I am ready." From the positioning of the kayaks to the finish of the capsize recovery should take about one minute during practice on calm water.

As I mentioned above, while this technique was once used quite often, it is not often used today for three main reasons: It takes more time to coordinate two kayaks to help; it no longer takes two paddlers to drain the water, due to bulkheads; and the last thing you want to do with today's lightweight paddles is use them to support the weight of a kayak while it is seesawed and full of water. However, if you did come upon a completely flooded kayak, this technique has proven itself.

Assisted Wet Reentry Capsize Recoveries

If you are comfortable doing wet reentries and have a pump (which all paddlers should always have), here are some assisted recoveries that can be done very quickly. These are perfect techniques if you need to get into your boat and paddle away from a dangerous area. Knowing how to paddle with a cockpit full of water is a great skill, especially with these techniques, if there is no time for pumping.

Wet Reentry Bow Assist

Have your partner move their bow near your cockpit. When ready, do your wet reentry and then wave your arms so your partner can do the Eskimo bow recovery. Once up, either pump out the water while your partner stabilizes your kayak or start paddling to get to a better location for pumping.

Wet Reentry Paddle Assist

Have your partner position his kayak for a paddle assist. Do your wet reentry, and when you wave your arms, you know your partner will be grabbing your wrist to place it on the paddle shaft. Remember, when you go upside down, the partner that was on your right side will now be on your left. Still wave both arms. After your hand is placed on the paddle shaft, roll up, pump, or paddle.

Wet Reentry Duo Assist

Here is a way for two swimmers to right each other almost at the same time. Get your overturned kayaks in a bow-to-stern setup with each bow near the other's cockpit. You can do this one at a time or try to perfect doing it with your partner simultaneously. When ready, do your wet reentry and reach for your partner's bow. Use it to roll up. When both of you are up, you can move your cockpits next to each other and rest on the other's deck and pump out the kayaks if you have the time. Otherwise, get out of this challenging area and raft up later for pumping. This is a nice alternative to the "all-in" recovery.

The All-In Recovery

Derek told me he came up with this recovery method when he heard about a Boy Scout troop that was hit with a sudden squall and the whole group went over. This is a great technique to have in your "bag of experience," but the immersion time for this method can be quite long. However, if the paddlers are dressed for immersion, the time factor isn't as critical. I would only use this option if no one in the group had pumps or paddle floats. It is much faster and more efficient if everyone in the group does their own solo recovery and then the first ones finished can help the others if they need it.

Again, this method was developed when kayaks did not have bulkheads or carry adequate float bags. Letting trapped air escape could mean the loss of your kayak due to sinking.

Assuming you all kept in contact with your kayaks and paddles, paddlers should pair up and tow their two kayaks together, keeping them upside down (no bulkhead concern). If there is an odd number of paddlers, one will have to wait until the pairs have completed their recoveries, which means longer immersion time. I would choose the warmest-dressed paddler to go last in this case.

Secure the paddles with leashes or deck elastics so you don't lose them. In the absence of either, tuck the paddles between your legs.

The delicate part of the whole operation is emptying the first kayak without losing the air trapped inside the kayak you use as the base. The two swimmers position themselves to face opposite ways, on either side of the kayak that we will call the "pivot boat." Underneath the water they each hold the cockpit coaming with one hand. This prevents the boat from tipping sideways and losing the supporting air trapped inside. We will suppose that you are on the right side, so your kayak will be the first one to be emptied.

As shown in Figure 2.11, you lift the bow of your kayak as high as possible into the air. Retaining your grip on the coaming of the pivot boat with your right hand, you feed or throw the overturned kayak across to your partner (Figure 2.12). Then, with the pivot boat underneath kept as steady and as level as possible, the top kayak can be seesawed carefully and emptied (Figure 2.13).

Once your kayak is emptied, you are faced with the problem of getting back into it without filling the pivot boat. You must form a bridge with the paddles across the two kayaks (Figure 2.14). The swimmer in the water on the far side acts as a counterbalance by putting weight on the paddles. This means that you can put your weight on the paddles at your side. The side reentry is the one recommended at this time. Your partner can counteract any pressure you may put on the pivot boat while you are making your reentry. The pivot kayak can now be emptied by means of a "T" recovery.

Figure 2.11 *Positioning the first boat for emptying. The paddles are secured either by paddle leashes or between the legs of the paddler of the pivot boat.*

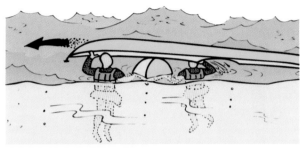

Figure 2.12 *The pivot boat is held firmly from below while the kayak to be emptied is lifted and pulled across into the seesaw position.*

Figure 2.13 *Emptying the first kayak across the pivot boat using a seesawing movement.*

Figure 2.14 *Entering the cockpit is easier if the paddles are placed behind the cockpit, forming a bridge as shown.*

Most of the tests I have done have been with kayaks with no buoyancy. This meant that any tilting of the pivot boat caused it to fill and sink. With kayaks even moderately full of buoyancy, the rescues can be completed quickly and efficiently.

During this recovery there will be an overturned kayak between you and your partner. Because of this you may be out of sight of one another. Therefore, in order to communicate, you will have to shout

If I had kayaks with bulkheads, all I would need to drain a boat is a simple bow lift using the other kayak as a support. Once the water is drained, I could use any number of methods to reenter.

It is good to be aware of different options if you ever find yourself in situations with inadequate equipment. Again, since many of the new recreational kayaks on the market are without one or both bulkheads, this "all-in" method is worth keeping in the back of your mind.

The Curl Recovery

The situation in Figure 2.15, known as a Cleopatra's needle, will of course never happen to you or those with you. Being the prudent person you are, your kayak and the kayaks of those who accompany you will always be filled with some form of flotation. Not everyone will be so circumspect, however, and it is a good thing you are able to cope with this highly difficult situation. It will probably fall to the assister to shout the instructions out to the person in the water.

1. The swimmer will have to stretch his leg down and hook his foot under the cockpit coaming of the sunken kayak. He will then raise it level with the surface.

2. With the cockpit coaming level with the surface of the water, the swamped boat must be maneuvered so that it lies parallel to the upright kayak.

3. The assister must hold the swamped boat level and in position while the swimmer swims around to the other side. He then throws himself across the foredeck of the upright kayak.

4. The swimmer reaches across and grasps the part of the cockpit coaming that is farthest away from him, with his palms upwards. (Figure 2.16)

5. The swimmer allows his body to slide back off the deck a little, while still retaining hold of the swamped boat. His elbows must come to rest on the foredeck, jammed tightly in place by the weight they are supporting.

6. All the swimmer has to do now is to hold the kayak level. His elbows should take all the weight. He should not try to lift.

7. The assister, who regulates the angle of his front deck by leaning over to the opposite side while using an extended paddle sculling brace, empties the kayak. This can be done in the normal or extended paddle position. As the cockpit drains, the swimmer can help rotate the flooded kayak to get more water out. They *are not* lifting. (Figure 2.17)

8. Once most of the water has been emptied out, the kayak can be flipped over into its upright position and any remaining water removed by reverting to a "T" capsize recovery.

Derek devised this system of emptying a fully swamped boat some years ago, after having the problem thrust upon him in the middle of Lake Windermere.

A word of caution, though: The curl is not easy and the strain on the foredeck of the rescuer's kayak is considerable.

Figure 2.15 *Cleopatra's needle*

Figure 2.16 *Grabbing the coaming*

Figure 2.17 *Curl method of draining water*

Anchoring an Assisted Capsize Recovery

During assisted recoveries, those involved in emptying boats have little control over their amount of drift. Any accompanying paddler must therefore be prepared to help by either towing the boats out of trouble or by acting as an anchor,

Figure 2.18 *Towing an "X" recovery out of danger while in progress*

holding everybody steady in one place while the recovery continues without interruption.

Under normal circumstances, any drifting can be ignored; lost ground can always be made up later. However, I can think of a number of situations that would benefit from some towing assistance; for example, rescues attempted near busy shipping lanes, surf, rocks, or dangerous overfalls (Figure 2.18). In strong offshore winds, the kayaks can be "anchored" to prevent them being blown farther out to sea or towed in towards the shore to gain more protection.

Summary on Assisted Capsize Recoveries

Numerous options were presented regarding assisted capsize recovery techniques. Once you have mastered the various components of the recovery techniques, you can put those components together in many different ways to suit your skill level, body type, equipment available, and the conditions around you. You and your paddling partners need to regularly practice your techniques so you can do them when needed.

When do you find out you can no longer perform a skill? The answer is simple: when you try to do it and you find you cannot. Skills are lost when they are not practiced. Eventually you will lose some skills just through aging. I would rather find out I can no longer perform a skill during a practice session instead of a real situation where I need it to survive or need it to help a fellow paddler.

After you mastered the techniques in calm protected waters, I recommend finding controlled "challenging waters" for practicing. The outside of a sea wall is a good place to practice as long as you can quickly get back to the sheltered side if your practice is not going well.

Solo Capsize Recoveries

The vast majority of paddlers paddle in groups. That is why assisted recoveries were covered first. However, paddling in a group does not guarantee that someone in the group will come to your aid, especially if conditions get real bad. If everyone in your group is just trying to stay upright due to the terrible conditions, getting assistance may not be an option. If you adopt the premise that you need to be totally self-sufficient when you go onto the water, you will be an asset to yourself and to the group. If you go onto the water and you cannot take care of yourself and assume the group will always be there for you, you may have a rude awakening someday. Learn how to take care of yourself and you will be better equipped to help others.

As mentioned earlier, the roll is the quickest solo capsize recovery technique. Since everyone eventually misses a roll, we need other solo options. Using the previously discussed components of a capsize recovery, we will review the different ways we can put those components together for successful solo capsize recovery methods.

The Paddle Float Recovery

Presently the paddle float recovery is the main solo recovery taught in sea kayaking classes, because if you wet-exit after capsizing, the use of the float provides support in the form of an outrigger. However, because of his vast experience in extremely rough conditions and believing "less than three on the sea should never be," Derek did not put as much faith in the paddle float recovery method. Here is what he wrote in his last book:

The paddle float is not really a rough-water rescue, although I have seen it done successfully in high winds and a steep unpleasant sea. The person I watched, however, was an experienced man who had no fear of the water conditions. The place was San Francisco Bay and the demonstration made me realize the potential of this comparatively uncomplicated means of solo reentry.

Any experienced lone paddler who finds himself in the water will probably revert to the reentry and roll. The novice, however, who finds himself alone and friendless while swimming next to his boat, whether by foolishness or force of circumstance, will have to think of some other method of getting back in again. Even though weather conditions may be calm, a gust of wind or some other unforeseen circumstance may catch a paddler unawares and cause a capsize. It is for just such a situation that I have included this method of unassisted reentry. Peter Dyer originally described the rescue in 1970, in the September issue of *Canoeing in Britain*.

Derek and I had many discussions about the reliability of the paddle float recovery. As he aged, he admitted that a skilled paddler could perform this recovery method in extremely rough seas and conceded it should be part of every paddlers "bag of experience." Following is a brief history of the paddle float.

By utilizing the paddle as a fixed outrigger and fastening some means of flotation to the extended blade, it was found to be possible for a lone paddler to reenter his kayak after it had been turned the right way up. Unfortunately, the original guidelines for this maneuver called upon the capsized paddler to remove his lifejacket in the water so that it could then be tied onto the end of the paddle. Because there were obvious dangers in this somewhat bizarre advice, the "Dyer outrigger method" was not given serious consideration by the majority of sea paddlers.

Under the name "Paddle Wing," a kayak designer who brought sanity to the system revived it in the United States. He recommended that a water container be tied onto the end of the paddle and suggested the soft plastic kind that has a carrying handle and a drain tap through which it could be inflated. An ingenious part of his idea was to fill the container a quarter full of water. The added weight would thus minimize the risk of a capsize on the opposite side.

The method was effective but clumsy. However, the whole idea was to be simplified even further by Will Nordby of California, who experimented with various air pillows and bags after he was involved in a capsize that he felt could easily have proved fatal. His friend Bob Licht of the Seatrek Ocean Kayaking Center helped with the tests and experiments, and the two men eventually presented their ideas to a manufacturer. The "paddle float," which resulted from their joint efforts, is best likened to an inflatable sleeve, consisting of a soft, strong plastic bag with double walls. A valve permits the walls of the bag to be inflated. Once the paddle float is slipped over the paddle blade, it cannot be removed until the air is let out again.

If you intend to use this method of rescue, ensure that your kayak is fitted with the necessary straps or shock cord elastics. To hold the outrigger paddle firm, these should be positioned immediately behind the cockpit, on both sides parallel to the gunwale. A double length of shock cord is the least that will hold the paddle in position. The best anchor is the specialized deck rigging made of non-stretch webbing, which is offered by some manufacturers.

How to Do the Paddle Float Recovery

1. Keep your paddle float secured under the elastics on the deck of your kayak. Do not store the float inside any sealed compartment. Taking a hatch cover off during a recovery could cause your boat to swamp.

2. After the capsize, position yourself on the downwind side of your overturned boat. This is in case the wind blows it away faster than you can swim after it.

3. This is a good time to keep in contact with your kayak by sliding one leg into the cockpit while the kayak is upside down. This frees both hands to allow you to put the float over one of the paddle blades (Figure 2.19 A). Inflate the float after it is secured to the paddle. Many newer floats have straps included to keep the float from sliding off and blowing away on a windy day.

4. Right the kayak as quickly as possible. Try to lift upwards as you flip the boat over to minimize the amount of water scooped by the cockpit. This could be a good time to try the bow lift, which may allow some water to drain from the cockpit, which will reduce pumping time.

5. If you have any pre-positioned elastics or fasteners, use them now and secure your paddle to act as an outrigger. Using deck rigging means you do not have to hold your paddle in place with one of your hands while performing this skill. We will continue as if you did not have the deck rigging.

6. Position your body close to the side of the kayak, aft of the cockpit. Hold the rear of the coaming and the paddle in the same hand. Hoist your body upwards and hook at least one leg onto the paddle shaft. Eventually you want both legs on the paddle shaft (Figure 2.19 B).

7. Bring one leg into the cockpit (Figure 2.19 C), carefully followed by the other leg (Figure 2.19 D). Keep your weight on the float side as you do this. This is not as easy as it may sound.

8. Rest over the paddle shaft and balance yourself. Do this by maintaining a slight lean on the float side. Then slide forward into the cockpit.

9. When ready, turn upright while constantly looking at your paddle float. You must keep your weight towards the float (Figure 2.19 E). If the weight shifts away from the float, you will go over with your paddle float, making a big arc in the sky called the "yellow rainbow," which means you must try again.

10. Once upright, use the paddle float to help you stabilize the kayak during the time you are pumping out the water and reattaching your spray skirt.

11. Before you paddle off, re-stow your pump and paddle float back to where they are accessible to be used again.

If the paddle float recovery is your main solo recovery, as it is for most sea kayakers, I highly recommend that you master it first in calm water and then perfect it in rough water.

Your pump and paddle float should be stored where you can get to it and re-stow it, while in your cockpit, on a rough day. There may be times when you need to use your paddle float for a rest period or to help stabilize another paddler.

Paddle Float Recovery with a Stirrup

There are few ways to use a stirrup with a paddle float, but doing so places a lot of stress on your

A

B

C

D

E

Figure 2.19 *The paddle float recovery*

Photo 2.17 *Paddle float recovery with a stirrup* WAYNE HORODOWICH

equipment. Some of the lightweight paddles on the market may not be strong enough for the challenge.

If you have secure deck rigging behind the cockpit, attach the paddle to it after you placed the float on the opposite blade and inflated it. You can then put the stirrup around the coaming as described earlier and climb into your cockpit.

If you have a fixed stirrup in your cockpit or on your deck, you can use it once the paddle is fixed on the back deck.

If you do not have solid rigging, you can loop the stirrup around one blade, by the neck, and pass the stirrup under the kayak and then loop the stirrup up over the paddle shaft on your side of the boat. Your stirrup will now be hanging down between the kayak and the paddle float (Photo 2.17). This method puts a lot of stain

on the paddle shaft. If you have a sharp-peaked deck, I would not recommend using this method. As in all stirrup recoveries, be sure not to get tangled in the stirrup when you get into the cockpit.

Wet Reentry and Paddle Float Roll

After years of teaching the traditional paddle float recovery where the swimmer climbs on the back deck, I have shifted my teaching to promote the wet reentry and paddle float roll as a more reliable and efficient solo recovery technique. Due to the lift from the paddle float, the paddler does not need to know how to roll without a paddle float.

Due to the energy expended climbing onto your kayak and the balancing needed in the paddle float recovery described earlier, this option

Photo 2.18 *Reentry and roll with a paddle float* WAYNE HORODOWICH

has you slipping into your overturned kayak and then using the paddle with float attached to right yourself. When upright you are holding your outrigger and are now ready to pump out the water.

As I mentioned earlier, Derek did not think the paddle float was very reliable in rough seas. Here is what he said: "Various methods of solo deep water reentry have been experimented with and the results have ranged from the humorous to the horrifying. Any sea condition that is going to eject an experienced man from his kayak is going to be too rough for rear deck 'hitching' even if the paddle can be fastened to the deck in the form of an outrigger. The only system that works every time for me in rough breaking seas is the R & R, that is, reentry and roll. It requires skill and nerve and on no account should it be practiced on the open sea alone."

My counterargument to Derek was, "If the paddler couldn't roll up when they first capsized and had to wet-exit their kayak, I don't believe their second attempt in rolling is going to be very successful. Their confidence is already compromised after blowing their first roll."

I do agree with Derek that the reentry and roll in very rough conditions has more benefits than climbing and balancing on your kayak. If you add the float to the paddle, the success of the roll is almost guaranteed.

This technique is exactly like the Eskimo paddle recovery except you will be using your paddle, with float attached, to right yourself instead of your partner's paddle.

After getting the float on the paddle and inflating it, do a wet reentry, keeping the paddle next to the cockpit between the boat and your arm with the float towards the bow. Once you are securely in your seat, reach up and grab your paddle with both hands. Push the paddle up towards the sky so you can move the float end out so the paddle is at a 90-degree angle to the kayak. Keeping the paddle shaft over the kayak, right yourself just as you did in the Eskimo paddle recovery (Photo 2.18).

I highly recommend mastering this option, especially for rough water. As always, I use my nose clips for any planned wet reentry. Once wet reentry is perfected, your breath-holding time is 5 to 7 seconds.

Sea Wings

Another flotation device that is great for solo recoveries and for stabilizing a boat being towed are dual float bags called Sea Wings (Photo 2.19). These two long, narrow floats (cigar shaped) attach next to the cockpit, one on each side. Pre-set clips need to be in place so the float tubes can be attached and then inflated after you capsize. Having the floats on each side increases the beam of the kayak and usually provides enough stability for most paddlers to climb back onto their kayak without it capsizing. The paddler can then pump out the water or just start paddling. Stability of the flooded kayak is not an issue with one of these floats attached on each side.

Photo 2.19 *Sea Wings provide stability in both directions. Here the paddler sits on her back deck just to demonstrate the added stability.*
WAYNE HORODOWICH

Unfortunately this device never caught on. I have seen the connecting straps get tangled, but if you practice using them, tangling is not really an issue. The extra inflation time is also not a big deal for most paddlers, unless they are hyperventilating due to the cold water. I will discuss the Sea Wings more in Chapters 12 and 13.

Scramble Recovery

A scramble recovery is any method the solo paddler uses to get back into their kayak while it is upright, without the use of any floatation devices. The two most common ways are over the rear of their kayak straddling the kayak as in the cowboy reentry (Photo 2.4) or a side reentry (Photo 2.1). If the paddler enters from the side, they need to have their belly (navel) directly over their seat. Once they are balanced over the kayak, they quickly flip over so their butt is in the seat with both legs hanging over the same side of the cockpit. Then they pivot in the seat, to be facing forward, with one leg on each side of the cockpit. When ready and balanced, they bring their legs back into the cockpit one at a time. Of the two scramble methods, most paddlers prefer to use the cowboy reentry.

Once in the kayak, the paddler needs to pump out the water to add stability to the boat. If it is too rough to just sit and pump, the paddler could get some forward speed to add stability and intermittently pump water out as they are moving.

The scramble recovery is generally used when a paddler needs to get their kayak out of its present location quickly. If they capsized near a surf zone, rocks, or a sea wall, it is wise to move away from the potential hazard. Once the kayak is in a less risky location, they can deal with emptying water.

Once during a surf competition, I jumped on my sea kayak after a capsize and just lay on it like a surfboard and paddled the kayak past the breakers so I could then do a paddle float recovery out of harm's way instead of getting washed ashore by the next big waves.

Tandem Recoveries

If you and your partner paddle a tandem kayak, you have certain advantages and disadvantages when it comes to capsize recoveries. The biggest challenge is that the tandem is heavier, especially when packed with gear and/or when it is flooded. The greatest advantage is having two paddlers. In actuality you have a built-in assistant. There is no such thing as a solo tandem recovery since there are two of you even though you have only one kayak.

Reenter and Pump

The quickest tandem recovery is the reenter and pump. After capsizing, get on opposite sides of the kayak. The person in the front stabilizes the tandem by holding their coaming. The paddler in the back climbs on and gets into their cockpit. The rear paddler then uses an extended paddle sculling brace on the side of the swimmer to allow the swimmer to enter the front cockpit without the kayak tipping over. If you do not have a reliable brace, this is a great time to use your paddle float.

Once both paddlers are in, the rear paddler can start paddling while the front one pumps out the kayak. They can switch pumping when one gets tired. The reason you start paddling is because a moving kayak is more stable than a stationary one. Since tandems are usually a lot more stable than single kayaks, the water must

be rough if you went over. Sitting still in rough water will be very unstable.

The stern paddler reenters first because they can better balance the kayak if they can see the person in front of them as they climb back on. It is very unsettling to have someone climbing on behind you.

You can also use a stirrup around the coaming to climb on since your partner in the water can counteract the force you are placing on the kayak. Again, having that second person in the water has its advantages and provides lots of options for helping.

Double "T"

If there are other kayaks there to assist, the double "T" may work as long as the tandem is not too heavy. Due to the extra weight, it may take two paddlers to drain the water. Just follow all of the steps for a "T" recovery with one addition: There is a second paddler next to the first assisting paddler. Their kayaks are in a bow-to-stern configuration. Think of it as two bars at the top of the "T." That extra paddler can help with the extra weight.

After the water is drained, the first assister stabilizes the tandem in a bow-to-stern configuration, holding the front coaming. The swimmers should enter one at a time.

Tandem Paddle Float Recovery

Since there should be a pump and paddle float for each paddler, you can do the paddle float recovery at the same time. If you do it from opposite sides of the kayak, you will end up with an outrigger on both sides. Having opposite outriggers provides enough stability that you can probably stand in your kayak, so pumping while sitting still is not an issue. After the water is out, have a picnic before you paddle on your way.

Dual Wet Reentry and Paddle Float Roll

Here is one if you and your partner like a challenge. You both do a wet reentry simultaneously and signal each other to right yourselves by both of you doing a paddle float roll. After a few practice tries, you will be surprised how easy this can be. The key is to do the roll at the same time. One person should bang on the kayak three times and then roll up together. Then do the pump and paddle as mentioned above.

Other Techniques

Paddle Swim

If you followed my advice and exit your kayak holding your paddle but your kayak was blown away from you, you can paddle swim to your kayak. Your other option is to abandon your paddle (you have a spare on your deck, right?) and just swim to your kayak. Keep in mind there is a lot of drag swimming in full immersion clothing while wearing a PFD and a spray skirt.

Photo 2.20 *Paddle swim* WAYNE HORODOWICH

When I first tried the paddle swim, it was awkward and slow going. I thought it was worthless. However, I kept at it. Over time I found I moved faster in the water with the paddle than by just swimming. As a side note, I am a strong swimmer. I swim at least four times per week, 2 miles at a time.

The key to the paddle swim is kicking your feet, which allows you to keep your head above water and keeping the strokes near the surface (Photo 2.20). If you dig too deep, the recovery is difficult. Play with this during pool playtime.

Paddling a Flooded Kayak

Since a kayak is a boat, it will fill up with water sooner or later, not counting capsizing. As I said in the equipment section, watertight and waterproof are concepts. When enough water enters the kayak, usually in the cockpit, it can upset your normal balance. You should learn how to paddle with a cockpit full of water before it happens as a surprise.

Remove your spray skirt, grab your partner's bow, and edge your kayak until the cockpit is half full of water. Grab your paddle and start paddling. The faster you go, the more stable you will feel. The water in your boat will slosh from side to side, especially in rough seas. That movement can capsize you. This is the time to use the supportive forward sweep stroke discussed in Chapter 3. The more you practice this skill, the less the water affects you because your body is learning how to react to the movement.

This feeling is similar to having a person lying on your back deck when you do a short-distance transfer as described in Chapter 12. If you choose to do a scramble recovery, you will be paddling with a boat full of water.

Dangerous Locations for Capsize Recoveries

Unfortunately there will be times when it may be too dangerous to perform any of the above capsize recovery options. Trying to do them in breaking surf can be extremely dangerous, as seen in Figure 2.20.

Capsizing in a sea cave, with breaking waves inside, makes it extremely difficult for another paddler to safely enter because the swamped kayak is being tossed around. Clipping on a tow-rope and swimming out to attach the other end to a waiting paddler may be your best option.

It may be best to let the swimmer ride through the tide race and collect them and their equipment in slower waters. That is another good reason to dress for immersion. Being able to ride out the race because you are well dressed allows more options.

We already mentioned doing a scramble to move your kayak out of harm's way (sea walls, cliffs, rock gardens, etc.) so a full recovery can be performed in more favorable conditions. Your goal is to help someone in need, not create others in need.

Figure 2.20 *Things can go terribly wrong when recoveries are attempted inside the surf zone.*

Playtime in the Pool

When you are learning a new skill, your body, aside from your brain, is being trained. As I said at the beginning of this chapter, I prefer teaching the components needed for capsize recoveries, and I have found the best place to really learn these components is in a swimming pool. Wear the same clothes you will use when on the open water. Jump in the pool and swim over to your kayak, then it is time to play and perfect the components. The water is warm and in many cases you will be able to stand. Since the sides and the bottom of the pool are hard, I recommend wearing a helmet as you practice.

This is a great place to practice swimming while in your kayak, the paddle swim, and the different wet reentry options. Play with your kayak. Climb all over it. Try standing in the cockpit. When you start perceiving these skills as playtime, a capsize recovery should not make you nervous, which means you will be more relaxed while on the water, which means less chance of capsizing.

When you feel competent doing the individual components, try putting them together in the recovery techniques described in this book. Mix and match reentries and different draining methods. Keep in mind that if you cannot do these skills here in the pool, there will be little to no chance for success on the open water.

I highly recommend the following training program: Perfect your skills in the pool. Then practice them and perfect them in calm, cold, protected waters. Then practice them and try to perfect them in controlled rough conditions. While in your training stage, you should be with other paddlers.

CHAPTER 3

STROKES AND MANEUVERING

For the sake of this chapter, a stroke is the way in which you use your paddle to move, stop, or turn your kayak. Maneuvering is a planned or regulated movement of your kayak. You use your strokes to maneuver your kayak.

Another definition of a stroke is what Derek may have experienced if he saw how I edited his book. Even though moving a paddle is really a matter of physics, every instructor has his or her own way of interpreting those movements and therefore teaches strokes based upon their own experiences and priorities. Since this is Derek's book, you should hear his presentation and thoughts on strokes. I will make my additions evident throughout as needed.

According to Derek, a kayak is a water vehicle powered by a person wielding a paddle. Every movement of the craft, in whatever direction, is due to the paddle being held in a certain position and moved in a certain manner. Since your blade provides resistance when you place it in the water, your kayak will either be moving towards or away from the point of placement.

When you watch an experienced paddler on the water, notice how the strokes merge. One fluid movement flows into the next. The paddler appears to be at one with the craft and the paddle. To reach this high level of competence, all these movements must be broken down into their separate components. It is these separate components that are the individual strokes.

The Paddle and Paddle Positions

Before we can name and describe the different strokes, we need to address the paddle so you can understand the different terms being used. I am assuming you have a paddle of sufficient length as described in Chapter 1.

The Paddle Blade

To make recognition easy, all the various parts of a paddle are distinguished by name. To help confuse the novice, however, some of the parts have more than one name! Familiarity will soon dispel any confusion because those parts that are referred to in the text are named in Figure 3.1.

The Leading Edge

In the following pages, repeated references are made to the fact that the leading edge of the paddle blade must be *high* for certain maneuvers (Figure 3.2). If the paddle is moved through the water sideways, with its leading edge high, the blade will act in a manner similar to that of a water ski. It will stay on the surface or at a chosen depth, but only for the duration of its forward movement. For example, plane your paddle

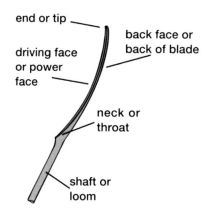

Figure 3.1 *Blade anatomy*

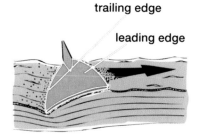

Figure 3.2 *Leading edge of the blade*

flat along the surface of the water. Keep the leading edge high, and the blade will skim across the water like a flat stone. Tilt the leading edge slightly *down*, and the blade will stop abruptly and sink.

You will see from Figure 3.2 that once the leading edge is high, the blade will stay on the surface or it will climb to the surface if it is underwater. This climbing angle can provide support to the paddler's weight.

It will soon become apparent to you as you perform some of some of the strokes that a slight alteration in the angle of the paddle will give you support as well as propulsion. As an example, forward paddling with a slight climbing angle

on your blade will give you enough support to allow you to lean over from side to side on every stroke. When conditions get rough, it is comforting if your strokes are supportive as well as propulsive.

The Basic Paddling Position

Whether you are paddling forward or backward, or performing one of the many different paddling maneuvers, the paddle is held in what is known as the basic (standard) paddling position. In this book, all instructions and illustrations assume that the paddler is right-handed and the paddles are set for right-hand control. You will, of course, adjust the information to fit your feather angle and control hand.

Hold your paddle with your hands slightly more than shoulder-width apart (Figure 3.3). Your palms should be on top of the shaft with your thumbs underneath, and your hands should be equidistant from the center of the shaft. The knuckles of your right hand are in line with the top edge of the right-hand blade. The power face is looking backwards. If your shaft is oval towards one end only, that will be the grip for your right hand.

Now try this simple exercise (Figure 3.4). Hold your paddle at arms' length. Grasp it firmly in your right (controlling) hand, while leaving your left hand relaxed. Start bending at the right elbow, allowing your paddle shaft to rotate until the left power face is correctly oriented to take a stroke.

Remember that your right, controlling hand moves the shaft by bending the elbow and perhaps moving the wrist a little depending on your feather angle. *The shaft does not move inside the fingers of the right hand.* In other words, no matter what weird contortions you may get the

Figure 3.3 *Basic paddling position*

Figure 3.4 *Simple paddle control exercise*

paddle into, once you return your hands to the basic paddling position, the paddle should be ready for the next stroke on your control side. You should not have to twist the shaft back into its correct position.

I feel obligated to add to Derek's comments here. The term *control hand* has been misinterpreted over the many years since Derek wrote his book. The control hand controls and maintains the indexing of the paddle. However, the hand that is closest to the working blade (blade in the water) controls the action of that blade, which is an important "truism" for good paddle manipulation. Once my left hand grasps the shaft for a stroke on my left side, my left hand controls all the movements of that blade even though I have a right-hand-controlled paddle.

The Extended Paddle Position

As a matter of course, it was quite natural for the Eskimo hunter to slide his hands to one end of his paddle, thereby gaining extra length and leverage to help with the variety of strokes and braces that he used as part of his daily work.

The modern paddler will also often find an advantage in the added leverage gained by holding the paddle in what is now known as the extended paddle (EP) position. It will help to give you confidence when practicing any of the supporting or bracing strokes, and it is especially useful for such maneuvers as turning a kayak in high winds. There are also a number of Greenland-style rolls that require the paddle to be held in the extended position.

Figure 3.5 shows the extended paddle position on the left side. The cupped palm of the right hand is supporting the lower corner of the held blade. The left hand is a forearm's distance from the neck of the held blade, and the knuckles of the left hand are facing backwards. The outer blade has its driving face looking down, parallel to the surface of the water.

Figure 3.5 *Extended paddle position*

You will notice that when this stroke is applied on the right side, the held blade will have its driving face towards you. Again, Derek's illustrations are for his 90-degree feathered paddle. The angle of the blade by your chest will vary according to your personal feather angle.

Edging and Leaning

Kayaks built for use on open water do not turn easily. You will be relieved to know that this has little to do with your level of ability. The answer is really quite simple: *Sea kayaks are designed to run straight*. To make turning easier, you must lean the boat over onto its side so as to place the more maneuverable part of the hull (i.e., the gunwale) under the water. There are two ways of doing this: edging and leaning.

Edging

Edging, or tilting, is the most controlled method of getting the boat over onto its side, and it is therefore kinder on the nerves of the novice.

Keep your body as perpendicular as possible, flex your hips, keep your balance, and dip the gunwale into the water.

The high-side knee, in Figure 3.6 the right knee, is raised and pressed upwards, either against the knee braces or underneath the cockpit coaming, hence the expression "knee-hanging." You should feel quite stable when you do this, and once you get used to keeping your center of gravity over the kayak, you will be surprised how far over you can dip the gunwale without losing your balance.

Leaning

This is when you allow your upper body lean to follow the angle of the lean of the kayak (Figure 3.7). The paddler and the boat become one unit, very much like when a cyclist goes around a corner. Because your weight is off-balance, you need some support from your paddle.

Most maneuvers will have a combination of edging and leaning. Remember, the more you lean, the more support you will need from your paddle. For the majority of kayak designs out there, the more you lean, the more turn you will get from your kayak.

Figure 3.6 *Edging, or tilting. Notice the paddler's right knee is raised, enabling him to knee-hang on the right side.*

Figure 3.7 *Leaning*

Your Paddling Engine

Although Derek will tell you to use your body while paddling, I wanted to expand on what he has to say. I mentioned earlier that the paddle is your propeller and your body is the engine. The water does not care how you derive your power when performing a stroke. I can tell you that your body and group members will care during a long paddle. I tell my students our engine has three different power levels.

Low power is when you paddle just using your arm muscles. Even though your kayak will move, it will be difficult to keep up with the group because your arm muscles are relatively small compared to other muscles in the body.

Medium power is when you are using torso rotation to move your paddle. Your trunk muscle can provide lots of power over longer periods of time compared to your arms. Using your foot pedals during the stroke gives your trunk support to allow rotation. In fact, you will even do a gentle push on the pedals when rotating your torso.

High power adds the driving force of your legs during the stroke. When I say driving force, I mean pushing off of your foot pedal in such a way that it drives the hip on the stroke side backwards, which means you are eventually straightening your leg during the power phase of the stroke. This driving force allows even more torso rotation. It is what racers do during their strokes.

While it would be nice to be able to maintain high power during the entire trip, it will be dependent upon your training. You need to be paddling at least three days a week to build and maintain paddling power. Your training retention will be minimal if you only get out once a week.

There will be no retention if you go out less than that. Therefore, use medium power for your general touring and go into high power for sprinting to help in a recovery, towing, or getting through surf zones and tidal streams.

The same applies to high-angle strokes. While they are more powerful and efficient, trying to maintain the stroke all day requires training because you are lifting your arms higher. This does not mean you should not do a high-angle stroke. What I am saying is, the more energy you put out, the more fatigued you get, and that is determined by your training. Your stroke style and how you use your engine should be able to last for the duration of your paddle on any given day.

The Forward Paddle Stroke

The paddle stroke we use for touring on the sea is based on the traditional racing stroke that was used before the advent of the "wing" paddle (see Chapter 6, Racing). It is an art form itself and was developed over many years as the most efficient method of propelling a kayak forward. In its purest form, however, it has only limited use when paddling on the open sea. As Figure 3.8 shows, the paddler leans aggressively forward. His back is unsupported. His right arm pushes forward and will finish up straight out at maximum stretch with his right shoulder twisted forward. During the stroke his right hand is relaxed, perhaps open, the fingers facing forward. His left arm pulls the paddle backwards, bringing the blade close to the hull.

Note the height of the upper blade. This is a sure beam-wind catcher. The lower blade is purely propulsive, giving hardly any support in rough conditions, due to the high stroke angle. While a

Figure 3.8 *The forward paddle stroke showing complete breakdown of movements*

Figure 3.9 *The forward stroke catch*

high stroke angle is very powerful and efficient, it does not provide the paddler with much support throughout the stroke cycle.

The sea kayaking forward paddle stroke may have to be continued over many hours, so it is a good idea to get comfortable. Sit in a relaxed manner with your feet on the footrest. In rough conditions you should wedge your knees up underneath the cockpit coaming, but for normal flat-water paddling, the legs can be almost straight (Figure 3.9).

The back should be supported in any way that suits the individual. I prefer a wide, padded backstrap so that the lower half of my body is braced between the footrest and the backrest. The body should be upright and with a slight lean forward. *Never lean backwards.*

The forward paddle stroke really consists of two parts, both of which occur simultaneously. They are the **pushing phase** and the **pulling phase**.

Figure 3.10 *The forward stroke power phase via torso rotation*

Figure 3.11 *The forward stroke recovery transitioning to a stroke on the other side*

The Starting Position

Hold the paddle with your right hand at a height approximately level with your ear. Your lower (left) hand places the power blade in the water, as far forward as is comfortably possible.

The Pushing Phase

Begin by moving your hip and the right side of your chest forward. At the same time, push your right hand forward at eye level, following the line of the gunwale. Avoid crossing your hand over towards the center line of the boat. During this forward push the paddle shaft is not gripped tightly but is cradled in the curved hollow between the thumb and forefinger. The fingers are relaxed and curved slightly forward. With *your wrist slightly dropped,* push the shaft by the *upper part of your palm* (Figures 3.9, 3.10).

The Pulling Phase

During the pulling phase the shaft is held firmly by the left hand. As this lower hand starts to travel backwards, the grip changes to facilitate a "pulling" action with hooked rather than clenched fingers and a *relaxed thumb.* This grip change, combined with a hip rotation, ensures that the wrist remains in an almost straight line in relation to the arm. Failure to relax the grip and *swing the body* will cause the wrist to bend to its limit. This is dangerous and could cause an inflammatory condition of the tendons known as tenosynovitis (otherwise known carpal tunnel syndrome, the "kiss of death" to paddling!). The action of tightening and relaxing the hands "milks" fresh oxygenated blood to the muscles and helps to prevent any tendency towards cramp.

Once the lower hand is pulled back to a position level with the hip, the upper arm is straight and the body is fully rotated forward from the waist. The upper forward hand, with the paddle, is brought straight down to coincide with the *rotation of the body* and the lower blade being clipped from the water (Figure 3.11).

In the instant before the right-hand blade touches the water, it is indexed into the correct angle for the catch by raising the left arm so that from the shoulder to the elbow, it is parallel to the water. In this manner the fully extended feathered blade will be presented correctly to the water. If the shaft is oval at the handgrip, this backward flick of the left hand will cause the paddle to fall into the correct position due to the cradling shape of the palm. However, this will not happen if the paddle is gripped too tightly.

This pulling phase is the most important in the whole stroke cycle. It is vital that the body and arm are fully rotated forward. The paddle must be dipped into the water cleanly, at boat speed and without a splash, in a position immediately outside the wave that runs from the bow.

The most productive part of the pulling phase is the time during which the immersed blade covers the first third of its backward movement. It is important, therefore, that the paddle blade is placed well forward. It is then propelled backwards with a vigorous pulling movement involving the shoulder, trunk, and leg muscles. This is also referred to as "trunk rotation." The pulling action ends when the lower hand is level with the hips. The speed with which this pulling blade is lifted from the water is governed by the rotation of your body.

Forward Touring Stroke

The paddle is placed farther out from the side of the hull than it is during the racing stroke, giving the stroke a slight sweep outwards rather than a downward plunge. The upper blade presents a more acute and therefore more favorable angle to any beam wind, with hardly any likelihood of the paddle being snatched or twisted from the upper hand by the wind. Moreover, because the paddle action is lower, it is less tiring on the arms and shoulders. One often doesn't take into consideration the weight of the arms, yet so much importance is placed on paddle weight.

As mentioned earlier, opening and closing alternate hands during the stroke cycle allows fresh blood and oxygen to circulate into the muscles, thus preventing cramp. It also helps to keep the hands from becoming numb in cold weather. Pressing on the footrest during the stroke cycle does the same for the muscles in the feet, legs, and thighs.

When worn by the paddler, the kayak is propelled not only by the movement of the trunk and arms, but also by the *whole body right to the tips of the toes*. During a forward stroke you are pressing on the footrest that is on the same side as the stroke. Paddling a kayak without a firm footrest makes it necessary for the occupant to brace with the thighs, without a firm support for the feet. This is inefficient from the point of view of propulsion and causes bad circulation, "pins and needles," and can lead to severe cramps.

Paddlers should be able to alter their forward stroke to suit prevailing conditions, such as an approaching danger, an adverse wind or tide race, or a need for speed.

In calm conditions, as a novice you should be able to paddle 3 or 4 miles without any problems.

If you grip the paddles too tightly, however, blisters may form inside your thumb. You may find 4 to 5 miles an ordeal at first, but after a few months of practice and if conditions are calm, you should be able to paddle between 20 and 25 miles quite easily.

Proficient paddlers can usually cope with distances of between 12 and 30 miles (depending on such things as age, general fitness, and muscle mass). Advanced paddlers should achieve significantly in excess of this. However, all these distances may be increased if a strong wind is favorable or cut down to a mere couple of miles, even for an advanced paddler, if conditions are bad.

Reverse Paddling

There will be many occasions when the quickest way to position your kayak will be by moving backwards. For instance, a member of your group may capsize behind you. Turning around in fresh winds can be a time-consuming business. Fortunately, some vigorous reverse paddling will get you into position faster and enable you to give more immediate help. You should use the back of the blade for any reverse strokes.

Unfortunately many paddlers propel themselves backwards by placing the paddle blades in the water vertically or, in other words, in the "slicing" position. This is unproductive and gives the paddler no stability (Figure 3.12).

When reverse paddling, especially in rough seas, the stroke should give you support as well as propulsion. For it to do this, the *back of the blade* should be presented to the water as *flat* as possible and at an shaft angle of about 45 degrees to the side of the boat (Figure 3.13). With practice you will be able to lean over as

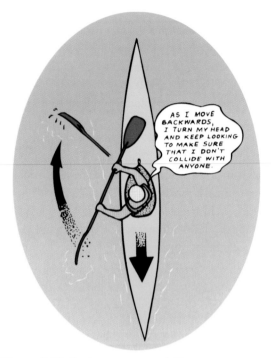

Figure 3.12 *Basic reverse paddling*

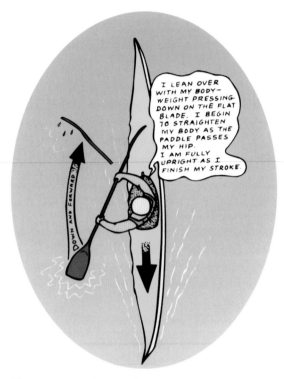

Figure 3.13 *Advanced reverse paddling. Note that the paddle shaft is parallel to the chest for shoulder safety.*

you press down and present the flat blade to the water.

Push down and forward as you sweep the working blade towards the bow. You then quickly transfer your weight onto the opposite side and repeat the stroke. Unlike the forward stroke, you press on the opposite foot pedal to get the support and power for the reverse stroke. What it really amounts to is that you will finish up paddling backwards by using a series of *supportive reverse sweep strokes*. In this way you will be supporting yourself as well as propelling yourself backwards. You will find that the power you exert is much greater and the stability much more reassuring than if you were to present the blade vertically to the water. A strong, powerful reverse stroke takes a good deal of practice to perfect. Use this lean and your *body weight* to

exert pressure *downward* and then *forward* during the stroke.

Warning: Over the years I have watched paddlers drive themselves backwards, with considerable violence, into other kayaks, speedboats, the heavy beams of wooden jetties, and concrete breakwaters. In light of these expensive and often painful mishaps, may I offer this advice: *When traveling backwards, look backwards!*

Stopping

Once, during a practice session out at sea, Derek was hanging upside down waiting for an Eskimo recovery (Figure 2.4, Chapter 2). The sea was choppy, and he had an unfamiliar partner. Time dragged by, as it tends to when you are holding your breath. After what seemed like a long time, he lost faith and dog-paddled up to the surface to get a gulp of air. Suddenly a kayak's bow flashed past his eyes as his head broke the surface. The pointed front end of the rescuer's kayak went straight through the deck of Derek's boat in a position level with his knees. Positioning himself for the rescue had taken longer than the assisting paddler thought. His concern for Derek, and the sight of his upturned hull, spurred him into high-speed action. In retrospect, perhaps they should have practiced emergency stops *before* the Eskimo rescue!

At full speed you will not be moving at much more than 5 mph. However, the combined weight of you and your kayak gives the mass considerable momentum. To stop your kayak from moving forward, it will take at least *four* paddle strokes and a surprising amount of effort.

The stopping stroke is identical to the stroke that is used for reverse paddling. The paddle blade is placed flat on the water behind you, at a shaft angle of about 45 degrees to the kayak's hull (Figure 3.14). As the blade bites the water, push it forward against the pressure of the water, then quickly change your stroke over to the other side and do the same again.

The first two strokes should stop you moving forward. The second two should have you moving in the *opposite direction*. Do not worry if your first attempts send showers of water over your bow as your paddle fails to bite the water. Keep practicing until you can stop quickly without looking at the paddle blades and you are able to use your body weight to press downwards on the flat paddle blade (Figure 3.14).

One usually does not feel very stable when sitting stationary in a kayak and bobbing

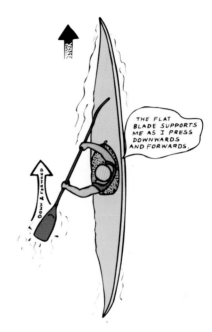

Figure 3.14 *Advanced stop*

around in rough seas. Even with little experience, you soon realize that you feel more stable in your kayak as it is moving, especially on windy days. Therefore, as you stop your kayak, you are essentially going from greater stability to lesser stability. With that in mind, wouldn't you want support from your stopping stroke? I find it amazing that the vast majority of paddlers choose to stop their forward momentum by placing their blades in the water on knife edge, as seen in Figure 3.15. Paddlers who choose to quickly stop their kayaks this way demonstrate the "intestinal wobble," which looks as if they are going to capsize at any moment. Try both methods and you will quickly feel which one feels better.

In all forward and reverse strokes, you should *keep your paddle shaft parallel with your chest*. Your blade should *not* go behind the front

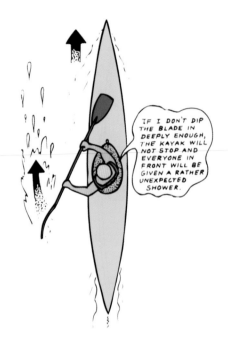

IF I DON'T DIP THE BLADE IN DEEPLY ENOUGH, THE KAYAK WILL NOT STOP AND EVERYONE IN FRONT WILL BE GIVEN A RATHER UNEXPECTED SHOWER.

Figure 3.15 *Basic stop (poor stopping technique)*

plane of your body. *This is an injury prevention warning.* The greater concern is during stops and reverse strokes. It seems to be an unsafe and nasty habit of paddlers to reach back without rotating their torso when placing the blade for these strokes. By doing so you are putting the working side shoulder at great risk for a strain. Once strained, it has a good chance of becoming chronic, especially if you continue unsafe blade placement.

If you look at your blade as you place it, you need to rotate your body to do so, which keeps the blade in the front plane. In addition, since you are looking back anyway, you will see where you are going if you are going backwards.

The Forward Sweep Stroke (Bow Sweep Turn)

The forward sweep stroke can be used to turn either a stationary kayak or one that is moving forward. It may be done either to avoid obstacles or as a corrective stroke.

The forward sweep is one of the easiest of all kayaking techniques and yet it is perhaps the most important. Because it appears to be an uncomplicated stroke, many paddlers tend to perform it in a slipshod manner. If your technique is bad, you will be wasting energy simply because it will take more separate paddle movements for you to obtain the desired result. Novices usually prefer to sit up straight during their first attempts at the forward sweep, but a kayak that is not edged is more difficult to turn. In a sea kayak you will not get the results you desire unless you tilt the boat over onto its gunwale, thus cancelling out the effects of a straight or pronounced keel. To do this your body must lean as well, which means getting some support from your paddle.

Lean forward. The paddle is placed as near to the bow as possible (Figure 3.16). The blade should be positioned so that the top edge is angled slightly outwards. As you start to sweep out, angle the blade even more, *keeping its leading edge high*. At the same time, tilt the kayak. Sweep the paddle out and around in a semicircle towards the stern. *Rotate your body* and pull the paddle around *with your arm straight*. As you pull with your arm, push forward with the foot on that side.

It is the angle of the blade that will provide lift and give you support. Your greatest angle of lean, therefore, will be during the first half of the stroke. Once your paddle passes the halfway

Figure 3.16 *The forward sweep stroke*

mark, your body can start to come upright. Finish the stroke when the paddle shaft is at an angle of 45 degrees to the stern.

The Recovery

The method of returning the paddle to its starting position is almost as important as the main stroke. Your most vulnerable time is when your body is twisted around and the paddle is closest to the stern. To prevent any chance of a capsize, do not clear the water completely with the paddle

Figure 3.17 *Skim the back of the blade across the surface to return the paddle to its starting position.*

when you remove it. With a forward rotation of the knuckles, flip the paddle over onto its back face and return it to the bow by skimming it along the surface. During the return the blade should hardly touch the water, but the paddle is ready to apply a low brace support at any time. If this return phase is done correctly, it is possible to maintain a considerable angle of tilt throughout the whole stroke cycle (Figure 3.17).

Extended Paddle Sweep

If you are turning a long, straight-keeled kayak in a high wind, you will find you have more success if you take advantage of the extra leverage afforded by the extended paddle position (Figure 3.5).

Correcting Course

There may be times when you find it difficult to maintain a straight course due to a side wind causing you to "weather-cock" (i.e., bow swings into the wind). To correct this tiresome problem, alternate your forward paddling stroke with a sweep stroke on the windward side. As you push your foot down on the stroke side, remember to knee-hang on the other (Figure 3.6)

The Reverse Sweep Stroke

The reverse sweep stroke (Figure 3.18) is used to turn a stationary kayak in a backward direction, or as discussed earlier, for going backwards. You may find it easier to turn your kayak by means of the reverse sweep than by using a forward sweep stroke. This is especially true where you have a strong wind pushing against your bow.

As a novice, you may be a little reluctant to lean over; however, as with the forward sweep stroke, once you increase your confidence you will begin leaning your straight-keeled kayak over on its side. In this way the curved gunwale once more acts as the new keel, and this makes turning easier.

In Figure 3.18 the stroke is illustrated on the right side. This will turn the kayak in a *clockwise* direction.

Twist your body around, edging the kayak slightly. Place the outer paddle blade with the back of the blade flat on the water, with a shaft angle of 30 to 45 degrees to the rear of the kayak. The knee on the opposite side of the stroke is hooked under the cockpit coaming (knee-hanging). With the paddle in this position, you should be able to put your weight onto the blade.

Figure 3.18 *Reverse sweep stroke. Combine this stroke with the forward sweep stroke to pivot the kayak in a complete circle.*

As you sweep it forward, the leading edge is slightly angled upwards. Press downwards and increase the angle during the short distance the blade travels forward. Reach out as far as you can. Think of the stroke as a sweeping outrigger. The pressure on the back of the moving blade will allow you to remain leaning out and put a considerable amount of weight into the downward and forward push. Throughout the stroke, you should be driving the hanging knee towards the working hand. It is important that you are sitting upright again as soon as the paddle starts to draw level with your body, i.e., when the paddle gets into a position at right angles to the boat's hull.

Do not be tempted to continue the stroke into a front quadrant, as there is little support for the blade in this position.

This is a very powerful stroke but the key to its success, in rough conditions, is due solely to the support angle of the blade as it is presented to the water.

The Draw Stroke

Now that you can move your kayak forward and backward, turn it and stop it, we need to discuss going sideways. There will be many instances when you will want to move sideways. Positioning the kayak for rescues must be done quickly, as any time spent in cold water can be dangerous. It is the draw stroke that will move you sideways faster than anything else.

Speed is especially important when positioning the kayak for an Eskimo recovery. Although the dangers of cold water are less during this particular rescue, it must be remembered that the paddler waiting for the assist will be hanging upside down, trying to hold his or her breath and perhaps feeling somewhat apprehensive.

Figure 3.19

Figure 3.23

Figure 3.20

Figure 3.24

Figure 3.21

Figure 3.25

Figure 3.22

Figure 3.26

In Figures 3.19 through 3.26, Derek talks you through the stroke as he would if he were demonstrating the movements to you on the water. Throughout the stroke the paddle is held in the *normal paddling position*. If you feel unsure and want to make things easy for your first couple of attempts, move your lower hand down the shaft and grip the paddle at the neck, where the shaft joins the lower blade. In this way you will get the "feel" for what the underwater blade is doing during the stroke. Revert to holding the paddle in the normal position as soon as possible.

Only experience will tell you how far to reach out to begin the stroke (Figure 3.19). With practice, you will be able to extend your reach by leaning the kayak well over onto its side. This will certainly give your stroke more power. However, you will also discover that the submerged gunwale digging into the water affects the stroke's efficiency.

As I draw the kayak towards the paddle (Figure 3.20), my knee on the opposite side to the stroke is exerting an upward pressure under the cockpit roaming.

Beware of "violining." This is a common mistake that occurs when the upper arm moves upwards rather than being pushed outwards and away from the body. There is no drawing power in violining because the submerged blade merely slices up out of the water.

Another danger is what I call "overrunning" the paddle. The dynamic part of the stroke is over but the kayak is still moving sideways with its own momentum. There is a need for caution when you twist the paddle. If the hull overruns the blade before you twist it, the paddle could pull you over into a capsize.

The Sculling Draw Stroke

The sculling draw (Figure 3.27) is used to move a kayak sideways. Unlike the draw stroke, the sculling draw has no return or recovery phase. The kayak is pulled sideways by a *continuous*, vertical, underwater sculling action. Because of this, the paddle can be moved into position to begin a different stroke without being taken from the water, and the angle of the stroke can be altered to support the paddler in bad conditions.

Turn the upper part of your body sideways in the direction in which you intend to travel. Hold the paddle as you would for stage 4 of the draw stroke (Figure 3.22). The sculling draw combines this paddle position with the sculling configuration of the high sculling brace (Figure 4.1, Chapter 4). You must knee-hang on the opposite side to the stroke, and your sideways movement can only be maintained by the continuous sculling action of your lower arm, wrist, and hand.

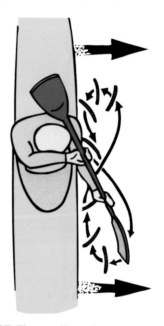

Figure 3.27 *The sculling draw stroke*

If at first you have difficulty in getting the paddle to do what you want, move your lower hand farther down the shaft to the neck. Place the palm of your hand on the back of the blade under the water. This will help you to direct the sculling action of the blade near the surface until you get the "feel" of the stroke.

Another approach is to start off by performing the sculling for support stroke. Without discontinuing this stroke, gradually move the lower blade in towards the kayak. The supporting figure-eight configuration is now being performed by your *vertically held paddle* and your kayak is moving sideways.

The One-Hand Scull

Sculling with one hand is a pleasurable and rewarding exercise for those *with some experience*. Before starting the scull, it is necessary to hold the paddle at or near the blade at the neck. The blade must be submerged and the paddle

Figure 3.28 *The one-hand scull*

balanced vertically. Moving the lower blade in order to scull will illustrate to you which hand does the controlling during the stroke. It will also let you see the small area into which the figure-eight can be compressed and yet still move the kayak sideways at a considerable speed.

Derek discovered that the one-hand scull is ideal for moving sideways away from the proximity of larger seagoing craft, while clutching a glass of whisky or a cup of hot coffee handed to him by some generous skipper (Figure 3.28).

Indoor Dry-Land Sculling Drill

Try sitting on a stool or an armless dining chair. Place the book with Figure 3.27 on the floor next to you. The figure-eight diagram applies equally to both right and left sides. Position yourself so that you are directly above the page, and then follow the movement with your paddle, either until you have mastered the movement or until your concerned friends have taken your struggling body to hospital.

The key to sculling is changing the angle of the blade before you move it in the opposite direction. This keeps the blade in a climbing angle. Trying to change direction and blade angle at the same time usually results in your blade quickly slicing away, leaving you vulnerable to a capsize.

Turning Strokes on the Move

The Stern Rudder

Using your paddle as a rudder allows you to steer the kayak while moving forward with a minimum loss of speed. This gives the paddler a delicate control over the direction of the boat. The stern rudder is one of the most important strokes in kayak surfing, but it can only be applied when the boat is moving forward (either by being paddled forward or carried on the face of a wave).

The paddle is placed in the water vertically and trailed at the rear of the boat with the back of the blade facing outwards. For the stroke to be efficient, the blade should be completely submerged (Figure 3.29).

To turn right: push the controlling blade outwards, away from the hull. *To turn left*: pull the blade in, towards the hull; the steering is limited on this side. *To go straight*: allow the controlling blade to trail with no sideways movement.

When you are running with a following wind out on open water, you may find you have difficulty keeping the boat straight. You can counteract the effect of small waves by incorporating a stern rudder into your forward paddling stroke. If the following waves are large and green, you may have to apply the correcting stroke more powerfully and for a longer period. If the changes

in direction are sudden, and the powerful "outpush" part of the ruddering stroke is the only way to correct, you may find yourself continually having to change sides.

Depending on the hull shape, the turn may be easier if the kayak is made to lean slightly *on the opposite side to the ruddering stroke*. You will discover this as you practice in your own boat.

This stroke affords very little support, and the blade cannot be leaned upon unless the kayak is moving very fast.

The Low Brace Turn (Low Telemark Turn)

The low brace turn (Figure 3.30) supports the paddler and turns the forward-moving kayak.

Paddle forward fast, then reach out with your right arm and present the *back* of the right blade to the water with a shaft angle of 45 degrees and its leading edge slightly higher than the trailing edge, just slightly above flat (a

Figure 3.29 *The stern rudder (steering stroke). Best results are obtained with the steering blade held completely submerged.*

Figure 3.30 *The low brace, or low telemark, turn. The kayak is moving forward fast. The paddler leans over on the turn and is supported on the back of the blade as it planes on the surface of the water. The greater the speed of the kayak, the farther the lean and the better the turn.*

vertical blade does not provide support). Your arm is almost straight, with the knuckles turned downwards. The angle of the blade is such that it planes on the surface of the water, enabling the paddler to lean right over onto the blade, thus getting plenty of support. The left arm is passed in front of the body, and the paddle is held at a low angle to the water. The kayak in the illustration should turn to its right, but if its hull shape is one that is likely to skid, the paddler may find that the boat is going to the left. With practice, there should be no need to change sides to correct this.

If you are using a whitewater kayak in surf or a following sea, you can finish up actually leaning down the face of the wave, the paddle stroke on the side of the turn. It may sometimes become necessary to change direction quickly, as on the face of a moving wave. Pushing downwards at the beginning of the stroke will lift the stern and jerk it sideways. The kayak can thus be turned sharply to zigzag on the face of a wave.

The High Brace Turn (High Telemark Turn)

The high brace turn is a high-speed turn performed in the high brace support position. Once the turn is completed, the paddle can be drawn in

towards the bow (Figure 3.31 B) and into a position from which it can move smoothly into the forward paddling stroke.

The high brace turn is both fast and powerful. The stroke's main application, therefore, is in surf or broken water. The turning qualities of short, rockered whitewater kayaks are such that as you perform the stroke, your paddle will remain stationary in the water while your boat executes a tight spin around the blade.

Paddle forward fast. Reach well out and rotate and place the paddle into the water behind you, with the leading edge high. The paddle shaft should be at an angle of between 30 and 70 degrees to the water. Lean your body over and tilt the boat so that you are supported on the "lift" of the blade. As you lean, knee-hang on the high side of the coaming and exert pressure on the water by increasing the angle of the blade, at the same time pushing it towards the bow.

Take note of the correct position of the upper arm in the illustration. The elbow is thrust forward, the wrist is thrown back, and the palm of the hand supporting the blade is facing upwards.

The quality of your turn will depend on how fast the kayak is moving forward, on the angle of tilt of the kayak's hull, and on the angle of the paddle blade to the water.

Figure 3.31 *The high brace, or high telemark, turn. "A" shows the planing angle of the paddle blade as it skids over the surface of the water. This angle supports the paddler during the high-speed lean-over. "B" shows the change in paddle angle as the turn nears its completion as the kayak slows down. Pulling the blade in towards the bow compensates for loss of momentum and leads into the next forward paddle stroke.*

The Bow Draw (Duffek Stroke)

The bow draw is one of the most commonly used variations of the basic draw stroke and is also the most important. This fast, powerful, tight-radius turn is more often used by white-water paddlers for "breaking out" into eddies or "breaking in" to the main stream. The speed of this turn, introduced into slalom racing by Milo Duffek, completely revolutionized the sport. Although its original application was ideal for the narrow confines of the slalom course, the stroke also has a twofold application for the sea kayaker.

The result of applying the bow draw will depend to a large extent on the type of kayak you are using. In a whitewater kayak, the response by the boat to the stroke is immediate and the kayak

can be spun around through 90 degrees within its own length. As the kayak completes the turn, the blade arrives in a position that allows it to continue without pause into the next forward paddling stroke. The speed of the turn and the subsequent follow-through makes it ideal for positioning and maneuvering in surf or among standing waves when speed is necessary and space is limited.

Sea kayaks do not have the same dramatic turning qualities as shorter boats, although their response can be improved if one is prepared to utilize the pivoting effect of a wave passing beneath the hull. I do caution you that a wrist strain is very possible if your kayak is moving too fast. I would never use this stroke if my sea kayak was surfing.

The bow draw can be used effectively when paddling close inshore among rocks. If a rock suddenly appears in front of your bow, you merely apply a bow draw. Although it will not appreciably turn the bow, it will pull your kayak bodily sideways, thus avoiding the rock without any interruption in your forward progress.

How far out you place the paddle at the start of the stroke will depend on the speed of the water flowing past the kayak. To put it another way, you will have to contend with the pressure of the water against the paddle blade. When performed, the bow draw appears as one smooth movement; it can, however, be broken down into three phases: the ruddering phase, the drawing phase, and the propulsive phase.

The ruddering phase: As the water moves past the hull, the paddle blade is placed into the water in a position approximately opposite your knee (Figure 3.32). The driving face is forward, at an angle of about 45 degrees to the kayak. The ruddering effect of the paddle blade locked into the moving water will turn the kayak (Figure 3.33).

The drawing phase: Immediately the pressure against the blade begins to ease off; continue the turn by drawing the blade forward and around in an arc towards the bow (Figure 3.34). Do this until the driving face is parallel to the hull. By this time you will have stopped turning.

The propulsive phase: At the moment when your paddle blade is parallel to the hull and about a foot from it, turn the shaft so that the driving face of the blade is now pointing towards the stern (Figure 3.35). Without any pause, you can now continue with your forward paddling stroke (Figure 3.36).

The result of your bow draw will be more dramatic if the bow of the kayak is already starting

Figure 3.32

Figure 3.33

Figure 3.34

to swing around. This will occur after a forward paddling stroke on the opposite side to the proposed turn.

Figure 3.35

Figure 3.36

In the illustrations, the paddler is sitting almost upright. However, by leaning the kayak over during the ruddering and drawing phases, the length and power of the stroke is greatly increased.

Known as the bow rudder, the ruddering phase of the bow draw is used as a separate stroke in its own right. As with the bow draw, sea kayaks do not respond well to this front ruddering action. When your sea kayak is moving forward, the bow is held in position by the water. That is why bow rudders can put a strain on your wrist. Using stern rudders is usually more effective and puts less strain on your joints.

Open Water Paddling

If you are paddling in open water, sooner than later, wind, tides, and currents will challenge you. Derek is going to share his experiences, which I am sure you will find helpful.

Wind Techniques

Beam winds come from the side, headwinds from the front, and tailwinds from behind. Quartering winds come on an angle. Keep in mind that the wind will also bring waves in the same direction as the wind (beam seas, head seas, following seas, and quartering seas). If there are swells coming from far away, they may be from a different direction than your local conditions. This really makes it exciting.

Beam Wind

Try to present the least amount of body resistance to the wind (Figure 3.37). Your kayak should be leaning towards the wind (Figure 3.38). Keep the paddle blade on the windward side low. In order to prevent very strong winds capsizing you, at the end of each forward stroke, let the back of the blade skim the water on the return (Figure 3.39). Keeping the blade low to the water keeps the wind from getting underneath the blade and lifting it (and you) up and over.

A strong gust could take the paddle out of your hands altogether. If you managed to hang on tightly, it could capsize you by whipping the paddle over in an arc. If a gust comes from the right, say, and the right-hand blade has been caught by the full force of a violent gust and is about to take off, do not hold on. Relax the grip with your right hand and let the paddle flip over onto your left side, allowing your left

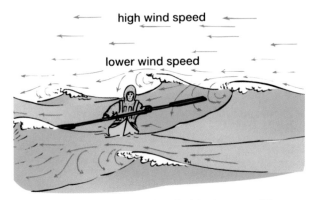

high wind speed

lower wind speed

Figure 3.37 *Wind eddies behind waves. The paddler keeps his arms low while paddling forward, especially on the windward side. He is sheltered to some extent by the wind eddying behind each wave. The danger of having the paddle snatched by the wind is greatest when he reaches the crest. He must keep his left-hand blade as low as possible as he travels forward; he does this by making the forward stroke on the right side so low as to be almost a sweep stroke.*

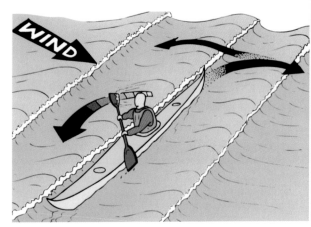

Figure 3.39 *Turning a kayak in a high wind. The kayak will not respond to a forward sweep stroke on the left side, so the paddler must lean into the wind and perform a reverse sweep stroke on the right side. As the kayak moves backwards, the "weather-cocking" action of the wind will help turn the kayak into the wind. The paddle may be held in the extended paddle position but care will be needed to avoid breaking it under the tremendous strain.*

Figure 3.38 *Paddling straight in a beam wind, correcting course. You are moving forward with a strong wind blowing onto your left side. The waves are close together. Just before the wave hits you, the paddle is angled, as it would be for a sweep turn. As you sweep the paddle back with your left hand, you will realize that the stroke is more of a propulsive paddle brace than a forward paddling stroke. In order to keep the kayak on a straight course, you must lean over into the wind and knee-hang on your right side.*

Figure 3.40 *Turning a kayak using a wave. The wave, passing under the hull, puts the bow clear of the water and gives a moving pivot upon which to turn the kayak by a forward sweep stroke. The paddle can also be held in the extended position for greater leverage.*

wrist to twist over with the loom. This way you will keep your paddle and you won't finish up underwater.

Use the top of the waves to help make it easier if you need to turn your kayak (Figure 3.40).

Headwind

If you are battling into a headwind, remember that although you may think you are making no headway, you'll be going forward a little at a time.

Lean forward and keep your head down to prevent the salt spray from lashing at your face and eyes. Try to shut your mind off from the flying spray and the white-tops breaking all around you. Get a nice rhythm going and punch your way through, always forward. Your body can do it. If anything lets you down it will be your willpower. When crossing the entrance to a bay, remember that any strong offshore wind will produce large waves once the protection of the land is left behind. A safer, though much longer, course will therefore be to hug the shore, leaving open crossings for calmer days.

lean into wind

Figure 3.41 *Localized downdraughts are sudden and violent and usually of a greater velocity than the wind that caused them.*

A gap in high protective cliffs or hills can cause any strong winds to accelerate due to a funneling effect, and therefore much stronger gusts can be expected and must be allowed for (Figure 3.41).

Tailwind

Tailwinds produce "following seas," which means the waves are coming at you from behind. The wind on your back will add to your paddling speed. Most of the time there is wind with following seas, but not always. The paddling effort is not constant in following seas because some of the time you will be surfing down the wave, and after it passes in front of you, you will be climbing up the back of it (Figure 7.3, Chapter 7). As the wave passes underneath, ease your efforts. Build them up again when the boat is in the trough, and aim to reach maximum when the hull is on the face of the wave slope. Ease off again as the crest is reached and passes underneath the boat.

Following seas can be fun or terrifying depending on your surfing abilities. You can also cover a lot of ground in following seas and a tailwind.

Quartering Wind

Quartering winds mean your kayak is going to feel more of the weather-cocking effect. This is where skegs and rudders are worth their weight in gold. If you have neither or there is a malfunction, you will be working hard all day trying to stay on course with ongoing corrective strokes and edging your kayak.

One strategy is paddling a zigzag course, which has you perpendicular and parallel to the wind instead of angled. It may mean more miles, but you may find it less frustrating and/or nerve wracking.

Turning Upwind or Downwind

Knowing that your kayak will weather-cock can help you if you have to turn in windy conditions. If your rudder or skeg fails, you will have to depend on your paddle. If you want to turn into the wind, paddle forward as you try turning and let the weather-cocking effect help bring your bow into the wind.

If you want to go downwind, do your turning strokes while reverse paddling. The stern will turn into the wind, which means your real bow will be heading downwind.

The Ferry Glide

When any boat is held at an angle to fast-moving water, or in the case of much sea kayaking, at an angle to the wind, it will move sideways across the main flow. In river kayaking this is called the "ferry glide" because of its association with flying ferries on fast-moving rivers. At sea, the maneuver is still loosely referred to as the ferry glide, although it would be more technically correct to call it "making an allowance for set and drift." This maneuver on open water can be a rather prolonged affair, and using it to travel across several miles is a very different matter from using it to cross a narrow river or even the narrows between two islands (Figure 3.42).

This is when the use of transit bearings (see Chapter 11 on navigation) really proves to be a blessing. A compass is almost useless in this situation, as the paddler has no means of calculating even the approximate speed of the wind when he is moving forward. The only way to ensure a straight ferry glide across the wind is by selecting transit markers.

When the paddler looks across a channel, the fastest-flowing water is always marked by a white-topped broken wave. If the strong current is opposed by even a moderate wind, it will produce a short, steep chop. This is because the waves are foreshortened or compressed by the wind, causing them to break. Therefore, beware when the tide changes against the wind during the crossing of a wide channel. It could produce conditions that might prove a nightmare, if not a complete disaster, for normal proficiency-standard paddlers. In windy weather be sure to make a specific note of what time the tide will be turning.

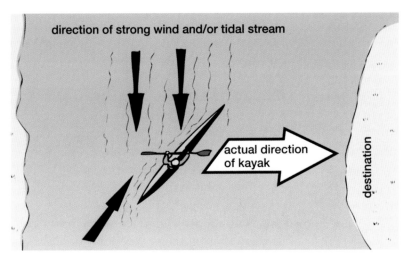

direction of strong wind and/or tidal stream

actual direction of kayak

destination

Figure 3.42 *The ferry glide. The kayaker paddles in the direction of the the black arrow tht is behind the kayak. If it is windy, he leans over to his left onto it. With luck the paddler may find landmarks, which will serve as transits, thereby making him aware of any drift off course.*

CHAPTER 4
BRACING AND SUPPORT

"Performing a roll is a sign of success. Having to roll is a sign of failure." This is one of Derek's many famous quotes. He strongly believed kayaking is a dry sport. Once you are a proficient paddler, you should never go over.

If you think about it, not capsizing is an admirable goal for many reasons. You are essentially eliminating immersion, you are reducing some of the reasons for being rescued, you are not taking time away from your planned itinerary, you are expending less energy, and you are most likely maintaining more body heat. The only downside to bracing is that you do not get a chance to practice rolling and capsize recoveries from unplanned capsizes, which is good training. However, I would not worry too much about that because sooner or later your brace will not work.

A brace is the technique used to return your body to a stable position, over your kayak, after your body has gone past its capsizing point. Your body's capsize point and the kayak's capsize point are two different points, even though you are taking the kayak with you as you go over.

The boat's capsize point is the point where you are holding your kayak completely on its edge, and if you let it go, it will fall upside down. If you let it go and it falls upright, you did not yet reach the capsize point. Once a kayak has gone past its capsize point, the technique used to right that kayak is called a "roll."

Once your body goes beyond its capsize point, it continues towards the water and it is taking the kayak with it. If you can recover your body before your kayak gets to its capsize point, you have performed a brace. Since you are attached to your kayak, that kayak will follow your body. Therefore, righting your body will right your kayak.

The moment beginners realize that a capsize is imminent, they instinctively drop their paddle and clutch the sides of their boat. This is a natural movement, but sadly not the correct one. They think, mistakenly, that the kayak is the only solid thing in a moving, watery, unstable world. It is in fact the *paddle* that would have been their means of support, and it is the flat side of the paddle blade, pressed onto the surface of the water, that would have prevented a capsize.

Reasons for Capsizing

Since a brace is designed to prevent a capsize from occurring, it is important to first review the main reasons a paddler does capsize. Anytime the paddler lets their center of gravity go beyond its capsize point in that given kayak, they will continue to go over until they hit the water. Capsizing on a calm day is usually due to carelessness or poor technique on the part of the paddler. Looking over to see the beautiful marine life is my favorite. If you overrun your paddle during a draw stroke, it is easy to go over.

Capsizing while performing a capsize recovery is not uncommon, usually due to losing your balance or your support slipping out of your hands. A panicked swimmer trying to climb onto your kayak can cause a capsize, especially if you are not ready for it. The same can occur anytime a swimmer climbs on your kayak, even if you are prepared for it.

Riding your kayak onto an obstacle—typically a floating log, rock, or other solid object—could throw you off balance. It is amazing how quickly you can go over when the sharp edge of your bow slides up onto a log that is barely at surface level. You are now balancing on the knife-edge. Your challenge is to back off of the log without going over. That supportive reverse sweep stroke (Figure 3.18, Chapter 3) would come in handy right now.

Outside forces that cause capsizes are the ones we are usually most concerned about, because we are not in control of them. We can only react to those forces. Paddlers can control the above-mentioned reasons for capsizing, if they pay attention. Wind, waves, and tidal streams are the outside forces provided by nature. Other moving boats or solid objects moved by nature could also knock us over. The forces that knock us over can cause the paddler to go over first or the kayak to go over first, or both at the same time.

Regardless of the reason, if you use the correct bracing technique, you should stay upright or get upright.

Components of a Brace

Regardless of the brace you choose to use, all braces have components that make up the entire

technique. Once you are past your balance point, for whatever reason, you have to place your blade, arrest your capsizing movement, and recover your body to a stable position.

Blade Placement

We have already established that the flat surface (either the front or back face of your blade) is what provides the most support. If you were to present the knife-edge of your blade for support, you would continue on your path to swimming because the knife-edge slices towards the deep. Therefore, you need to get your blade into position as efficiently as possible.

Proper blade placement is dependent upon proper hand position. In order for a brace to be reliable, you need to get your blade in proper position without thinking. You will only have time to rotate your wrist to position your blade. Therefore, as mentioned earlier, keeping your top knuckles even with the top knife-edge of the working blade is essential for reliable blade manipulation. When your knuckles are even with the top knife-edge of the working blade, you can move your blade into a high or low brace position. Sculling braces require that same grip in order to change the blade angle as you scull.

The flat face of the blade momentarily stops on or near the surface when it first hits the water. It will continue to sink if there is weight pressed on it, such as your body weight. The resistance of the blade is affected by the size and shape of the blade. Wider blades generally provide more resistance.

If you present the power face to the water, it is a high brace. A low brace has you presenting the back face of the blade to the water.

The distance of the working blade from the cockpit will also affect the support you get from your paddle. The farther the blade is from the kayak, the more support you get. That is the main advantage of extended paddle braces.

The faster you get your blade to the water's surface, the sooner you arrest your movement, which means less recovery distance. Therefore, quick blade placement is important and more efficient because it means less body recovery.

Blade Movement

If your blade is stationary, you will have momentary support. That support eventually disappears as your blade sinks. As it sinks, the tip of the blade is eventually pointing down, which means it is slicing tip first towards the deep. This stationary brace is commonly referred to as a "slap brace." As a side note, if you were to intentionally slap the water with the flat of the blade, that sudden impact gives a solid feeling of support, even though it is momentary.

If you were to properly move your blade, after it is placed on the water's surface, you will have support as long as the blade is moving. That movement requires the leading edge of the blade to be higher than the trailing edge (Figure 3.2, Chapter 3). If you placed your blade slightly behind your cockpit and did a supportive reverse sweep stroke (sweep brace), the duration of support is greater than keeping your blade in one spot (slap brace) and just pressing down on it.

If you were to move your paddle forward and backward, while keeping the leading edge higher than the trailing edge, that continuous movement is called "sculling" (Figure 4.1). The sculling motion was first described in the sculling draw stroke section in Chapter 3 (Figure 3.27). The blade movement is the same except that during the sculling brace your paddle shaft is parallel to the water rather than vertical, as it is during the

Figure 4.1 *The sculling brace (sculling for support)*

sculling draw. Therefore, continuous sculling of your blade can provide you with endless support. Keep this in mind.

Arresting the Capsize

Arresting the capsize means you are stopping the body movement from continuing. That can only be done with some type of external support. Your paddle, used as a brace, provides that support. If there is a solid object within your reach, that too can be used to arrest your capsize.

Once you have stopped your capsizing movement, you still need support to keep it arrested, because your body is hovering over the water. If your support disappears, your capsize movement will continue. If you have continuous support (sculling brace or solid object), you can hover as long as that support is there. That same continuous support can also allow you to recover your body to an upright position once again balanced over your kayak.

Body and Boat Recovery

Body recovery is the most difficult part of learning a brace. This is where students make it or not. Blade placement is learned very quickly. It is learning how to move your body to get back over your kayak that presents the challenge.

There are a few ways in which you can get upright after arresting your capsize. You can just focus on your body and try to bring that up, knowing your kayak will follow. You can focus on moving your kayak first, with the body following. Doing both at the same time is your third option.

The support you have at your disposal could dictate how you get upright. If you have momentary support, as in a slap brace, your recovery has to be quick. The present-day method of body recovery, during a slap brace, has the paddler righting their kayak with a hip snap, also known as the hip flick (Figure 5.2, Chapter 5), with the body following and the head coming up last. If a paddler tries to recover by leading with his head (body before boat) while using a slap brace, the brace does not provide long-enough support to allow the body and boat to get upright before the blade begins to sink. The slap brace needs to be explosive, and all the movements must be coordinated.

Some call this technique the "head dink" method because the paddler is actually snapping their head to the side, as part of the hip snap. The hip snap, which is discussed in greater detail in the rolling chapter, is an essential component of rolling a kayak. In fact, this slap brace movement is the same action as performing a "C to C" roll (described in Chapter 5), which is a favorite of whitewater kayakers. Those who can roll usually have no difficulty performing slap braces. However, my experience has shown me that those who cannot roll their kayak rarely develop reliable slap braces.

If you have longer support from your blade, you can recover your body more slowly, which I

find more students can effectively do, especially if they cannot perform a roll. Using a sweep brace and/or a sculling brace provides longer support. In addition, your body recovery follows the movement of the paddle during the sweep, which is a somewhat circular movement.

When you are hovering out over the water and you place your paddle on the surface slightly behind your cockpit and then sweep it forward with a climbing blade angle, your body will automatically follow your paddle towards the front of your kayak. As your body moves towards the bow, start moving it towards the centerline of your kayak. When the blade has run its course, your body should be over the kayak with a slight lean forward.

Rather than the explosive movement of the slap brace, you have now gotten upright with a steady fluid motion. I highly recommend you begin your bracing career using this technique.

The other advantage to using this method is the possibility of moving into a sculling brace if your first forward sweep did not provide enough support to get you upright. If you were almost upright, just sweeping your paddle back could give you enough support to get back over your kayak as you follow the paddle back. This method is unlike the slap brace, where you have one shot. Once your blade sinks during a slap brace, it is too low for the average person to recover it for a second attempt.

Blade Recovery

A brace is completely finished after you are upright and your paddle is ready to continue to a stroke or another brace. After you are upright over your kayak, it is common to find your blade is still submerged due to the force you placed upon it while trying to get upright. How you recover your blade (retrieve your blade from the deep) can be the difference between staying upright or going back over.

If your blade is underwater, it will probably still be flat. If you try to pull that flat blade towards the surface, the resistance is enough to pull you back over. Turning your blade so it is on knife-edge will eliminate the resistance as you pull the blade out of the water. Just a slight rotation of your wrist will change your blade angle. Remember, your blade dives deeper with slap braces, so this last step is important to complete that kind of brace.

During sweep braces your blade is usually right on or very near the surface. Sweeping it out of the water with a climbing angle on the blade is a nice, smooth way of recovering your blade.

Types of Braces

There are two main categories of braces: high braces and low braces. While you are performing these braces, you can hold your paddle in a normal grip, a slightly extended grip, or a fully extended paddle position. The grip position does not change any movements of the brace. Just a reminder, you get more support and leverage as the blade moves farther from your kayak. While extending your paddle does give you more support and leverage under normal circumstances, you will not take the time to change your hand position on the paddle shaft if you are going over. If you were already in an extended position, using the paddle that way makes sense.

The most useful times for using extended paddle braces are during your learning phase. This way you get more support to help you as you learn your body movements.

High Braces

A high brace uses the power face of the blade, which puts your hands higher than your elbows (Figure 4.2). The key is you are using your power face. It has nothing to do with how high you lift the paddle.

Figure 4.2 *The high brace*

High Slap Brace

Figure 4.3 shows how you would perform a high slap brace. As you go over, bring the paddle down smartly onto the surface of the water. As you

Figure 4.3 *The high slap brace in normal paddle position*

Figure 4.4 *The high brace in extended paddle position*

Photo 4.1 *High sweep brace starting at the stern and then sweeping to the bow with a climbing blade angle* COURTESY OF THE USK PHOTO LIBRARY

feel the capsize movement halted by the paddle blade, you can flick the kayak back into the upright position with the hip snap movement. After you are up, you can rotate your hand forward so the blade is turned on knife-edge and is sliced upwards out of the water.

Figure 4.4 shows the slap brace in an extended paddle position. Again, this is a good way to begin learning body and boat coordination because of the extra support. It also shows the knife-edge recovery of the blade.

High Sweep Brace

Photo 4.1 shows the paddler rotating his body to place the blade on the water off the rear of the kayak with power face down. After the blade touches the water, the paddler sweeps the blade towards the bow and follows it forward with his body. He finishes with a slight lean forward over his front deck. His blade was easily lifted off of the water's surface at the end of the sweep.

The high sweep brace can also be done from bow to stern. It depends on your body location as you go over. If you go from bow to stern, you will end up over your back deck with a slight lean backwards.

As you can tell, this brace is nothing more than using your forward and reverse sweep strokes, with a climbing blade angle as you sweep. The main difference is your blade is placed almost flat. Once placed, you immediately sweep with that climbing blade angle and recover your body accordingly.

High Sculling Brace

Figure 4.1 shows the sculling action of the blade during a sculling brace. Remember, the hand closest to the working blade controls that blade. The paddler is still hovering over the water. He can get his body back over his boat by incorporating the hip snap or sweep method.

Photo 4.2 *Over-the-shoulder sculling brace*
WAYNE HORODOWICH

If you find that the blade begins to sink and your support is lost, it is either because your paddle angle is too steep or you have lost the planing angle on the driving face of the supporting blade.

Doing a sculling brace, for extra support, when stopped and bouncing around in rough water is a good way to keep from capsizing. You are gently leaning to the side of the sculling brace and will find this provides a feeling of stability in those conditions.

Performing an over-the-shoulder high sculling brace provides support while leaving one hand free for any number of tasks. Again, it provides additional support in rough conditions (Photo 4.2).

Low Braces

When you use the backside of your blade, it is called a low brace. In this case your hands are usually lower than your elbows (Figure 4.5).

Figure 4.5 *The low brace*

Low Slap Brace

The low slap brace is performed just like the high slap brace except you are using the back of the blade. The only difference is the blade recovery movement. This time you rotate your knuckles up to get your blade on knife-edge for recovery.

Low Sweep Brace

Figure 3.18 (Chapter 3) is essentially the reverse sweep stroke. You perform the same movement but make sure your paddle is placed flat to the water. Once it is placed, you sweep the blade towards the bow with your body following. As your body comes over the front deck, your blade should be coming off of the water.

If you did not quite make it all the way up and you need longer support, you can quickly flip the blade over and start sweeping backwards (with climbing blade angle) to continue your support. By doing so you have changed from a low sweep brace into a high sweep brace, which can become a high sculling brace if you keep sculling the blade forward and back.

Low Sculling Brace

A low sculling brace can be done, but the vast majority of paddlers end up slicing their blade underwater when they move it in the bow-to-stern direction. This is mainly due to not lifting their elbows high enough during the stroke. Therefore, unless you perfect this skill, I would not count on using it. The low sculling brace is the same as the high sculling brace except you are using the back of the blade. Most paddlers find the high sculling brace more reliable.

Shoulder Safety

The shoulder joint is the most moveable joint in the body. It is a ball-and-socket joint, and unlike the hip, the socket is very shallow. This wide range of movement and the shallow socket means it can easily be dislocated and/or strained. Unfortunately shoulder dislocations seem to occur during bracing or rolling. Reaching up and out during a high brace raises your chance of injury. When performing a high brace, you need to keep your elbow well below the level of your shoulder, as seen in Figure 4.2. Here we see the paddler performing a high brace on a medium wave with the correct arm position. If you keep your elbows lower than your shoulders when doing high braces or rolling, you significantly reduce your chances of getting a shoulder injury.

If you want to get injured, just copy the guy in Figure 4.6 who is reaching up and out. You can see his working elbow is higher than his working shoulder. When the wave hits him and/or when he pulls on his paddle, his shoulder is in danger of slipping out of place. When you lift your elbow higher than your shoulder (in an extreme high brace position), the head of your humerus (arm bone) can be pulled out of the joint by the muscles you will be using to pull on the paddle. Keep your elbows pointing down to avoid injury.

If you want to reach out with your high brace, make sure the elbow is lower than the shoulder.

Figure 4.6 *Reaching up and out to brace with your elbows near or above your shoulders is asking for trouble. I commonly refer to this movement as a "dislocation brace."*

Once it gets level to or above the shoulder height, you are at risk.

The main reason trained paddlers reach up and out is trying to do that last-second save when their body is already hitting the water. Without realizing it, putting your paddle on the surface when your body is already in the water gets your elbow closer to the level of your shoulder. In those cases, I recommend just going over and setting up for your roll or Eskimo recovery or wet exit.

As for low brace dislocations, I have yet to hear of any in paddling. The way your arm rotates during a low brace makes the shoulder joint more secure. Even though Figure 4.5 shows the elbow nearing the level of the shoulder, the shoulder is more secure because of the rotation I just mentioned.

Which Brace to Use

Now that we have reviewed the different braces at your disposal, which one should you use? I personally believe you should use the brace that will be most efficient for the position you are in when you realize you need a brace. That being said, when I watch paddlers brace in unexpected situations, they seem to go to their favorite brace even though it may take longer to get into the position.

I have seen paddlers in a perfect position to do a low brace change their paddle into the high brace position. That extra time meant they went farther over. If they would have immediately arrested the capsize with a low brace, they would have been upright with less energy.

It is common to have a favorite or "go-to" skill. It is also common to constantly practice the skills we do best. Seriously, who likes feeling uncoordinated? Keep in mind that all new skills feel awkward at first. The more skills you can perform correctly and reliably, the more options you have at your disposal.

Once I started teaching sweep braces instead of slap braces, my beginning students demonstrated a sharp increase in reliable bracing skills. I have put together an incredibly effective progression for learning bracing in my *Bracing Clinic* video, which focuses on the sweep braces. I primarily teach the slap brace after a student has learned how to roll.

When you start to feel you are losing your balance, you need to quickly decide which brace will be most efficient, assuming you can do different braces. If you only have one brace, your choice is simple, but it is limiting.

Before you get to your body's capsize point, arresting the movement is the key. Once your body is past that point, arresting and recovery are needed. As you are going over, your body is going straight to the side or it may have a slight lean forward or backward. If I am in a forward position, I use my high sweep brace from bow to stern. If I have any back lean, I use my low sweep brace from stern to bow. If I fall directly to the side, I will use either of the above with the deciding factor of how close my body is to the water. It is difficult to get into a low brace if you are too far over.

That being said, the best demonstration I have ever seen for bracing shows how far over you go before your blade hits the water when comparing a high brace and a low brace. The low brace is right there. You can stop most capsizes if you do a low sweep brace the moment you feel you may lose your balance.

Helpful Learning Tips

The first skill to develop, which is quickly learned, is moving your paddle into high and low braces. Do a high then low blade placement on your right side and then try it on your left side. Then mix it up going from side to side as fast as you can while placing the paddle correctly. Once you feel you can correctly place your blade, it is time to move on to the meat of the brace.

As I mentioned earlier, the body recovery portion of the brace is the key to the brace and the hardest part to learn. Therefore, try practicing the movements without the boat at first, then practice those movements while resting on your partner's kayak or the side of a pool or dock. Some folks like using their paddle float, on the end of their paddle, during the learning phase.

When you are ready to try it in your kayak with your paddle, use the extended paddle braces first because of the added leverage and support. If you are successful, start moving your hands along the shaft towards normal position as your successes continue.

It is also a good idea to have your partner nearby so they can help you up with an Eskimo recovery. You will be saving a lot of energy and frustration. The average number of times of capsizing and wet-exiting a novice experiences before giving up for the day is four. If you stay in your kayak (using Eskimo recoveries) and have your nose clips on during practice, you can go on for a long time before you get tired or too frustrated.

Body position when practicing is important. If you start in proper paddling position, upright with a slight lean forward and feet secure on your foot pegs, you will have greater success. Lying back reduces hip movement. Remember, do not reach up and out when doing high braces. As always, dress for immersion and wear your PFD while practicing.

Learning how to brace takes time and a lot of practice. Once you learn your braces, they need to be practiced regularly if you want them to work when you need them.

If you develop reliable bracing skills, you may never capsize again, which, as Derek notes at the beginning of this chapter, is a sign of success.

CHAPTER 5
ROLLING A KAYAK

The roll, defined in the chapter on bracing and support, is the technique used to right a kayak that has gone past its capsize point.

When this book was first published, "Eskimo roll" was the generic term used for righting your kayak with your paddle while you remained in your cockpit, as "Eskimo" was widely used at the time to describe the natives of the north. However, there are so many different names for the northern natives that calling any one roll an Eskimo roll is truly inaccurate. Since the term was originally used in this book, the first on the sport of sea kayaking, it only perpetuated the inaccurate naming of what is commonly known as the "screw roll" today (Photo 5.1).

There are numerous ways to roll a kayak. In this chapter Derek will be explaining and reviewing some of the more popular ones. He even drew the illustrations so you can see it from the paddler's perspective (fish-eye view) when turned upside down.

Again, rolling is the skill of righting the kayak after it has capsized. It is hardly surprising that the northern natives invented this system of self-rescue. The water in the Arctic being as cold as it is means any swim may well be the last. During the winter in some areas, the natives actually laced their sealskin anorak tightly onto the manhole rim, making an exit from the kayak impossible and a roll the only way of ensuring survival.

During extreme conditions out in the open sea, a bailout could prove hazardous, not only for the man in the water but also for his companions, who might be stretched to the limit themselves in dealing with the situation. Furthermore, any rescue would be virtually impossible in very

Photo 5.1 *Derek performing the screw roll. He said of the conditions, "I thought the water in San Francisco Bay would be warmer than that in the North Sea—but I was wrong."*

rough seas or high winds, or inshore near cliffs during a heavy swell or over reefs at sea. A coaching colleague once had the rather horrifying experience of being swept along sideways, upside down, in the blackness of a sea cave, and having to roll up with the broken ends of his kayak jammed against the rock sides. In circumstances such as this, any other type of rescue would obviously be almost impossible.

A roll is a great skill to have because it gives you more options. It also builds confidence and can improve your whole attitude towards the sea and rough-water kayaking. However, it does not mean you are a failure as a paddler if you cannot roll. Remember, everyone swims sooner or later. All of us have missed rolls and will miss them again. What is important is the ability to get back into your kayak unassisted and be able to continue paddling after a capsize. The advent of reliable thermal protection has reduced the necessity for rolling due to fear of exposure, which was the reason native paddlers developed the roll. A swim is no longer a death sentence due to exposure if you dress properly for immersion.

In my opinion, based upon my own informal survey of sea kayakers, 80 percent of those I have met cannot perform a reliable roll. I define a reliable roll as being able to roll up after an *unexpected* capsize. Setting up for roll and performing it with a planned setup does not qualify as a reliable roll in my book. I also know incredibly proficient paddlers who have great bracing skills and can handle extremely rough conditions, but they could never master the roll. The fact that they cannot roll does not mean they are not excellent paddlers. There are a few of them I would want with me if I were going out in challenging conditions, because they can handle themselves and I know they would be able to assist me if needed.

Figure 5.1 *Another way to skin dive*

There are also much happier uses for a good rolling technique. It is necessary for any high degree of competence in surf work. And when you are armed with a face mask on a warm summer's day, it gives you a window into a world that is denied to everyone else except divers (Figure 5.1).

While I am a "do it yourself" kind of guy, I can tell you that learning to roll is best done with an experienced and qualified instructor. Good instruction will reduce endless hours of frustration and save your shoulder from an injury. In addition, learning in a warm pool is a bonus. Wearing a face mask or a nose clip makes the experience even less unpleasant by giving you a clear view while upside down and preventing water from shooting up your nose.

The Hip Flick (Hip Snap)

The key component of rolling a kayak is the hip flick, or hip snap. The number one reason for missed rolls is trying to roll up headfirst. Your goal should be righting the kayak first, with a hip flick, and then let your body follow.

Even though this skill has been named the hip flick, your hips are not causing the movement—your trunk muscles and thigh muscles are. The result is the movement of the hips.

1. Hold onto the side of the pool or anything else, which will give you a firm handhold (Figure 5.2 A).

2. Lean over and dip your head into the water (Figure 5.2 B). As you lean, remember to "knee-hang" (Figure 3.6, Chapter 3). Hook your upper knee under the cockpit coaming and then pull the kayak over onto its gunwale with a flick of your outer hip.

3. Bring the kayak upright again with another flick of your outer hip (Figure 5.2 C). Your head should leave the water about the time the hip movement is finishing.

An efficient hip flick brings the kayak upright due to the fast twisting action of the lower trunk. At the end of the flick, enough momentum is gained to pull the body out of the water and help return it to its upright position.

When practicing your hip flick and before starting to roll, make sure that you and the kayak are as one. A tight, snug-fitting molded seat, thigh grips, knee supports or bars, and a well-adjusted footrest are needed to make sure you "wear the boat" rather than just sit in it loosely.

For sea kayaking it is not necessary to be able to roll on both sides since it is rare there will be

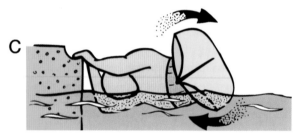

Figure 5.2 *The hip flick*

any obstacles blocking you. Regardless of which side you go over, once you are upside down, just get into your normal starting position and roll up on your favored side.

The Pawlata Roll

In my opinion, the Pawlata (extended paddle roll) (Figure 5.3) is the best roll to teach a beginner. Many of my coaching colleagues would support this view because the screw roll, the most important roll of all, is a direct progression from the Pawlata. But as long as you can roll the first time every time, the particular technique used

So you want to roll. Well, are you sitting comfortably? Good. The paddle is on your left side. Hold the nearest blade at the top corner, thumb downwards, fingers inside. Don't reach too far forward with the right hand; the knuckles should be uppermost looking away from the kayak. The outward edge of the forward paddle blade can be tilted slightly towards the water. Are you ready? Right, take a deep breath and capsize. Turn the page round now, and keep holding your breath!

Fish Eye View

angle of sweeping blade

Wait, open your eyes, study the picture. Try to orient yourself—good. Don't panic; it's only water. Bend your body and push your face towards the surface. Push your hands upwards towards the surface. You are trying to get your body and hands as close to the surface as possible. Now swing out with your right-hand blade, the outward edge tilted upwards as it planes out in an arc along the surface. Keep that right arm almost straight. The left hand pushes up out of the water and forward.

Figure 5.3 *The Pawlata roll*

You should be in the position shown as your head breaks the surface. Your right bicep should have just brushed past your nose. Push down hard—you have just completed your first Pawlata roll.

Figure 5.4 *The Pawlata roll—human's-eye view*

is irrelevant. The main advantage of the Pawlata roll is the leverage and additional support you get from the paddle in the extended position.

If you have difficulty with the Pawlata, think about the following:

1. The angle of the blade as it moves from the kayak must be such that it planes out and along the surface.

2. You must lean forward.

3. The roll should be executed with great vigor.

4. Don't try to roll before you are upside down.

5. The forward arm is swept out to the side in an arc by the straight arm, not pulled downwards.

6. Remember you are also pulling up on the knee that starts farthest from your paddle. When you come up, that knee will be closest to the paddle. The hip flick is done slowly during the Pawlata roll.

7. Don't forget to push the left arm forward and to the surface; otherwise, the blade will hit the side of your hull and you will not be able to sweep the forward blades outwards.

8. After the sweep outwards with the right hand, the upper part of the right arm should brush past the nose and over the head as you break the surface (Figure 5.4). Failing to do this is the most common reason for an unsuccessful roll.

The Screw Roll

The screw roll (Figure 5.5 A–F) is probably the most important roll of all, because the basic position of the hands on the paddle loom remains unaltered. Sometimes the paddler becomes unsure of their hand position in relation to the angle of the paddle blades. That is the reason for oval shafts or raised grips. If in doubt, the paddler can move the nearest hand quickly along the loom until it reassuringly touches the blade in a recognizable position, and then put it back in place for the commencement of the roll. With practice it will not be necessary to move the hands from the normal paddling position. Because the leverage is shorter, a higher degree of skill is required for this than for any other roll. Specifically, your hip flick needs to be more explosive.

It is during the performance of this roll that we discover another advantage of using the longer, narrower sea paddle. The roll is made easier because the upper blade does not have to be pushed up as high to clear the bottom of the kayak. The blade, which in the meantime is sweeping outwards on the surface of the water, is also at a better angle for the downward stroke of the roll proper.

1. Before capsizing, set up your paddle on the deck of your kayak. If you are going to roll up on your right side, begin with your paddle on the left side of your deck. (Figure 5.5 A)

2. Wait until you are completely upside down. (Figure 5.5 B)

3. Reach both hands to the surface and lean as far forward as your flexibility allows. (Figure 5.5 C)

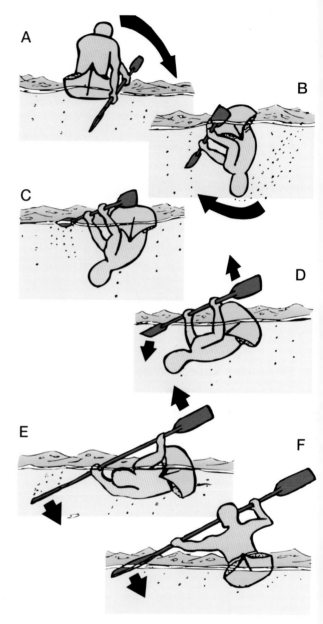

Figure 5.5 *The screw roll step by step*

4. Start sweeping the paddle along the surface with a climbing angle on the working blade. At the same time begin your hip flick. (Figure 5.5 D)

5. Continue sweeping while saying your mantra, "Head up last." (Figure 5.5 E)

6. If you have done everything correctly, you should be upright when your blade passes by your cockpit. (Figure 5.5 F)

A variation of the screw roll is called the "C to C" roll. Instead of the blade starting at the bow and sweeping towards the stern, you move your blade in the air until the paddle is at 90 degrees to the kayak (Figure 5.5 E). Then in one explosive movement, you pull down on the paddle while you do your hip snap so the boat comes up first with your head coming up last (Figure 5.5 F).

Shoulder Safety When Rolling

Reaching too far out and/or too far behind the front plane of your body could result in a shoulder strain or, even worse, a shoulder dislocation. The paddle shaft should be parallel to your chest during this maneuver. Therefore, good trunk rotation is a necessity for saving your shoulder, as mentioned earlier when performing sweep strokes and high braces.

Other Rolls

Here are some other rolls that Derek included in his last edition: the King Island roll, the Steyr roll, the Eskimo storm roll, the vertical storm roll, the Greenland roll, and the hand roll.

The King Island Roll

A King Island, or Alaskan, roll is shown in Figure 5.6. This is done with a single paddle blade. Note that when the paddler is in the inverted position, the paddle is held at arm's length downwards. Because of its angle, the blade takes a rising path towards the surface during the sweep around and finishes up in a position behind the man. The remaining forward sweep, bringing the man upright, reminds one of the European Steyr roll illustrated in Figure 5.7.

While hunting in the rough waters of the Bering Sea, a man could be caught by a sudden capsize. If unable to roll up with his paddle, he could withdraw himself up into the roomy body of his kayak and wait until his comrade paddled to his assistance and turned him upright again. A skill used by a hunter who has lost his paddle is to attempt a roll using his throwing stick, and sometimes in desperation even attempting to use the blade of his knife.

The paddler sits in the middle of the large manhole with his back unsupported. He hooks his knees under the first thwart forward of the cockpit. This roll is a good one for a tired paddler; it is a gradual roll, spreading the righting action over a longer period. The paddle is held out in front of the body horizontally, and the paddle blade sticks out to the left. The kayaker is now in the position for the capsize.

Fish Eye View

The arms can be extended during the capsize or immediately afterwards. To roll up, the paddle is swept forward as indicated; the leading edge of the blade planes towards the surface during its sweep around. This must be done with some speed to gain lift towards the surface. The change of direction for the forward sweep must also be executed quickly, so as not to lose the momentum of the rising sweep around. This roll can be done successfully with a double-bladed paddle.

Figure 5.6 *The King Island roll*

The Steyr Roll

Hold the paddle as if for the Pawlata, then lie back along the rear deck, with the right arm either above the head as in "A" or across the face as in "B." This is a most uncomfortable position, especially for the left hand. You will also feel unstable. Twist the top half of your body to the left, then capsize on that side.

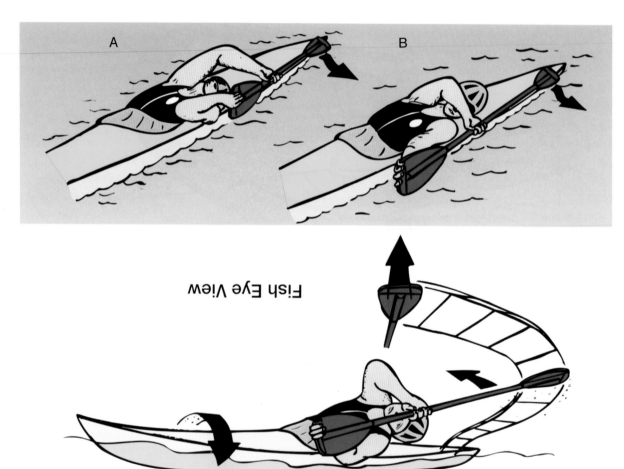

Wait until you are hanging upside down and your head is twisted back, looking at the rear of the kayak. Push your right hand and arm across your face and out to the side. Push down as the paddle sweeps out, and you will rise to the surface. Much less effort is needed for this than is needed for other rolls, but it lacks popularity because the preparatory position or "windup" is a difficult one to adopt underwater.

Figure 5.7 *The Steyr roll*

The Eskimo Storm Roll

This is a true Eskimo roll as used by the Eskimos of the Angmassalik area of Greenland. The starting position, or "windup," is rather like the Pawlata, except that the forward paddle blade is at an angle of 30 degrees from the side of the kayak.

Fish Eye View

Lean well forward and push upward with the right hand, so that the forward paddle blade is about a foot above the surface. Now pull down violently. You will rise very quickly. The paddle goes down vertically for about a foot, then starts to plane outward as the roll nears completion.

Figure 5.8 *The Eskimo storm roll*

The Vertical Storm Roll

Use the same "windup" position as for the Eskimo storm roll.

Fish Eye View

The blade when pushed above the surface is in a vertical position. The edge of the blade nearest the water is angled slightly outwards from the kayak so that although the blade bites down very deeply, 2 to 3 feet, it will eventually slice outwards and down for maximum support.

Figure 5.9 *The vertical storm roll*

The Greenland Roll

It has been thought, quite wrongly, that because a kayak is very unstable when the right way up, it is easy to roll when upside down. It is obvious that the bottom hull shape, apart from its narrowness, exerts very little influence on the kayak when it is being rolled. However, if the deck has a "banana" shape lengthwise, when the boat is upside down it will try to turn on its side, upon which it will normally readily float. This action is assisted by the buoyancy of the kayaker's body. Boat and man finish up at an angle of about 45 degrees to the surface of the water (B), the kayak in many cases showing an almost flat bottom to the sky. In this position the man is ready to start the roll.

A

The paddle is held alongside the kayak with the blade in a vertical position. The blade angle is altered as it leaves the side of the kayak. It is then planed outwards. This can bring the man to the surface, or the roll may be finished off by a quick forward blade scull, the paddle finishing on or near the surface of the water.

Figure 5.10 *The Greenland roll*

The Hand Roll

The ultimate in kayak rolling is the no-paddle roll, otherwise known as the hand roll.

1. An assistant is needed at first. He stands on your right-hand side. (Figure 5.11)

2. Lean well back in the cockpit to touch the back of your head on the rear deck.

3. Place the knuckles of your right hand well behind your left ear, palm outwards.

4. Capsize on your left side. Keep your head touching the back deck.

5. Your partner will put his upward-facing palm in a position where it touches your downward-facing palm. Hook your fingers into his.

6. Sweep your arm violently in a wide arc towards the bottom of the pool and follow through until your right arm is fully extended sideways.

7. As you break the surface, fling the left arm forcibly over sideways; this will assist the momentum.

This exercise will give you confidence. Next try the same with a table tennis paddle or a polystyrene float (Figure 5.12). You can assist the first part of the roll by dog-paddling to the surface first on the right-hand side. With your head on the back deck, quickly fling your right arm downwards and around with great force, throwing your left hand out as a counterbalance to help the last part of the roll.

Conclusion

Once you have learned to roll, by any of the methods described, practice at every opportunity, especially in rough conditions. Surf is ideal because a failure means only a short swim.

Always keep calm when you are upside down. Worry makes your heart beat faster; this takes more oxygen, which is unobtainable. So keep cool and think about something else. You will be surprised at just how long you can happily hold your breath: You should be able to do so for about 30 seconds, if not a little longer. The time will depend on many factors—some physical, some

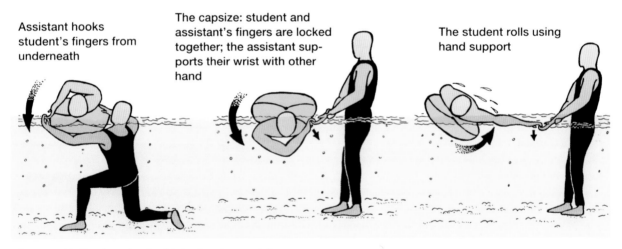

Assistant hooks student's fingers from underneath

The capsize: student and assistant's fingers are locked together; the assistant supports their wrist with other hand

The student rolls using hand support

Figure 5.11 *The hand roll with instructor assistance*

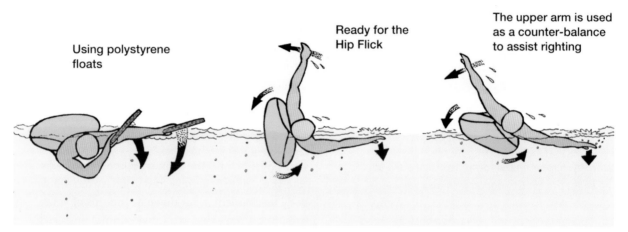

Figure 5.12 *Hand roll practice using floats. The floats are gradually reduced in size until only the hands are used.*

psychological, and some environmental (the temperature of the water is a major factor).

Some people have taught that one's time under water can be lengthened by hyperventilation, which is not recommended. Over-breathing increases the endurance time by removing carbon dioxide from the body and delaying the time at which its concentration builds up again to the point at which it produces an irresistible stimulus to breathe. The over-breathing does not appreciably increase the amount of oxygen stored in the body, as the hemoglobin of arterial blood is almost saturated with oxygen even during normal breathing.

If you exclude carbon dioxide from your body for too long, you will lose the desire to breathe, and after doing the longest underwater hang on record, you will quite painlessly lose consciousness and subsequently drown. Hyperventilating for rolling practice is dangerous and unnecessary.

Again, in all rolling practice, it is vital to have qualified instructors near at hand in case of trouble.

CHAPTER 6
RACING

Derek was very proud to be the first to include a detailed chapter on the racing stroke in a sea kayaking book. This entire chapter is in his own words.

I suppose our attitude towards physical activities is always the same. At first we just want to be able to do something. Then, once we feel we are becoming reasonably competent at something, we want to see just how good we really are compared to everyone else. In the early stages we naturally tend to match ourselves, almost unconsciously at first, against our immediate paddling partners. I should give you a word of caution here. You may find that your tendency to always want to be out in front does not particularly endear you to your friends; indeed, you may soon discover that your desire to constantly keep that tiny bit ahead of your companions renders you totally friendless. Fortunately for your social life, and for the general safety of the group, the time will come (the sooner the better) when you will look further afield for these challenges.

This is when you will discover racing. I'm not talking about the International Olympic stuff here. I'm referring to the type of fun races put on by clubs, stores, and organizations, who offer prizes of various kinds, ranging from small amounts of cash to items of equipment that have been donated by sponsors (you might even pick up a free kayak).

Racing has a lot going for it. It's obviously very physical, and the training you need to dedicate yourself to is aerobic and utilizes your whole body mechanism, right down to the tips of your toes. But it has other attractive components such as glamour, color, and excitement. Sometimes there is even an element of danger, although organizers try to keep this to a minimum.

For me personally, it's not merely the actual race that appeals. The whole circus is a delightful thrill, from driving my car into the race parking lot to fastening the kayak back onto the roof at the end of the day. As I look for a place to park, I can see all manner of different craft being unloaded. Nowadays you would see quite a number of narrow racing skis adding to the colorful scene.

All competitors have to register, and while standing in the line, you will notice that everyone seems to know everyone else. There is excited banter as stick-on numbers or perhaps brightly colored numbered vests are collected. It is this lively atmosphere that starts to kick in the adrenaline. There is no shortage of humor, as there is always someone who makes the startling discovery that the white numbered circle they have been allocated refuses to stick to the deck of their boat. Long forgotten holes are discovered, and the cry for duct tape is heard. Others, meanwhile, are searching their tool kits for pliers in order to string together wayward rudders. One race I have entered on several occasions demands that all competitors carry certain items of safety equipment before they are allowed to enter. These items include two hand flares, a repair kit, a first-aid kit, a towline, and a large plastic exposure bag. Under the eagle eye of the scrutineers, most competitors discover they lack some item or other. Fortunately, the trade anticipates this and is on hand to supply the need—at a price.

The joy of these informal, fun races for sea kayaks is that people can turn up with just about any kind of kayak or ski. So long as there is a class for your type of kayak and it passes the eye of the scrutineers, all you have to do is put your name down to gain your position on the starting line. The paddles and buoyancy aids that competitors use are the normal everyday touring kind, and the skills required to win are simply being able to maintain your normal touring stroke faster and longer than anyone else.

Starting can be hilarious. Trying to get fifty or a hundred competitors to stay in position for a "straight" line start can try the patience of any organizer. Personally, I prefer the Le Mans–type start. In this, the kayaks are lined up on the sand at the water's edge. At the sound of the gun, horn, or whistle (sometimes even a distant dog bark!) everyone sprints down the beach. Kayaks are then snatched up and dragged 20 yards or so to the water's edge. Depending upon the rules, spray skirts will have to be fitted before pushing off from the beach.

I remember one memorable massed start I took part in. Our kayaks were all lined up right at the water's edge. I was number 13, and I had my strategy all planned. With water lapping against the hull, I placed my kayak as near to the water's edge as possible. All I had to do was jump in and push off from the sand. That was the plan!

As I stood, leaning forward into the start position, adrenaline coursing through my veins, the starter/organizer took the opportunity to launch into an infuriatingly lengthy preamble, running over the details of our island-hopping course and the marker buoys that had been placed at strategic points to help us find our way around. He went on to outline the duty of the numerous rescue craft. There was even a moment when I thought he would mention them all by name. He droned on and continued to enlighten us on the morning's weather forecast, the wind speed, and the temperature of the water. I never actually heard him finish. All I could think of was run down, jump in, and push off!

Suddenly the gun went off and I was away like a startled greyhound. I sprinted down the beach and jumped into my boat well ahead of everyone else. Just as I reached to put on my spray cover, I realized that everyone on both sides of me had picked up their boats and were running past me and on into the water, which had now receded some 20 yards. Unfortunately, I had not noticed that the tide had been going out and the boats had been left high and dry! Thankfully, things did improve after that and I gained first place.

Time moves on and although we can still race our touring sea kayaks, the fast, narrow racing skis have introduced the wing paddle racing stroke to the sea kayaking scene.

The Racing Stroke

The racing stroke I am about to describe is performed with what is known as a "wing" paddle (Figure 6.1). The cross-section of a wing blade echoes the cross-section of an airplane wing. It has a broad leading edge, while the top curves away to a fine trailing edge. If the wing blade is presented vertically to the water at the commencement of the stroke and then moved outwards, the dihedral angle will cause the blade to "fly" forward with no slip towards the rear and therefore no loss of power (Figure 6.5).

Let us look at this new stroke in stages. I have drawn in an imaginary floating marker, positioned exactly where the paddle enters the water for the catch. This will help you appreciate the position of the immersed paddle blade throughout the stroke.

Because a high-speed cyclic motion has to be maintained, racing paddles should weigh as little as possible.

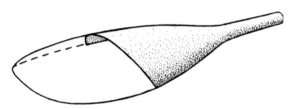

Figure 6.1 Wing paddle blade, cutaway cross-section of a right-hand wing paddle blade. The original wing paddle blade was developed by Stephen Lindeberg of Sweden in 1985–6. Extensive testing was carried out using both conventional blades and wings, and it was found that though it was slightly slower off the start, overall the wing was more efficient if the correct technique was used. The Swedish team used the wing before anyone else, and had exceptionally good results. British paddler Jeremy West realized the potential very quickly when winning the 500m and 1000m at the Montreal World Championships.

A few years after the wing was introduced, a Norwegian called Rasmussen improved the design by adding a slight twist to the blade. This reduced vortexing, thus improving its efficiency. There are now hybrids of this design produced all around the world, and all sprint and most marathon paddlers use the wing shape.

Phase One

Figures 6.2 and 6.3 show the position of my body just before my upper arm is thrown forward and I present the paddle to the water in the "catch" position. In reality, I fall onto the paddle blade as it enters the water. This is also known in racing circles as the bent shaft position (BSP). Barney Wainwright, BCU's Sports Science Officer, first described it to me: "The Bent Shaft is when the paddle is bent due to the stress put on it during the 'catch.' This is almost impossible to see except in some photographs and only during high, forceful efforts. It is akin to a pole vault when the pole is locked into position and the athlete is driven up and forwards. In the same way, your blade is locked into the water and you are driven up and forwards, thereby reducing drag. This is a conceptional model to visualize during paddling and really only applies to racing."

What you are trying to achieve, therefore, is to bend the paddle shaft by the combined tension of the pulling and pushing arm. It is the blade's compression against the water that triggers the locking tension in the shoulder on the stroke side.

Anyone looking at you from the side should see your back in full view (Figure 6.4). Just as walking forward on land can be described as a continuous falling action arrested by alternate feet, in a similar manner, consider the forward racing stroke as a series of capsizes arrested by alternate "catches."

Viewed from above, the apparent and actual path of the paddle becomes clear (Figure 6.5). The stroke can start only when the paddle blade is vertical in the water, i.e., when the paddle shaft is as vertical as it is possible to get it.

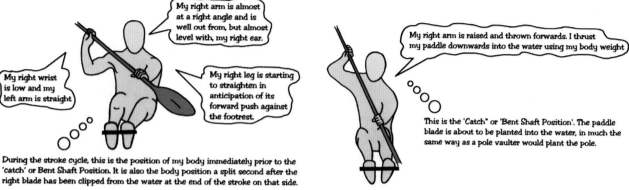

Figure 6.2 Phase 1.1

During the stroke cycle, this is the position of my body immediately prior to the 'catch' or Bent Shaft Position. It is also the body position a split second after the right blade has been clipped from the water at the end of the stroke on that side.

Figure 6.3 Phase 1.2

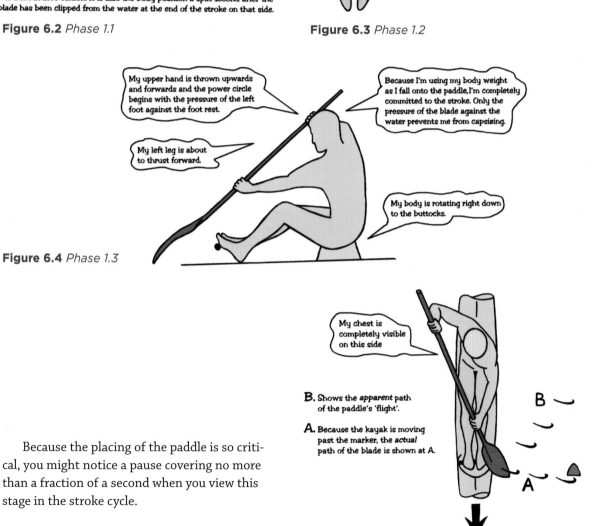

Figure 6.4 Phase 1.3

Because the placing of the paddle is so critical, you might notice a pause covering no more than a fraction of a second when you view this stage in the stroke cycle.

Figure 6.5 Phase 1.4

Phase Two

Fantastic though this may sound, your aim is to pull the weight of your buttocks off the seat. If you are paddling correctly at this stage of the stroke you should feel that your body together with the boat are being lifted out of the water. Concentrate on rotating your body vigorously forward. In this way the line of power down from the pulling side shoulder to the opposite hip will maintain the tension. You should try to imagine that your shoulders and the paddle are hanging on strings like a wooden puppet. This is only possible if you maintain the pressure against the paddle blade and *keep the kayak accelerating all the way throughout the stroke*. The tension from the pressure applied to the footrest is transferred to the stroke shoulder. At the same time the lower hand pulls against the paddle as it "flies" outwards. Remember that powerful legwork is vital to the structure of the whole stroke (Figure 6.6).

If you present the paddle to the water efficiently and maintain a constant pull on the paddle blade during phases 2.1 and 2.2, your body weight will be transferred from the kayak to the paddle. In this way you will lighten your boat as it moves forward. The more powerful the swing forward, the greater the force, which locks the blade in the water. Remember to keep your pulling arm almost straight throughout the stroke (Figure 6.7).

Looked at from above, it can be seen that the paddle shaft is kept parallel to the line of the shoulders. Notice that during the stroke, there has been no slip backwards on the part of the paddle blade in relation to the marker buoy (Figure 6.8).

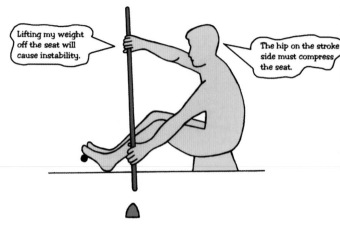

Lifting my weight off the seat will cause instability.

The hip on the stroke side must compress the seat.

Figure 6.6 *Phase 2.1*

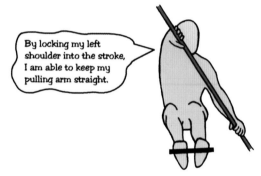

By locking my left shoulder into the stroke, I am able to keep my pulling arm straight.

Figure 6.7 *Phase 2.2*

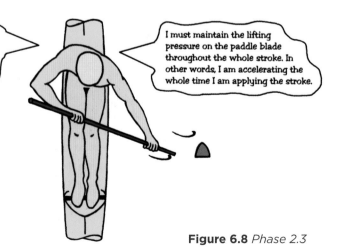

I am throwing my right arm forwards as my body rotates. At the same time, I am trying to keep my shoulder almost parallel to the paddle shaft.

I must maintain the lifting pressure on the paddle blade throughout the whole stroke. In other words, I am accelerating the whole time I am applying the stroke.

Figure 6.8 *Phase 2.3*

Phase Three

This is the final stage of the stroke cycle. The kayak has been pulled forward, towards the locked blade, and then moved past it. It is vital that the kayak is kept straight and level, so you must *avoid any bouncing, snaking, or rocking from side to side.*

You must rotate your lower body towards the pulling blade in order to counteract any turning effect that your pull on the paddle may have. You must recover quickly between the strokes so that there is no time for your body to sink backwards and downwards and thus allow the kayak to settle back into the water.

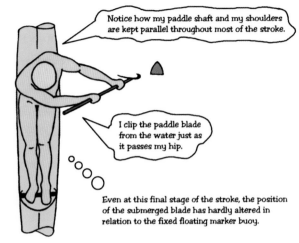

Notice how my paddle shaft and my shoulders are kept parallel throughout most of the stroke.

I clip the paddle blade from the water just as it passes my hip.

Even at this final stage of the stroke, the position of the submerged blade has hardly altered in relation to the fixed floating marker buoy.

Figure 6.10 *Phase 3.2*

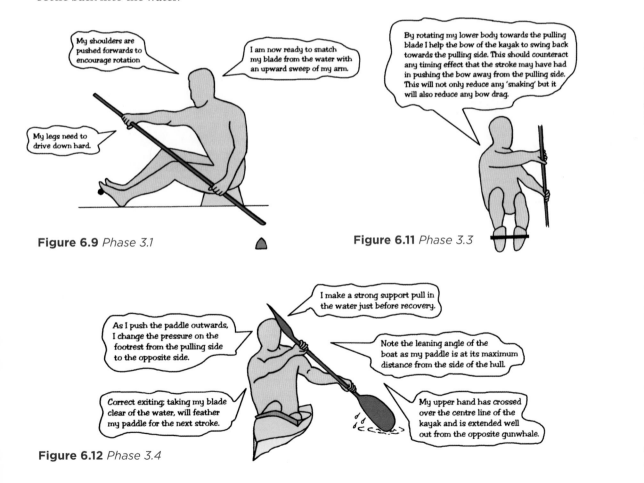

My shoulders are pushed forwards to encourage rotation

I am now ready to snatch my blade from the water with an upward sweep of my arm.

My legs need to drive down hard.

Figure 6.9 *Phase 3.1*

By rotating my lower body towards the pulling blade I help the bow of the kayak to swing back towards the pulling side. This should counteract any timing effect that the stroke may have had in pushing the bow away from the pulling side. This will not only reduce any 'snaking' but it will also reduce any bow drag.

Figure 6.11 *Phase 3.3*

I make a strong support pull in the water just before recovery.

As I push the paddle outwards, I change the pressure on the footrest from the pulling side to the opposite side.

Note the leaning angle of the boat as my paddle is at its maximum distance from the side of the hull.

Correct exiting; taking my blade clear of the water, will feather my paddle for the next stroke.

My upper hand has crossed over the centre line of the kayak and is extended well out from the opposite gunwhale.

Figure 6.12 *Phase 3.4*

Mastering the racing stroke will not be immediate, but with practice you will come to appreciate how all your body movements interact with the kayak.

Conclusion

In this chapter I have presented to the everyday touring paddler the racing stroke as used by international competitors. I must warn you that racing kayaks and the equally fast racing skis have an unstable cross-section that is designed for speed and speed alone. Unfortunately for you as a touring paddler, stability is an important consideration, so if you jump into (or onto) one of these missiles in an attempt to impress your friends by rocketing over the horizon, be prepared for a wetting.

Photo 6.1 *This picture, taken at the Marathon World Racing Championships in Nova Scotia in 2000, bears close scrutiny. The front group of paddlers from left to right are Ivan Lawler (GBR), Greg Barton (USA), Tomas Jezek (CZE), Conor Holmes (GAP), Dolph Te Linde (NED), Manuel Busto (ESP), and Istvan Salga (HUN). The race had only 16 kilometers to go, and to ensure a good result, a good position at this stage was vital. In this race the competitors chose not to wear spray skirts. In rougher conditions this may not be the case.*

This is a good photograph to show the lateral movement of the wing paddle. However, note that by the time the paddle has reached this point, the face of the blade is angled well back, meaning that there is little propulsion in the forward direction available. By this stage of the race, fatigue will have set in and the paddling technique will not be at its most efficient. Top arms will have dropped quite low, and the paddle will stay in the water a little too long. BARNEY WAINWRIGHT (PHOTO AND CAPTION)

Photo 6.2 *Anna Hemmings pictured at the Marathon Racing World Championships, Stockton-on-Tees, UK, 2001. She had a good position in the boat, sitting upright but leaning slightly forward, which enables more body weight to be put on the blade at the next catch. Good rotated position after finishing one stroke will enable a lot of rotation during the next stroke. As can be seen, the line of the shoulders is virtually parallel with the paddle shaft. The right leg has already fully extended and now the left leg is ready to push against the footrest just before the left blade enters the water. Anna is using a drinks system in which the fluid reservoir is fixed to the boat. Even in these moderate conditions in the UK (19°C), fluid intake is important and is taken on early, as can be seen here, 8 kilometers into the race. For races over one hour, the consumption of fluids is essential to avoid dehydration and offset the depletion of carbohydrate stores in the muscles and liver, both of which will decrease sustainable work rate and performance. If the environmental conditions are very hot and humid, fluids may be needed for events shorter than one hour. A beverage should contain between 4 and 8 percent carbohydrate depending on whether preventing dehydration or providing energy is more important. Fluid intakes of 0.5 to 1.0 liter per hour may be required depending upon the environmental conditions and the intensity of work. For races or activities of longer duration, it may be necessary to use a carbohydrate-electrolyte solution containing sodium. This will help to replace sodium lost in sweat and increase the thirst drive, making the paddler drink more frequently.*
BARNEY WAINWRIGHT (PHOTO AND CAPTION)

Photo 6.3 *Greg Barton was a four-time Olympic Gold medal winner. In the stroke cycle, viewed from the left side, he is about to present the left blade into the catch position. His back is fully visible, and he is still pressing down hard with his right foot.* BARNEY WAINWRIGHT (PHOTO)

First, you will have to spend some time getting used to the racing boat's tippyness. Then you'll have to go out, purchase a wing paddle, and come to terms with its peculiar handling characteristics. As I previously explained, the wing is designed for traveling in the "flying" direction through the water. However, the minute you try to normally perform any of the basic strokes that include draws, sculls, or braces, you will have

only limited success and you could well finish up swimming. The problem is that by attempting some of these strokes, you will be forced to put the wing into a position where you are actually trying to make it fly backwards. This could make for a very unhappy day and make you wish you had worn your immersion clothing.

If you want to try for a little extra speed, it is quite acceptable to use a wing paddle with your touring kayak. Remember, however, that because a touring boat is wider than a racing boat, your forward stroke will start much farther out from the center line of the boat. Therefore, the length of your outward "flight" will be shorter. Because stability is not a problem, as you plant your blade for the "catch" in your touring boat, you will not have the advantage of capsizing your body weight onto the paddle blade.

Caution: When you finally buy your wing paddle, please do not be tempted to immediately thrash off into the middle distance at high speed. Athletes train for this kind of thing, and they build up their speeds and distances gradually.

In this way their heartbeat and respiration keep pace with their performance. Any untrained paddler who sprints off at high speed and who attempts to maintain this for as long as possible will soon begin to pant for breath. This means that they will be sucking in an excessive amount of oxygen to the detriment of carbon dioxide. It is the carbon dioxide in the air that you inhale that triggers your involuntary breathing mechanism, so if no carbon dioxide goes into your lungs, you will not want to breathe. This is called hyperventilation, and it's very dangerous. The result of this strenuous effort is that you will very probably black out. It once happened to me

Photo 6.4 *A kayak race held by the Port Burwell Eskimos during HBC Governor P. A. Cooper's visit in 1934.* H. BASSETT

many years ago when I was training for a cycle road race. I'd been pedaling furiously and then suddenly I woke up with a very sore head and my nose buried in the tarmac amidst a good deal of blood. The good news is that in a kayak, your landing will be softer. The bad news is that the results could be more permanent.

Remember, a life vest may prevent you from sinking, but it won't prevent you from drowning.

In addition to possibly passing out due to overexertion, greater stress is placed upon your upper extremities when you start using the wing paddle. After my first one-hour training session, I felt great. Two hours later, I could not bend my elbows without significant pain. I never realized how much impact was placed on my joints because the paddle did not back slip during the stroke. It took a month of training (three or four paddle days each week) for me to grow into my wing paddle.

CHAPTER 7
WAVES

During all your happy years of sea kayaking, waves of one kind or another will be your constant companion, so every paddler should know something about the waves he or she is likely to meet (or which are likely to meet the paddler). By looking at a map or chart and equating certain coastal features, such as depth and shape of the sea bottom, with certain weather conditions, it is possible to anticipate roughly the type and character of the wave you will meet, even if you cannot foretell its size and ferocity. Looking at a chart and noting the various submarine gradients makes it possible to know whether a certain beach will be suitable for different kinds of kayak activities. That is, will you be able to surf, will you be able to land at all, and will the surf be dangerous?

Waves are caused by the wind. All waves have two things in common: a **crest**, the highest part; and a **trough**, the lowest part. **Soup** is the name given to the wave after it breaks (Figure 7.1).

Wind moving across still water immediately produces ripples, which are the smallest waves, with only a split second between one crest and another. Wind blowing across water flowing at the same speed will produce no waves, and wind blowing against the tidal stream produces steep standing waves. The expanse of water the wind

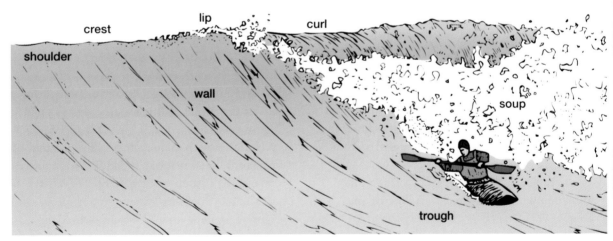

Figure 7.1 *A surfing wave. As the water breaks, it tumbles over from the top and down the slope. For the whole of its life cycle, this is the finest form of surfing wave. Both the breaking wave and the "soup" it creates lack the violence of the dumper or the storm waves. If the wall of this water was steeper, the "curl" would topple over and form a "tube."*

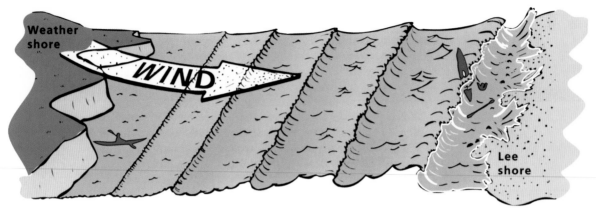

Figure 7.2 *Sheltering in the lee of the cliffs on the weather shore, wind and water conditions appear suitable for the trip to the island. However, conditions in the open sea are quite different and a landing may be impossible.*

blows over, the amount of time it blows, and the speed at which it blows all influence the size of the wave. The unobstructed distance over which the wind travels creating waves is **fetch** (Figure 7.2), and the greater the fetch distance, the more opportunity the wind has to create larger, more powerful waves. Some waves travel faster than others, and as they move along across the oceans for hundreds, sometimes thousands, of miles, other wave patterns join them on their journey. It is little wonder that the sea often looks confused.

When these waves do form in a synchronous pattern, they can form **sets**. These sets often have predictability, so launching and landing can be made easier if you study the pattern and the timing. In addition, these swells can be helpful to the experienced paddler if they are coming from behind, which is called a **following sea** (Figure 7.3).

When waves from distant storms come towards shore, you see them as **swells**. The ocean just appears to be moving up and down. If you are in water that is deep enough, swells are not a threat. However, if you are in windy conditions, the local waves you will be experiencing will be irregular, with no pattern, and have short wave intervals. These local waves are called **seas**. This is very confusing to the paddler and often not very stable for the novice. It is said, "You can relax in swells, but need to pay attention in seas."

Storms hundred of miles away will create a swell, and it is this undulating movement of the sea that, when it reaches our coasts, causes surf to break on our beaches and pound on our rocks. Although the swell or wave moves a stationary kayak up and down, the relative position of the boat on the surface of the water alters very little (Figure 7.4).

Notice the orbital movement of the water particles. When the kayak is paddled and moves forward, the surface movement of the water particles has a definite influence on its progress (Figure 7.5). Long undulating swells hold no danger for a kayak, but if the wind blows strongly enough and the height of the waves increases to more than one-sixth of their wavelength, the tops fall over themselves, forming whitecaps. The

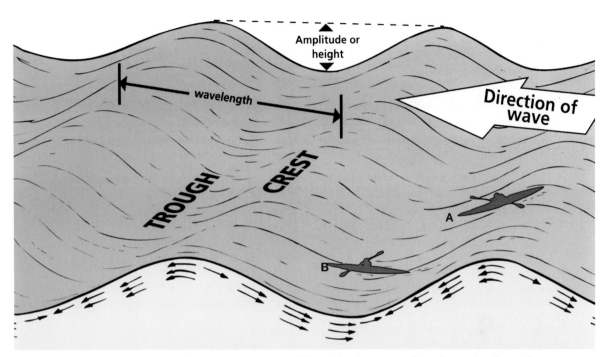

Figure 7.3 *Formation of unbroken sea waves. Paddler A is almost surfing down the face of a wave, while paddler B is retarded in the trough. This is the dreaded "following sea" of the novice. The wave will catch up to paddler B and throw him forward. This type of following sea is a godsend for the experienced paddler on a long sea trip, although surfing experience may be needed at the end of the journey.*

kayaker who is out at sea in a swell, and perhaps in a high state of tension, may find it difficult to judge the height of the waves. Remember that when you are on top of one crest, another crest, the height of which you are trying to estimate, may be on its way down again. Waves tend to look much larger and more menacing when viewed from the trough (Figure 7.6).

As previously mentioned, water particles move with a circular motion. As a wave reaches shallow water it slows down, and when it gets into water one and a half times its height (called its **critical depth**), the frictional resistance caused by the bottom makes the crest topple over, producing a broken wave (Figure 7.5).

Figure 7.7 shows how the swell rolling in parallel to itself is slowed down near the shore, while the outside of the swell marches on at its original speed, producing what is called a **refraction curve**. This refraction gives kayakers and board

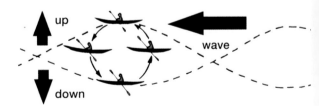

Figure 7.4 *Track of a stationary kayak. After returning to the crest from the trough, the kayak is almost in the same position.*

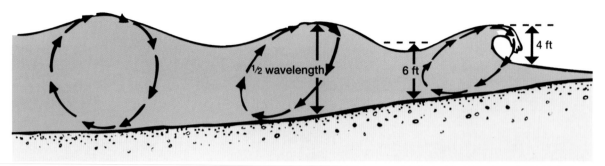

Normal circular orbital movement of wave particles before wave reaches shallow water

Orbital movement begins to become elliptical as the wave approaches shallow water. This is caused by the frictional resistance or bottom drag, and usually occurs when the depth is half the wavelength

When the depth is approximately one-and-a-half times the wave height, the wave begins to break

Figure 7.5 *Orbital movement of wave particles*

surfers the graduated surf suitable for experts and beginners alike, and also the breaking "shoulder," which is the delight of surf kayak paddlers.

When you paddle out from a protected harbor, remember that the swell that does not affect you while you are in the sheltered area between the piers is quite a different matter when you reach exposed water around the piers and beyond. This is because waves are reflected from piers and cliffs, and as Figures 7.8 and 7.9 show, the crashing together of two wave patterns can produce the haystack effect of **clapotis**. Clapotis

can also be produced by waves being refracted around an island (Figure 7.10).

A **dumping wave** (Figure 7.11) is caused by a steeply shelving bottom. The wave reaches its critical depth quickly, peaks up and breaks suddenly, dragging with it sand and small stones that rise up inside the curl. Wave and stones then crash down with tremendous impact, smashing craft, filling eyes and ears, and sandblasting the battered paddler. The breaking of the wave is almost explosive because the air trapped and compressed inside the breaking curl exerts

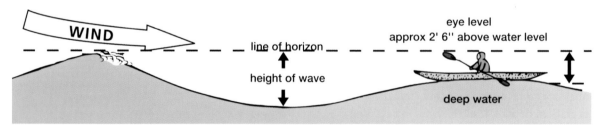

Figure 7.6 *Paddler judging the height of a wave. If the waves are higher than one-sixth of their wavelength and the wind is blowing, the tops will fall over in whitecaps.*

Figure 7.7 *Refraction curve off a headland. As the parallel swell approaches the shallow water of the point, the wave lines are slowed down inshore, while in the deep water the swell tries to continue as before, producing what is called a refraction curve.*

Figure 7.8 *Waves strike the pier and are reflected back; these superimpose themselves on the original wave pattern. The trough of one may be cancelled out by the crest of another; or, if a crest meets a crest, the wave height may be higher.*

Figure 7.9 *The crashing together of the two wave patterns producing a high, vertical, broken wave is called clapotis. This type of area offers an exciting and challenging playground for experienced and skillful paddlers.*

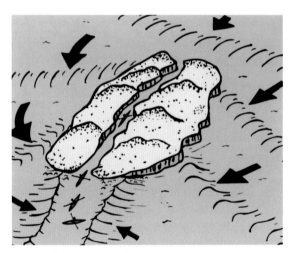

Figure 7.10 *Wave refraction round an island*

tremendous pressure. This is undoubtedly a most dangerous type of wave. Landings and departures through such waters should be made with extreme caution.

More deadly than shore dumping waves are the **storm water waves** shown in Figure 7.12. These are huge, pounding, crashing waves whose area of breaking extends far out to sea. Occasionally some parallel order of approach can be noticed in the waves, but mainly the pattern is confused. Close inshore, at what I shall call the **secondary break** area (point C in the illustration), the surf may look manageable for kayaking, but even the inshore soup here generates

Figure 7.11 *Dumping wave. Air is trapped at point A as the wave breaks. Note the water draining back out to sea at point B. This is the undertow.*

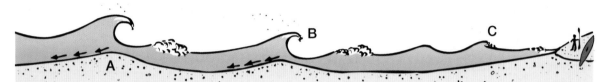

Figure 7.12 *In the area of primary break at points A and B, the waves are breaking a quarter to a half mile out to sea, creating a powerful undertow more associated with inshore "dumpers." In normal conditions the presence of the shallower water at A and B would remain unknown. Point C marks the area of secondary break and provides a dangerous playground for paddlers.*

power tremendous enough to capsize and inhibit rolling. The paddler and his boat can be forced backwards as he tries to paddle out, his kayak stabbing viciously into the sand with a back-breaking jerk. A paddler may roll up and find he is underwater.

Viewed from the level of the beach, the **primary break** at points A and B may be hardly visible, as the illustration has a foreshortened look, with the waves appearing to pile one on top of the other. Only by climbing higher up the beach can one obtain a better view of the whole situation. The primary break is the area of the fearsome, dumping, deepwater waves, which because of their great height now break over depths, which would normally have no influence on the surface swell.

Each of these deepwater dumping waves forms its own dreadful undertow. Rescue in this area is very difficult, if not impossible. Storm water is not for recreational kayaking and should be avoided, and even the secondary break should be treated with great caution.

The type of wave that surf kayakers travel many miles to ride is shown in Figure 7.1. These waves can be very large, but because of their shape and because the break topples gently over from the top, they are quite manageable. Found on beaches that have a long, even, gradual slope, these surfing waves do not usually have an undertow.

A **rip** is a phenomenon consisting of water moving at a different speed from that of the water adjacent to it. Water that has come ashore

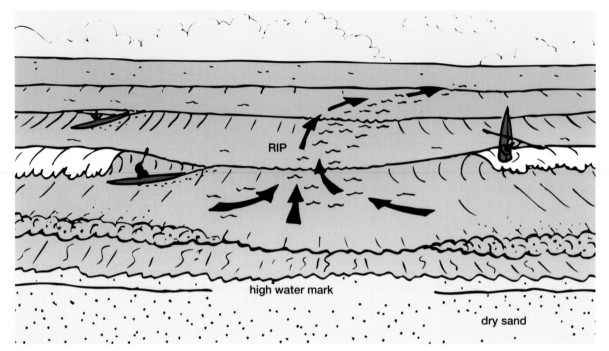

Figure 7.13 *High tide*

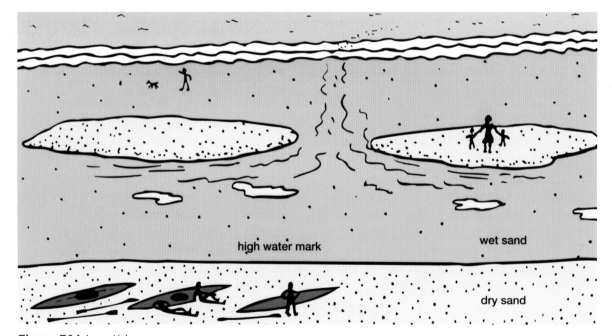

Figure 7.14 *Low tide*

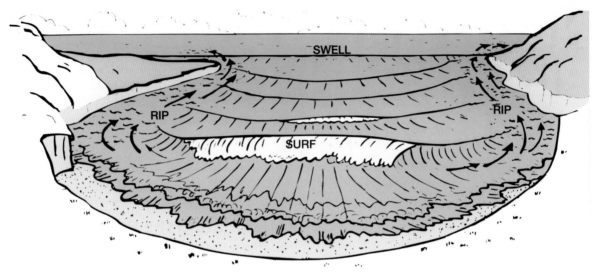

Figure 7.15 *Wave refraction and rips in a bay. When surfing in a bay, use the surf in the center, then use the rip as a quick and easy way out again. The swell refraction is caused by the sides of the bay.*

as surf is taken back out to sea by rips, as shown in Figure 7.13. On the beach at low tide, deep channels may be seen (Figure 7.14). At high tide these channels form rips taking water back out to sea in large volumes at 1 or 2 knots, faster than you can tow a kayak back to shore if you capsize one. Rip channels, which provide a swift means

of getting out through surf, can also be found at the sides of bays (Figure 7.15).

If you are swimming, it is almost impossible from your position at water level to know that you are in a rip. If you are in a kayak, you will have to inform any swimmers as to the correct direction in which to swim clear.

CHAPTER 8
NEGOTIATING AND PLAYING IN THE SURF ZONE

The "surf zone" begins where the ocean meets the shore. It ends when the paddler is well past the breakers where the rolling seas only lift their kayak up and down, but do not launch it forward. The shore can be a sandy beach, a jetty, rock gardens, or cliffs. For our discussion we will assume a sandy beach.

The ability to handle breaking waves, to run with them, battle out against them, and take them on the beam, is probably the best training anyone can have for tackling rough water out at sea. "Surfing" is when you take advantage of the steepening wave and catch a ride in your kayak. However, surfing is just a specific skill in sea kayaking. There are many men and women who love the sea and paddle on it to a very high standard, but who prefer not to enter the world of surfing. In fact, skilled paddlers can launch and land through surf zones and never surf a wave, which is an admirable goal to achieve due to the control and experience the paddler needs to have.

On a long trip, in a fully loaded kayak, a surfing mishap could destroy your kayak due to the weight of the contents. Once that mass gets moving, any sudden stops could shatter the kayak. That is not what you want on a multiday trip. Learn how to get through a surf zone under control.

Negotiating the Surf Zone

For the sea kayaker, launching and landing through surf is a necessary skill. Even though playing in the surf will be discussed at the end of this chapter, our primary focus is to help the sea kayaker get through the surf zone without surfing. If you want three hours of comprehensive instruction, my award-winning video *ABC's of the Surf Zone* is available on the USK website.

The Wave

The details of wave formation are discussed in Chapter 7. For the purposes of this chapter, what we need to know is that as a wave (swell) approaches shore, that wave will begin peaking up and increasing in height because the water is getting shallow. As the wave's face increases in height, it resembles a steep hill. If a kayak is on that hill face, it will slide down the hill (surfing) due to gravity (Figure 7.1, Chapter 7). While this is fun, the action does not stop there. When the wave gets too high to support its own weight, it collapses (breaking wave) and there is a wall of white water now moving towards shore, consuming any kayaks in front of it.

As that whitewater wave moves towards shore, it decreases in size until it hits the beach as surging water. If your kayak is on the beach side of the breaking wave, that wall of white water will eventually deposit you and your kayak near the shore, stopping when your head is dragging in the sand.

As a side note, waves travel faster than one can normally paddle. They also travel with their friends. As soon as one passes over you, its good friend is following closely behind. When you hear the weather report say the wave interval is 8 seconds, that is how long it takes for the next wave to hit you.

Taking a Beam Wave Hit

The key to successfully negotiating the surf zone is learning how to take a hit from the whitewater wave and learning accurate timing. This is where you are told to take a surf class from experienced and qualified instructors, not only for your own well-being, but also for those innocent beachgoers who could seriously be injured by your uncontrolled boat smashing into them, aside from the risk the lifeguard must take saving you from your own folly.

The most important skill to learn in the surf zone is how to take a side hit from a wave. When the beam of your kayak is hit by the white water, it forcefully pushes the boat sideways. How your kayak is tilting when impact occurs will determine what happens next. If your hull is flat, you will get knocked over towards the beach. If your hull is facing the wave, you will be rolled over towards the beach even faster. However, if you present your deck to the wave (hull towards the beach), your kayak has an excellent chance of being side-surfed to the beach, if you can remain upright. Staying upright is accomplished with the proper use of your paddle.

This is what happens in slow motion: As you sit in your kayak, with proper edging, the force of the wave moves the boat sideways from under you and your upper body is now capsizing towards the wave. If you use your paddle as a brace (Figures 4.2 and 4.5, Chapter 4), the dynamics of the water pushing up on the blade can keep you upright. Once you master this skill, the surf zone becomes a fun play area.

Wave Simulation Drill (Stirrup Pull)

Before you get in the water to practice the side hit, there is a drill I developed to help you get the feel of being hit from the side by the whitewater wave. You will need calm shallow water, your kayak, a stirrup, and a partner. The purpose of this drill is to let you experience the same forces that will occur in the surf zone, but in a user-friendly location. This drill moves the kayak out from under you just as the wave would do, except it is pulled out rather than pushed out.

Once you are positioned in your kayak with the stirrup around your cockpit area, as seen in Photo 8.1, edge your kayak away from your partner. Since your partner will be pulling your kayak, the simulated wave would be coming from the opposite side. Remember, the wave pushes you. Hold your paddle in either high or low brace position, and look towards the oncoming wave. When your partner yanks on the stirrup, you will feel the boat move out from under you. If you maintain the proper edge and brace, as needed, you should remain upright as your kayak moves sideways.

If you go over, your partner is there to roll you quickly to the surface to do this again and again until you do it instinctively. In our surf classes at UCSB, the success rate of students staying upright when hit by their first whitewater

Photo 8.1 *Stirrup pull to simulate getting hit broadside by a wave* WAYNE HORODOWICH

wave went from 50 percent to over 90 percent after using this drill.

While this makes the learning easier and less risky for the boater, there is a safety concern for the helpful partner. Since the paddler is watching the simulated wave (and not you), they have no idea the bracing movements of their paddle could be hitting you as their boat moves towards you as you pull. Therefore, it is up to you to protect yourself. Wearing your helmet and PFD will give you some protection, and using your hands and dodging as needed should protect your face.

Surf Zone Drills

Properly dressed for repeated immersions and wearing your helmet, get in your kayak and paddle out to where you are not touching bottom with your paddle. Keep your kayak pointed into the oncoming whitewater wave. Your goal is to learn the timing and feel the force of oncoming waves hitting your bow. Paddle forward as needed to counteract the force of the wave so

you are not surfed backwards. Move forward and backwards in that whitewater area while learning to take on larger waves. This is where those supportive forward and reverse strokes are useful.

After you feel comfortable taking hits on the bow, quickly turn around and do the same, taking hits to your stern. Keep your kayak stern pointing into the oncoming waves, which means you are constantly looking behind you. Again, your goal is to counteract the forces and not be surfed towards shore. You want to control your movement in the surf zone when your kayak is perpendicular to the waves.

When you feel up to it, turn your kayak sideways (parallel) to the whitewater wave. Edge your kayak by lifting your shore side knee (knee-hang) and get ready with your brace. If you did well with the stirrup drill, you should have no problem taking the hit and side-surfing to shore. It is important that you maintain the proper edging after the hit because your boat is still moving sideways. If you flatten the hull, you will flip over.

Of the two parts, edging your kayak is more important than the brace. If you edge incorrectly, your brace will not help you. You can only brace if your kayak is not rolled over, which occurs with titling the kayak deck towards the wave.

A reminder about shoulder safety: Do not reach up and out when bracing into a wave, especially a high brace. If the wave is small, your paddle will end up on top of the wave automatically. As the waves get bigger, you just brace into the wave in a "shoulder secure" position. If you reach up to place the blade on top of a tall wave, you are vulnerable to a shoulder injury, as mentioned in Chapter 4 and shown in Figure 4.6. Your blade gets upward lift from the wave when side-surfing in the white water, regardless of where it is placed relative to the height of the wave.

Launching from a Flat Beach

When you feel confident that you can take a beam, bow, and stern hit from a whitewater wave and stay upright, you are ready to do a full launching and landing.

Before you get in the kayak to launch, spend time on the beach looking at the waves, timing them and looking for patterns. The purpose of watching waves, whether launching or landing, is to identify where the waves are breaking and *not* being where a wave breaks on top of you.

I prefer using a plastic kayak when first learning my surf zone skills. In fact, I recommend using a plastic whitewater kayak because they maneuver more quickly, but a sea kayak will do just fine. Place your kayak on the beach after watching how far the waves surge up the shore. Choose a lull, climb into the cockpit, and position yourself while the boat rests on the sand. Secure the spray cover *with the release strap on the outside*. The next wave washing up the beach should

put enough water under your hull to enable you to push off and paddle into open water.

On a very flat beach it is possible to sit in your kayak ready for the big moment, only to find that the sea appears to have receded. Should this occur, there are some who advocate knuckling down towards the water using a hand on either side of their kayak. I prefer to use an upright paddle on one side and, by leaning over, put my flat palm on the other. Then by a series of lifts and ungainly forward jerks, I make my awkward way to the water's edge, leaving a trail in the sand reminiscent of that of a one-armed mermaid (Figure 8.1).

Figure 8.1 *Launching from a flat beach. Spot the car keys!*

Photo 8.2 *When launching from a flat beach, remember to time the waves so that you paddle through the smallest of the set. Here Brian Henry paddles out from the shores of Vancouver Island. Any equipment carried on deck must be well secured.* CURRENT DESIGNS

It is rare to be able to launch and continuously paddle past a breaking wave without stopping along the way or getting smashed by it. That means you need to get close to the breaking waves while holding your position through whitewater waves hitting you (Photo 8.2). When you feel the time is right, sprint forward and get over the steepening wave before it breaks. Keep going until you are in deep-enough water where you will not be surfed forward by the incoming waves.

With experience you will be tackling quite large waves. When that day arrives, do not raise your paddle above your head; rather, keep on paddling straight through with your head down.

Landing on a Flat Beach

Many paddlers feel launching is easier than landing because they are facing the waves and are just counteracting the forces. When landing, you are going with the flow and against it at different times.

The hardest part of landing is getting close enough to the breaking wave without surfing it. That means you will be where the wave is steepening and the stern of your kayak is lifted up by the wave. At that location you need to back paddle so you do not surf down the face of the wave. If you back paddle enough, the wave will pass under you.

Photo 8.3 *Derek allows a wave to pass underneath before heading in to the beach. Notice he is leaning and bracing towards the wave.* HELENE HUTCHINSON

165

The closer you can get to the point just before the wave breaks, the farther ahead you can get of the next incoming wave. Since wave energy dissipates as it gets closer to shore, the farther you are from the breaking wave, the less force you need to counteract.

Just as in launching, you do not want to be where the wave breaks on you. Your goal is to paddle in just behind the breaking wave (Figure 8.2, paddler 2). As you follow that wave in, another wave that just broke behind you will catch up to you. At that point you need to reverse paddle your stern into the whitewater wave to keep from getting launched forward. You want to land under control (Photo 8.3).

After counteracting that whitewater wave, follow it to shore. If it is a long surf zone, you may encounter a few whitewater waves on your way in. Since you cannot paddle faster than most waves, you will have multiple waves catching up to you. Counteract as needed. Sprint yourself up onto the sand and get out before the next surge sucks you back out. You can use your hands and paddle to keep your kayak from sliding back. Once out of the kayak, quickly drag it up above the surge area.

This landing method is often called the "in-out landing" because you are going in and out as you work your way to shore. I have two friends who prefer doing the in-out landing going in backwards. This way they can face the waves instead of constantly looking over their shoulders. It is a personal choice.

Launching from a Steep Beach

Flat beaches usually have longer surf zones but are easier for launching and landing because the wave is not breaking right on the beach. Steep beaches have a shorter surf zone, but the waves crash right near the shoreline. This makes for a lot of energy being released right where you launch.

Study the surf as it rolls into the beach. If it is coming in wave sets, there will be a number of large waves, then usually a pause with much smaller waves. Sometimes the swell may even die out altogether. Then far out to sea the dark ridge parallel to the horizon can be seen as another big set marches majestically towards shore.

Timing and speed are the keys in launching from a steep beach. If your timing is wrong or if you are not fast enough getting off of the beach, you will find yourself like paddler 3 in Figure 8.2. Even though your bow will be pointing out to sea when launching, the disastrous results will be the same if you are where the wave breaks on you.

In a launching of this kind, it is better if the most experienced person goes last. When the others are ready in their kayaks with their spray covers on, he can hold each one steady, time the waves for the lull, then push them out. When his turn comes, he holds himself steady on the steeply sloping beach, and as the last surge comes up the beach from the last big set or group of waves, he pushes himself off, using the water as it runs down the slope. He must beware that it does not twist him sideways, beam on to the next approaching wave. If this does happen, it is no time for a heroic paddle brace. He should jump out quickly if he can, get clear of the kayak, and leave it. To stay with it may result in an injury.

Landing on a Steep Beach

The three men in Figure 8.2 are all in different stages of negotiating the nasty dumping shore waves on a steeply sloping beach.

Paddler 1 got as far up the beach as he could on the surge of water from the broken wave. He stopped himself being sucked back into the next

Figure 8.2 *Landing in dumping surf*

wave by holding himself on his paddle and his hand. Then, very quickly, he jumped out, grasped his kayak and paddle, and ran up the beach out of the way of the next bone crusher.

Paddler 2 sat watching the waves. Every time one came up behind him, he back-paddled so as not to be hurled forward on the face of the wave. When a big set died down, he paddled forward very hard on the back of the wave, shown in the illustration. This will carry him up the steeply sloping beach, and he will follow in the path of paddler 1.

Paddler 3 hasn't managed things so well. Although he landed well, he threw his paddle to shore while the surge was still going up the beach, and then when he was half out of the cockpit, the water started to come back down the slope again, taking him with it into the next curling wave.

The Lazy Boy Landing

I am a fan of economy of effort. If there is a long surf zone, I get past the breaking wave and then turn sideways to the next oncoming whitewater wave. I edge accordingly and ready for my brace, and let the wave side-surf me towards shore.

While I am side-surfing, I stay balanced over my kayak, maintaining my edge, so I can almost lift my brace off of the foam. This balance allows me to paddle forward or in reverse, while going sideways, if I need to avoid an obstacle I am approaching.

When I get near shore, I do a draw stroke to let the small whitewater wave go under my kayak. Then I turn my kayak so I can land bow first on the beach.

Side-surfing in with the energy provided by the whitewater wave saves me from doing the in-out routine.

Capsizing in the Surf Zone

If you do go over in a surf zone and cannot roll up, a quick wet exit is recommended. Get to the bow or stern of your kayak, the one closer to the waves, and push it to shore. Never get between the shore and your kayak. If you have a rudder, try to pull the bow into the waves, because holding near the rudder could cause injury. The kayak moves faster if it is upright, but you may not be able to reach the bow if it is too high above the water. In that case, leave it upside down.

As you push you kayak towards shore, while still holding your paddle, realize that waves will be coming over you. Hold your breath as they pass. Your kayak will be pushed forward; hold on if possible. I keep a bend in my elbow to act as a shock absorber. As the boat is pushed forward, my arm straightens out. By the time my arm is straight, the wave has usually passed. If my straight arm is being forcefully pulled by the kayak, I let go of the boat to avoid a shoulder injury.

When I grab the end toggle, I never have my fingers in any loops. If the kayak were to spin, it could close on my fingers and cause severe damage.

When I get in the shallows, I stand up and empty the water before going to shore, unless it is a steep beach. On a steep beach, you don't have to worry about swimming in the surf zone. You and your kayak will be thrown ashore. Get out of the way.

Emptying Out a Kayak in a Surf Zone

After swimming your kayak towards shore, stand in about a foot of water and flip your kayak onto its right side. If you do this quickly, you shouldn't

Figure 8.3 *Emptying a kayak in shallow water*

scoop too much water into the boat. Now lift the bow upward and twist the boat upside down. Most of the water should drain out (Figure 8.3). Any water that is left in can be removed by using your pump or sponge.

Surf Zone Reminders

Always wear a helmet when going through a surf zone. Stay clear, by a long distance, of bathers and kids on the beach. Kids and dogs will run to you. Your kayak is a lethal weapon when it is being surfed by a wave, and it covers lots of distance quickly when it speeds along.

Rudders and skegs can get damaged if left down in a surf zone, when they hit bottom. Disconnect all paddle leashes in a surf zone. Secure all items on your deck and in your cockpit before launching and landing. Waves will clean decks if the items are not clipped on. If you capsize in the surf zone and wet-exit, you do not want items floating out of your cockpit.

Never be on the beach side of your kayak when in the water. Never put fingers into loops in a surf zone. Paddle strong and fast with determination whenever you are in a surf zone.

Surfing

Surf is the white water of the sea. It is exhilarating and exciting, but it can be dangerous if not treated with respect. Surfing utilizes the basic sea kayaking skills: the stern rudder, low and high telemark turns, and the paddle brace. With just these basic skills, a high standard of surfing skill can be yours. Being able to roll is highly recommend but isn't required. However, those who cannot roll get exhausted quickly from constantly swimming their kayaks ashore after capsizing.

Sea kayaks can be used, but specialized surf kayaks, with planing hulls, are more responsive and allow more difficult maneuvers (Figures 8.4, 8.5). Over the years the kayaks used for surfing have become more specialized. In 1991 and 1993, when I was Captain of the U.S. Surf Kayaking Team, our kayaks were long and narrow, which at best could do 180-degree turns but could not do 360-degree spins that the shorter surf kayaks do today (Photo 8.4).

Since an entire book can be written about surf kayaking, we are just going to do a brief overview of this specialty.

Figure 8.4 *Derek Hutchinson design surfing kayak*

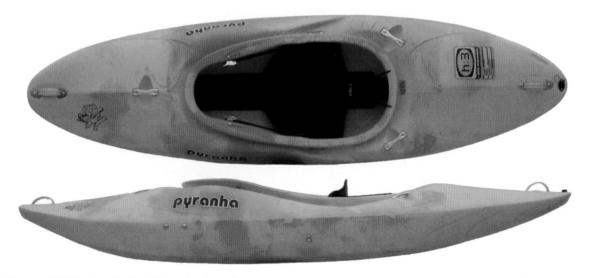

Figure 8.5 *Planing hull whitewater kayak*

Photo 8.4 *Wayne Horodowich surfing a wave at the 1991 World Championships in Thurso, Scotland. That same wave folded a teammate's kayak because he didn't get over the wave lip in time. The bottom was a slab rock shelf, not sand.* USK PHOTO LIBRARY

Surfing Maneuvers

There are numerous maneuvers that can be done in your kayak while flying down the face of a wave (Figure 8.6). Although we can surf our kayaks, we cannot match the speed and maneuverability of a surfboard. In addition, a surfboard does not side-slip down the face of the wave, like kayaks do, because they have a skeg on the bottom of the board. On the flip side, some surf kayaks can do 360-degree spins while surfing down the wave, due to their planing hull and turned-up ends.

Bottom Turn

The most basic maneuver is called the bottom turn (Photo 8.5). The kayaker surfs down the face of the wave and turns near the bottom using a rudder or a low brace turn. If they stay at the bottom of the wave, that same wave will break over them and send them towards shore (Photo 8.6). If they edged and braced correctly, they will be side-surfing. If not, they will be heading to shore upside down.

Instead of getting swallowed by the wave, the paddler can brace into the wave face and climb

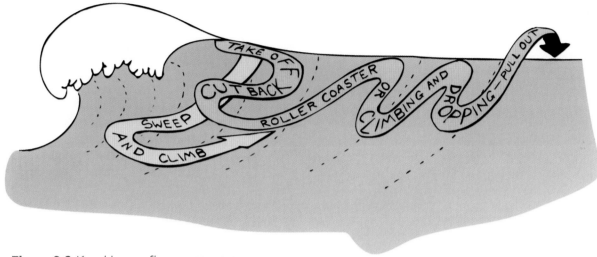

Figure 8.6 *Kayaking surfing maneuvers*

Photo 8.5 *This is a good example of a planing hull. Note that the kayak is not leaning over despite the leaning action of the paddler, Rusty Sage, who is performing a vigorous stern rudder.* JENNING STEGER, SL PRODUCTIONS

Photo 8.6 *Clive Kerswell working hard to stay in the slot at the Northern Surfing Championships, 1993.* ERIC CHACKSFIELD

their boat up and over the wave before it breaks, then paddle out and catch another wave.

Cut Back

The cut back is just as it sounds. As you surf along the wave, away from the shoulder of the wave, you can you turn your kayak on the down side so you are surfing back to the shoulder of the wave. You will want to do another cut back before getting to the shoulder.

Roller Coaster

The roller coaster has the kayaker going up and down the face of the wave.

Surf Acrobatics

If your kayak has enough volume, such as a sea kayak, that buoyancy can launch your boat into the air if it gets submerged deep enough. Here

are some maneuvers that take advantage of that buoyancy. It is important to note that many a bow and stern have been smashed in during the pursuit of catching some air.

The Loop, or "Endo"

If you surf for long enough, the day is bound to arrive when, quite accidentally, the nose of your kayak digs in and before you realize it the whole thing goes end over end. You have just done your first loop. At the end of the day, you'll tell your admiring friends all about it and how easy it was.

What makes the kayak do this? When a wave is critical and steep and you surf your kayak straight down the face, it will plunge down to the bottom of the wave, burying its bow deep. You will not have to paddle forward to make it do this. Thus at an angle of about 60 degrees, all forward movement is arrested at the bow, while the moving wave still pushes the rest of the kayak into an upright position called the "loop." The bow of your kayak may touch the bottom (a pole vault) or it may stand on end and use its own buoyancy for support. The rest of the kayak then falls over, completing the loop.

Although it all looks quite horrific to the uninitiated, it is the stern of the kayak that performs the large arc through the air, not your body. Your head travels perhaps only in an arc of 3 or 4 feet while the loop is in progress, because when the boat stands on its end, the wave carries on, giving you a soft bed to fall upon. Thus you will not finish your loop way down below in the distant trough, but on the back of the wave.

If you lean forward, as you will if you prepare yourself for a roll, your head will hardly travel any distance at all (Figure 8.7).

Figure 8.7 *The loop, or endo. Lean well forward and end up in the roll position. You will be over and up before you know what happened.*

A loop can be done as a finale to a run when the wave is about to break, or the paddler can wait at the break-line, catching the waves when they are too steep for a run and allowing the bow to plunge into a loop.

The Flick and the Pirouette

The upright loop position can also be the start of other exciting maneuvers. By reaching down onto the water with the paddle blade and performing a quick push and hip flick, you can turn the kayak so that as it falls back down, it will be facing out to sea again and you won't even get wet (Figure 8.8). This is a spectacular trick, and it can be improved upon.

With the kayak standing upright on its bow, stand on the footrest, your body at right angles

Figure 8.8 *The loop and flick pirouette*

Photo 8.7 *Derek Hutchinson performing a pirouette at the Northern Surfing Championships during one of his energetic periods.* DEREK HOLMES

and the paddle held slightly to the left side. Straighten your body quickly, your head traveling in the direction of the back deck. As you do so, fling around both arms, holding the paddle across to the right and violently twisting around to the right from the thighs. With practice the boat will spin round and round in a pirouette (Photo 8.7).

This is an extremely difficult trick, requiring a lot of practice. One of Derek's friends in Bristol, a winner of many surfing prizes, can do this without a paddle, having dispensed with it at the beginning of his run down the wave. If necessary he can do the loop, pirouette, and roll, all without a paddle.

The Reverse Loop

This is the forward loop in reverse, quite simple and requiring perhaps less courage than the forward loop because your body tends to be nearer the water during the actual loop and it is your back that is presented to the water, not your face and front.

Watch out for a reverse pole vault. This can cause you to jerk backwards, leaving the footrest and jarring your spine against the coaming. A backstrap is handy there, although I prefer to have inflated buoyancy protruding into the rear of the cockpit with a polystyrene bath float jammed between it and the seat to absorb any shock.

The Eskimo Loop, or Reverse Loop and Flick

This is probably the most graceful trick in surf acrobatics (Figure 8.9). As the kayak is running backward down the wave, the stern will begin to dig in. Just before it reaches the vertical position, the paddler winds up into the screw roll position. He then rolls into the wave, rotating the kayak vertically on its point through 180 degrees. As the front end of the kayak continues in its arc through the air, the paddler will be completing his roll and, hopefully, will find himself continuing his run on the same wave, this time forward.

Figure 8.9 *The Eskimo loop, or reverse loop and flick*

The Pop-Out

This is sometimes called a "skyrocket" (Figure 8.10). With practice it is possible to maneuver the kayak to the crest of a large wave. The boat will drop down the steep face and, with great force, will bury itself and you down inside the wave. Like a ping-pong ball in a bucket of water, the kayak is forced skyward, with any luck completely out of the water. While in this airborne condition, you can execute a flick or pirouette and shout in exuberance or perhaps just admire the wonderful view.

BCU Lifeguards

With their knowledge of surf techniques and skills, kayakers offer a relatively fast method of reaching anyone in distress in open water. They can travel much faster than a swimmer and arrive far less exhausted. The use of a kayak (Figure 8.11)

Figure 8.10 *The pop-out, or skyrocket*

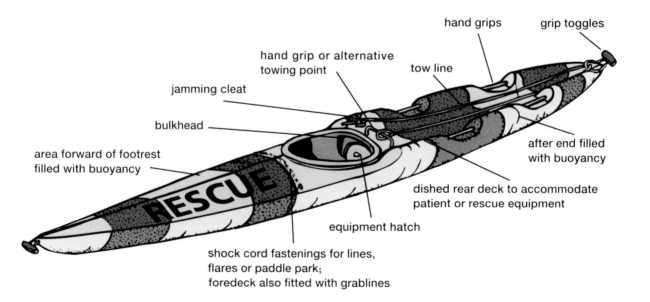

hand grips   grip toggles

hand grip or alternative
towing point   tow line

jamming cleat

bulkhead

after end filled
with buoyancy

area forward of footrest
filled with buoyancy

dished rear deck to accommodate
patient or rescue equipment

equipment hatch

shock cord fastenings for lines,
flares or paddle park;
foredeck also fitted with grablines

Figure 8.11 *A rescue kayak*

also enables lifeguards to patrol beyond the surf line or within it if necessary. In this way they can be a welcome addition to any existing rescue facilities, such as inshore rescue boats and rocket lines, and augment the reel and line team while in no way replacing it.

The BCU Lifeguards was originally founded to operate in times of flood and natural disaster. It has now moved away from its original concept and sets a high standard in the field of beach and estuary rescue, and lifesaving and patrolling techniques.

One of the main purposes of the BCU Lifeguards is to train young people in kayak handling skills so that they in turn will be able to go to the assistance of anyone in, on, or under the water. The training is rigorous, as the risks involved are not inconsiderable, and covers a wide and varied program. It is constantly changing as a result of experience, changing conditions, new equipment, and more advanced techniques.

All lifeguards are trained in the following:

- A high standard of kayaking ability, i.e., BCU proficiency tests and coaching awards
- Royal Life Saving Society and Surf Life Saving Association methods and awards
- First aid
- Signaling
- BCU Lifeguards methods of rescue using a combination of kayaking and lifesaving techniques varying from unit to unit depending upon local conditions
- Patrolling methods, which also vary from unit to unit depending on local conditions

CHAPTER 9
TIDES AND TIDAL STREAMS

Since this chapter was written by the late Derek Hutchinson, you will find many references to the United Kingdom. That being said, tides and tidal streams couldn't care less about countries and borders. Water movement due to the gravitational pull of the moon is the same around the world.

Paddle your kayak on the largest lake in the world, and if the wind doesn't blow, the water will be calm. The big difference between the largest of great lakes and some small sea bay is this: The sea is a live, living thing; it does not need wind to make it violent because its waters are continually in restless motion—in some places with quiet subtlety, in others with great speed and noise. Unlike the weather, however, the behavior of water movements is much easier to predict. Any kayaker who has watched and studied water as it flows down a river, around rock, and past obstructions on the bank should be able to apply his or her experience to the movements of the sea around our coastal areas. When a tidal stream surges around a headland or rushes between islands, its behavior is almost the same, although on a larger scale, as that of water in a river. This is an excellent time to suggest you take a whitewater class to hone your skills in moving water.

Let us look at tides and their causes, at some of the sea conditions associated with them, and

at the resultant movements of the sea, which are generally referred to as **tidal streams**. Very briefly, the moon acts like some huge magnet upon the earth. As the earth turns on its axis, it draws the sea and gives the tides a rhythmic rise and fall. The moon pulls the water nearest it, while the water on the opposite side of the earth also rises. Therefore, twice a day every part of the world has a **high tide** and a **low tide**. When it is high tide on the eastern coast of North America, it is low tide around the British Isles. When the tide is rising it is said to be **flooding**, and when it goes down it is **ebbing**. There are approximately 6¼ hours between high and low water. If it is high tide at 07.00 hours one day, the following day it will be at 07.52, a difference of about 50 minutes each day.

Twice every month, when the moon has its greatest influence on the earth's waters, a little after new moon and full moon, **spring tides** occur (please note twice a *month*, not twice every spring). Tides will rise higher and fall lower then, and tide races and overfalls are more violent. Tidal streams run faster, thus giving more help or offering more resistance to paddlers. The water will uncover rocks and wrecks that are rarely seen, or flood the tiny area where you were going to stop for lunch.

Halfway between each spring tide, when the moon has the least effect on the oceans, we have what are called **neap tides**. Any epic crossings or expeditions are best planned to coincide with these.

Because the moon's track around the earth is elliptical, it is nearer the earth at certain times than at others. When nearest, it is said to be in **perigee**, when farthest away, in **apogee**. When it is in perigee at almost the same time as a spring tide, the highest and lowest tides and the fastest tidal streams will occur.

Because the coastline of the British Isles is so indented and broken, it is important to remember when planning expeditions that although the tide may be out where you are, it could well be that a few miles away the tide is still moving and has in fact some 2 or 3 hours to go before slack water occurs. There is also a lag between the time of high water at the mouth of an estuary and the time of high water 5 or 6 miles inland. Heavy rain and melting snows can also affect the time of the flood.

At high and low water the tide remains more or less still—that is, slack—for a short amount of time, but in some places the water is never really slack. The rate falls off and the water then tends to flow at right angles to its original path. If the area is particularly bad, slack tides may create huge, uneasy upsurges and swirls as if the water is trying to decide what to do next. Anyone who has paddled over the position of the whirlpool in the Gulf of Corryvreckan at high tide will have been much aware of this.

It is not the movement of the tide up and down the beach that most affects us as kayakers during our paddling, but the tidal streams caused by the enormous amount of water that pours around the northern tip of Scotland and up the English Channel to fill the North Sea. As the tide floods and forces its way between islands,

it increases in speed, swirling round headlands and emptying bays and estuaries. The narrower the gap between the pieces of land, the faster the tidal stream flows (Figure 9.1). This is particularly forcibly illustrated in the tides around the west coast of Scotland, with its islands, sea lochs, and narrows where the flood rushes up one side of an island only to overtake a slower-moving tidal stream or collide with another fast tidal stream going in the opposite direction. Such complex tidal streams, when coupled with bad visibility and unstable weather, make Britain's coastal waters some of the most dangerous in the world to navigate.

There are tide and current tables readily available on the Internet that will give you all the information you need for specific bodies of water. For instance, if you wish to paddle across the Sound of Jura, the tables will tell you the west-going stream begins +0410 HW Oban, which is some 28 miles to the north. You therefore add 4 hours, 10 minutes to Oban's HW time to find out when the west-going stream at the Sound of Jura begins, thus making the adjustment, which is necessary to stop yourself from being swept away in the wrong direction.

Let us suppose it is high slack and the tide is starting to ebb. At first the water moves slowly, then gathers speed until it is running at its fastest when it is halfway between high and low water, after which it gradually slows down again until it reaches low slack. The same speed change occurs when the tide starts to flood until it reaches high slack once more.

The speed of the tidal streams at any stage of the tide cycle can be estimated fairly accurately by the ratio 1:2:3:3:2:1, where hours 3 and 4 have the greatest tidal speed. In rivers and estuaries the rate flow may not conform to the 1:2:3:3:2:1

H. W. Dover

3 hours after H. W. Dover

6 hours before H. W. Dover

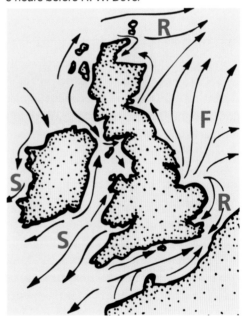

3 hours before H. W. Dover

Key: *S = slack   R = rising   F = falling*

Figure 9.1 *Tidal streams around the British Isles*

rule and the water may be at its greatest speed soon after the tide has started to run. The rise and fall of the tide is sometimes worked out by applying the rule of 12ths: 1/12, 2/12, 3/12, 3/12, 2/12, 1/12. Again, hours 3 and 4 will have the greatest water flow.

If a kayaker wishes to cross, for example, a mile-wide strait and the tide is running at more than 2 to 3 knots, he would do well to wait until the stream slackens off, thus saving himself a strenuous and prolonged ferry glide. It must be remembered that in any channel, the water moves fastest at the center. If the channel is several miles wide, as in Figure 9.2, it may be easier to leave point A while the tide is still running and arrive at the center of the channel at slack water, and then paddle on to point B after the water has started to move again in the opposite direction. Because of the distance involved in long crossings such as the English Channel, it is difficult to work the tides successfully, so that any course line must be rather a dogleg.

Along the south coast of England, tides can be very complex because when it is HW (high water) at one end of the channel, it is LW (low water) at the other. This can cause peculiar local conditions, such as the prolonged low-water condition at Portland that is known as the "Gulder," or the one at Southampton where the first flood rises normally for about 2 hours after LW, then rises very slowly (almost slack) for about 2½ hours, after which the main flood tide runs for about 2 hours until HW. Then to complicate matters, it falls a little for about an hour until it rises again for over an hour, creating another HW. So if you are paddling in the Solent, get some local information from the Sea Kayaking Centre at Calshot or do your homework *well*.

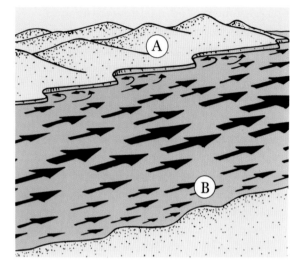

Figure 9.2 *Movement of water through a strait. The broad arrows indicate the fastest-flowing water.*

If we know the time of high tide at a major port such as Dover, the time at which other parts of the coast will have high water in relation to it will always be the same, or remain constant. After reference to a table of tidal constants—a list of times, which must be added to or subtracted from the high tide at Dover—it is easy to find out exactly what the tide is doing in a particular place at a particular time.

Tidal constants are marked on the maps in the *Automobile Association Members Handbook*, and HW London Bridge and Dover are also given in the *Times* and the *Daily Telegraph*. If the homework is not done properly for your trip, you might find yourself arriving at your lunch stop to be confronted with a sea of mud and slime, your only company being rotting cycles and pram frames, old tires, and the pleasant tinkling sound of the local sewer discharging into the mud. The Wye, the Solway Firth, and various tidal stretches of large industrial rivers such as the Thames, Tees, Mersey, Tyne, and many others, exhibit similar unpleasant characteristics at low tide. In such a situation you have few choices! Until the tide rises you can either read a book or you can set off dragging your kayak behind you, probing the mud in front with your paddle. If the mud gets too deep, you would be well advised to sit on your boat, grasping your paddle firmly, and jerk and kick your way to the nearest solid landing. Setting off to wade over a large expanse of mud, the depth of which varies from a few inches to an unknown number of feet, could at best be unpleasant and at worst prove fatal. So take care and work out your landing times correctly.

As the tidal streams travel around the British coast, whitewater conditions, sometimes of quite gigantic proportions, can be formed. A headland jutting out into a fast-moving tidal stream can cause the water to accelerate off its end, forming a **tide race** (Figure 9.3), which may extend for some considerable distance. Water rushing through narrows may produce roughly the same sort of water turbulence (Figure 9.4).

Headlands usually have underwater shallows extending well out to sea. Water rushing over these underwater shelves produces what is called an **overfall** (Figure 9.5), the water falling and tumbling over itself and producing steep and sometimes breaking waves, very close together. In some places the same effect can be seen when fast tidal water passes over slower-moving deep water going in either the same direction or the opposite one, creating what might be called a false bottom and producing a large standing wave going nowhere, like something out of a whitewater paddler's nightmare. One such wave seen off the west coast of Scotland by several independent, reliable witnesses has been estimated to be 8 to 12 feet high. The chart marking in this area shows the water to be about 400 feet deep.

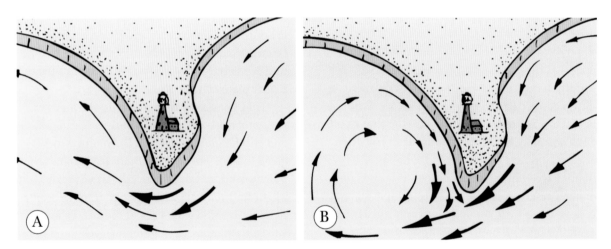

Figure 9.3 Water behavior off a headland. Although the tidal stream is running around the headland in A, it should be possible to negotiate the point. But if the opportunity is missed and the tidal stream runs at its maximum, it could produce a fast and dangerous back eddy as in B, which when it meets the tide race could produce large eddies and whirlpools.

Figure 9.4 *Behavior of water when passing between islands. Note the buildup of water at the upstream end of the islands accelerating into a race, where the fast water hits the slower tidal stream, which is itself starting to move faster because of the constrictive effect of the islands. The increased tidal speed will form an overfall as the flowing water reaches the point where the depth starts to fall away again after the shallows around the islands.*

Where two tidal streams or races move at different speeds, the meeting of these two bodies of water produces a **tide rip**. Off surfing beaches, rips are produced in a different manner (see Figures 7.13–7.15, Chapter 7).

Do not confuse tidal streams with currents, which are in fact thermal changes in the water. A good example is the Gulf Stream, which is warm and travels to the British Isles from the Gulf of Mexico at about 3 mph. If it wasn't for this warm current, Great Britain's waters would be frozen over every winter and we really would be emulating the Eskimos in more ways than one.

One final word! As a seagoing paddler you must make the tidal streams work for you and

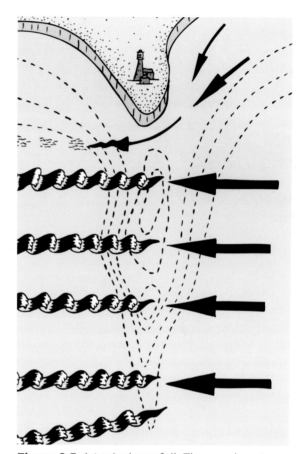

Figure 9.5 *A typical overfall. The rough water associated with this can extend 3 or 4 miles out to sea. The safe passage for a kayaker would be close to the headland unless there is heavy surf, in which case he must paddle just outside the surf line. However, the paddler must not forget the rough water caused by the race (Figure 9.3) off the headland, and unless he likes wild conditions, he may have to wait till the tide eases. Overfalls provide good training grounds for advanced sea work.*

not against you. There's an old sailing ship maxim: "Water goes off all promontories and into all bights." This still applies to yachts, and

Photo 9.1 *A kayak paddler may be considered the master of a small powered craft able to go where others dare not venture. This is the view from the "bridge." Some effort was needed to paddle against the tide rushing between the rocks. The seal gave a good impression of a depth charge as we paddled through the gap.* DEREK HUTCHINSON

how much more so must it be necessary for you, the kayaker, as you propel your kayak either with or against the wind and sea by the strength of your arms and body and nothing more. You are lucky in that your craft draws only a few inches of water and you can halt your progress towards rocks infinitely quicker than a yacht on the same path. A path extremely close inshore or around headlands is no problem to you (Photo 9.1), and using small back-eddy streams in small bays means that you can, even at an adverse state of the tide, get some help from the water which is forever denied to larger craft.

CHAPTER 10
WINDS AND WEATHER

Although many references to the United Kingdom are included in this chapter, written by Derek, weather is weather no matter where you go. You should learn the weather patterns for your particular paddling locations. The weather stories in this chapter are Derek's.

As far as the sea kayaker is concerned, wind is your greatest nemesis. Rain, sleet, hail, fog—all these are water off a paddler's back, but wind is a different matter. It is the whistling, tearing, shrieking wind that grasps at the fluttering, jerking paddle blades. Flying spray fills smarting eyes and lashes the face. It drains the strength gradually at first; then, as realization comes that progress forward is almost nil, demoralization and the seeming futility of the fight take away the will to go on. Arms that are still physically strong suddenly feel weak. The kayak becomes almost impossible to turn. The discovery is made that the constant crashing of the sea over the bow and along the deck is gradually filling the boat, finding its way through the spray cover, which is impossible to remove in these conditions to mop out. Body heat just seems to be snatched away. If ever paddling on the sea had an enemy, the wind is it.

Winds do not arrive from nowhere, and we can be reasonably prepared. The following are useful aids:

- Radio weather forecast
- The Internet or weather apps
- Knowledge of clouds and weather lore
- Check of the barometer
- Bad-weather cones or flags outside the coast guard station
- Phone call to the local weather center or coast guard station
- Knowledge of previous weather conditions for the time of year
- Intuition

Clouds

Cirrus
Fibrous and feather-like, these are the highest clouds of all. They herald the approach of a frontal weather system and are sometimes called "mare's tails." If they are arranged in a haphazard manner or if they start to dissolve, fine weather is indicated. However, if in parallel streaks feathering up at the ends, this probably means high winds, blowing in the direction of the streaks.

Cirrocumulus
Cirrocumulus are spread over the sky like the ripples in wet sand on the beach. They cast no shadows and are usually an indication of fine weather, but the wind could be strong. This type of cloud, nicknamed the "mackerel sky," is associated with the cirrus cloud in that both are very high and both indicate the approach of a front.

Cirrostratus

This is a milky white sheet covering the whole sky. The sun shines through very weakly, while the moon will have a halo.

Altocumulus

These appear in isolated formations of waves or lines and are rather like the "mackerel sky" in appearance, although lower. They are a light or medium gray color depending on the direction of the sun. When the cloud is castellated—i.e., piled upwards in a castle-like structure—this could mean thunder.

Altostratus

Forming an even gray cloud sheet covering the sky, these tend to give the sun a dilute watery appearance.

Stratocumulus

These big, soft, gray clouds give an overcast effect. The weather should be dry and settled.

Stratus

This is an even layer of cloud, really a high fog. The weather will be mild, warm, and damp.

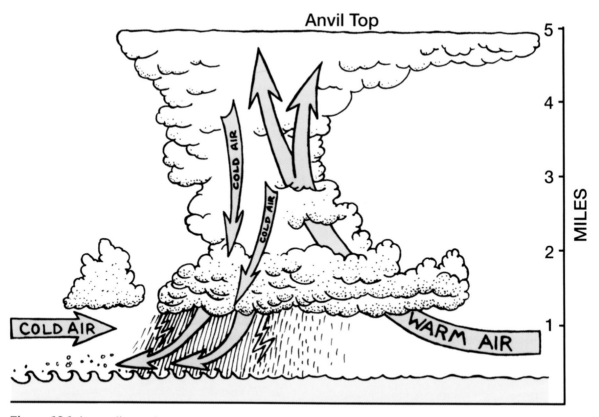

Figure 10.1 *An anvil-top thundercloud is formed as warm air is forced upwards by a cold front. The downdraft or wind sheer can cause winds of over 100 mph.*

Nimbus

These are big, black rain clouds, ominous in appearance. As nimbostratus they form a heavy layer of rain cloud.

Cumulus

These huge white clouds are like giant balls of cotton wool. Fractocumulus, small broken clouds, mean fair summer weather.

Thunderheads

These are very high mountainous clouds. The summit of the towering mass often forms itself into an anvil top, which is the classic shape for a bad-weather thundercloud (Figure 10.1). These monstrous clouds have a considerable vertical development, sometimes as high as 6 miles.

The updrafts inside these clouds rise rapidly, often reaching over 100 mph (160 km/h). This large volume of condensing water vapor causes more of the droplets to collide, giving us those large raindrops, which are so characteristic of thunderstorms. However, if the darkening of the sky, the torrential rain, and the thunder and lightning are not enough, there is worse to come. Those powerful updrafts inside the cloud are also the cause of vicious, explosive downdrafts called microbursts. These microbursts cause even larger raindrops to fall, and when this blast hits the surface of the sea, it can create winds of up to 100 mph (160 km/h). I think this is one of the most frightening things that can happen on the water.

A microburst can knock down a large sailing vessel level with the surface of the sea with disastrous results; it has also caused very large aircraft to crash onto airport runways while landing. As far as a kayaker is concerned, it can blast you and your group out to sea, even if you are paddling only a few yards from shore. On open water, it can also capsize a whole group of unsuspecting paddlers and render any kind of rescue almost impossible.

I remember once off the coast of Maine being hit by one of these horrific downdrafts. Luckily, I had seen the storm coming and I had already got most of my group to shelter; unfortunately, somebody capsized and I then had to talk my frightened and inexperienced companions through a deepwater rescue. To prevent them from being blown to oblivion, I fastened my towline onto the rescue group and paddled backward into the wind and towards the shore, all the time shouting out the necessary instructions.

Additional Warning Signs

Here are some more visual signs in the sky:

- If clouds start and get lower, it means bad weather is coming.
- If you see the rising sun breaking above a bank of clouds, beware of wind.
- If the clouds at sunrise have a nasty purple look, it is going to be stormy and windy.
- When the sun sets in a copper sky (bright yellow), look out for wind.
- A halo around the moon or sun after a fine spell means wind.
- If the clouds high up are moving in a different direction from those lower down, or in a different direction from the wind at ground-level, the wind is going to change in their direction.

Squalls

Wind speeds given in weather forecasts refer to the average sustained wind speed, not to gusts, which can take the form of squalls. A squall is a brief, violent windstorm, usually with rain, hail, or snow. When a squall is stretched across the sky, heralding the approach of a cold front, it is called a line squall, which should not be confused with the isolated squall cloud. To give a violent downdraft these clouds must have a considerable vertical development. If the squall cloud is above you, the heavy cold air can rush out of the cloud in one almighty initial blast, which can capsize a whole group of unprepared paddlers. This is the squall front.

I remember being about a mile off Holy Island, Northumberland, watching a squall approaching. The breeze was soon livened by a few outriding gusts. The sea seemed to be tumbling and falling towards us. Then suddenly there was a howling, streaming wind and white-tops all around. The raindrops were so close together that sea and sky seemed to be one. The paddler in front of me was outlined by the spray bouncing off his head, shoulders, and kayak. We seemed to be beaten down as we leaned on what appeared to be a solid wall of wind, sea-spray, and rain. Suddenly it started to ease, the drops of rain seemed smaller. I could lift my head up and see again. In a matter of minutes it had gone as swiftly as it came and we watched the ominous wall of rain retreat into the distance. If you can brace yourself and warn your group to prepare themselves, once the violent blast is over, the rest is almost an anticlimax. Continuous squalls can, however, upset a planned journey.

Lightning

The lightning that is associated with thunderstorms is dangerous, so get off the water and seek shelter as soon as possible. In the USA on average one hundred people are killed by lightning every year. In Britain the average is only four. In order to find out how far away the thunderstorm is from your position, wait until you see a flash of lightning. Count the number of seconds between the flash and the thunderclap, then divide by five to get the distance in miles and three for the distance in kilometers.

Once on shore you can help insulate yourself from a strike that travels through the ground by standing on your PFD and crouching down. It is also a good idea to spread out the group so one strike does *not* hit the entire group. If there is a strike, those who were not hit could assist those who were struck.

Create Your Own Local Weather Charts

Over the years a number of readers have commented to me that they feel that my weather overview in this book is too narrow, and that even though this is an international book, I give only the weather scenarios for the British Isles. Of course, what I have given you is merely an example of what you should all be doing for yourselves—that is, doing a breakdown month by month of your local weather patterns.

I can think of many examples. Let us say you want to go paddling in Baja, Mexico. You will find that winter is the best time, but even that has its problems. During the day, the hot air of the desert inland rises up, leaving low pressure near to the ground. This sucks in the air from the sea, causing fierce onshore winds. Unfortunately, these start to blow predictably every morning around 10 a.m. Because of this, the only sensible time to paddle is during the first four hours of the day. This means getting up at around 4 a.m., packing dew-soaked gear in total darkness, and then paddling off at 6 a.m.

In the Bay Area of San Francisco, something similar happens during the summer months. The sun heats up the inland valleys, causing westerly onshore 30- to 40-knot winds to blow every afternoon under the Golden Gate Bridge. The winter months therefore give more settled weather for paddling. Remember that the fogs in the Bay Area are notorious. During the summer months in the Chesapeake Bay area and the states adjoining it, you will hear a Heat Advisory broadcast (it is interesting to note that more people in the United States die from heat than from any other natural disaster, including earthquakes, floods, and tornadoes). The sudden thunderstorms in these areas are as severe as any I've seen anywhere.

So, dear reader, there you have it. Everywhere is different. I once paddled on Pyramid Lake in the Nevada desert. It was July and we had *snow*! Next time there is a lull in your paddling program, do some research and produce a month-by-month weather breakdown similar to this one of mine. Choose either your local area or the area in which you intend to paddle.

The weather chart below is based on monthly surveys over a period of one hundred years. It could be called the Historic System of Weather Prediction. There are variations in the weather, but on average certain weather conditions occur again and again. Reading this chart may well give some indication of what you might expect when planning trips and expeditions months in advance.

Wherever you are in the world, make a point of drawing up your own weather chart for the year. Here the first six months of the year for my location as an example.

Jan.	Violent storms. Low pressure with high winds can often build up huge seas. Good boat-building weather.
Feb.	Very bad weather. Hail and snow. Varnish some paddles. Visit the National Canoe and Kayak Exhibition.
Mar. 1–10	"Many weathers." Storms and gales. This is the stormiest period in Britain. Kayakers in the North and in Scotland face much stronger winds than those in the South.
Mar. 11–20	Much less stormy. Sometimes very fine with settled conditions.
Mar. 21–31	Storms and gales. Low temperatures. Possibility of snow, so try the ski slopes.
Apr. 1–15	Unsettled weather. Moderate storms and gales. Prevailing winds are W/NW.
Apr. 16–22	Season of the "anvil top" thundercloud, although it can be bright and sunny.
Apr. 23–30	Unsettled weather again, perhaps snow, sometimes the odd gale.
May 1–10	Slightly higher temperatures. There can be some cold winds, usually from the N/W, and the occasional night frost. So into the loft and check the camping gear.

May 11–22   Usually a cold period. Winds can be strong from the north.

May 23–31   A little warmer. The winds have dropped, but this time of May has produced some heavy thunderstorms with flooding. Good for whitewater kayakers.

June 1–10   Changeable and cool, but the weather starts to improve towards the 10th.

June 11–30   Usually fine and warm, sometimes very hot. Don't forget the dark glasses and sun cream. Watch out for thunderstorms, and perhaps a squall.

The Barometer

Make a habit of checking your barometer. I was brought up in a home where the barometer was tapped every morning and evening. It gives an instant indication of air pressure, so let us see what happens when you observe it.

Starts to rise after being well below its normal for the time of year, the first part of the rise may well bring very strong winds or severe gales from the north. If it keeps on rising, it will bring fair weather.

A quick rise means the good weather may not last and the wind may come from the north.

A steady rise means good weather is on its way. High pressure brings an anti-cyclone, which means good weather is here and is going to continue. Light winds blow in a clockwise direction. During the summer months, the anti-cyclone brings hot fine weather with very little cloud. In winter, the still air brings fog and frost.

A quick fall means a storm is on its way, so don't go far offshore.

A steady fall means bad weather is on its way but taking its time.

A fall while a southerly wind is freshening, and backing to the southeast means the wind could veer and produce a westerly gale.

A fall during southeasterly winds could bring a gale. However, southeasterly gales do not last long.

A fall during southeasterly winds while the temperature starts to increase could make the wind veer to the south and southwest.

A fall while the wind is backing to the south and southwest is a sure sign of bad weather.

Constant low pressure brings unstable and changeable weather with thick, heavy clouds, gales and storms, and big swells. This is a depression, which we in Britain know and love so well. Low-pressure systems travel very quickly.

The Beaufort Wind Scale

When we left the world of Fahrenheit and started measuring temperature by Centigrade, it was all very confusing. Tell me the temperature is going to be 40°F, and I know what I'm going to take when I go kayaking. But if told I'm going to experience 20°C, I know not whether I am going to sweat or shiver. In the same way, I am one of those people who was brought up on the Beaufort Wind Scale. If I hear that a Force 6 is due, I know exactly what the wind will feel like on my face, and what it will do to the water and the boat. But if I am told that the wind will be blowing at 30 mph, I honestly don't know what it means until I convert it to Beaufort. So for poor mortals like me, here is the Beaufort Wind Scale, modified somewhat for the kayak paddler.

THE BEAUFORT WIND SCALE

Beaufort No.	Speed (mph)	Term	Grading	Conditions (these will depend on whether wind is on- or offshore or sheltered)
0	0	Calm		A nice quiet paddle is indicated. Do some fishing; spear a few flat fish. Long trips by coracle possible.
1	1–3	Light air	Very easy	A few ripples. Still good for fishing. Take the open Canadian out.
2	4–6	Light breeze	Easy	Feel wind on face; little wavelets. Take the open Canadian back in.
3	7–11	Gentle breeze	Fairly easy	A few scattered white-tops. Flag flutters straight out on coast guard station.
4	12–16	Moderate breeze	Moderate	Proficiency standard: should start for sheltered water unless an onshore breeze.
5	17–21	Fresh breeze	Moderate	Lots of white-tops. It's hard work into the wind, difficult for the inexperienced. Proficiency standard: tackle this only in sheltered water or near shore.
6	22–28	Strong breeze	Difficult	Rescues will be difficult. Warnings issued to small craft. Seas getting big; white-tops and spray. Proficiency standard: man will be in trouble.
7	29–35	Moderate	Very difficult	You *must* be strong and experienced; your equipment should be good. Seas are big. Kayaks difficult to turn. Very difficult to make headway. Wind catches at paddle blades. Foam is blown off in long white streaks, lots of spray. Communication very difficult.
8	36–43	Gale	Dangerous	Experienced man may handle this in sheltered water. In the open sea, paddlers are extended almost to the limit. Seas are piling up and breaking continuously. Wind catches the kayak on the crests. It's a fight all the time. Communication almost impossible unless very experienced. Each paddler must look out for himself. Rescues impractical.
9	44–51	Strong gale	Extremely dangerous	Fight for survival in open sea. Huge, breaking spume-swept waves, close together. No rescues. Communication: hand signals (if you can spare the hand). Try a prayer. I find these work.

Note: Winds of almost hurricane force can be coped with if the waters are sheltered, and the fetch and therefore the waves are small. In the open sea or on unprotected water, even winds of Force 3 can create problems for the inexperienced paddler.

The question of whether it is safe to venture out to sea does not entirely depend on wind speed, since the degree of danger or risk inherent in any wind speed can be heightened or lessened by the particular circumstances. The area being exposed, a large existing swell, the wind against the tide—all are factors that can increase the risk. This means that in some circumstances a Force 5 or 6 could be a foolhardy gamble for a paddler with little advanced experience, whereas with a sheltered area, a flat sea roughened only by the high wind, and the wind blowing with the tide, even a Force 7 or 8 could be quite a reasonable proposition.

When a wind is said to be veering, it is changing direction in a clockwise manner. When it is said to be backing, it is changing direction in a counterclockwise manner.

Weather Forecasts

The late-night weather forecast on television is always worth watching. Radio, on the other hand, still provides the most widely used forecasts, because it keeps the listener informed at frequent intervals throughout the day. However, most of these forecasts are for the folks on land. Even the forecasts normally found on the Internet focus on the weather over the land. As a kayaker you want to get the marine forecast on your VHF radio.

These forecasts open with a short summary of general weather conditions. A forecast is given for each of the sea areas for the next 24 hours, including the direction and strength of the wind, visibility, and general weather. After the forecast for the larger sea areas comes a similar one for the coastal areas, and the barometer pressure is given in addition to information as to whether it is rising or falling. When the wind reaches over 40 knots, a gale warning is broadcast. The BBC helps us by interrupting its programs as soon as the information is received. If a gale is **imminent** it will arrive in 6 hours; **soon** it will arrive in 6 to 12 hours; **later** it will arrive in over 12 hours.

In North America, continuous VHF weather forecasts are transmitted by the NOAA in the United States and by the coast guard in Canada.

The Coast Guard

The coast guard is always very cooperative and will give information over the telephone. Apart from the local weather and wind speed, they can also be relied upon to give the height of the swell, which often proves useful.

Do not forget that although the coast guard may tell you that your trip is ill advised when the weather is bad, they are not allowed to officially advise you that conditions are suitable for your trip. Thus if things go wrong, and they often do, the onus rests firmly on your shoulders, not theirs. Even the shoulders of the coast guard are not that broad.

When the coast guard advises against a particular trip because of prevailing weather conditions, they base this advice on a wealth of experience. Unfortunately, they have no idea of the potential of a kayak in rough seas handled by a good kayak man. So while proficiency-level paddlers would do well to take their advice and find a piece of sheltered water somewhere, advanced kayakers must fall back on their considerable personal experience, considering all factors, together with the coast guard's advice, and make their own decisions accordingly.

Remember that the advice given by the coast guard is designed to keep you alive and to allow the lifeboat crews to carry on their normal daily occupations without interruption. They cannot be wrong, even if you spend your day languishing on the beach, wishing that you had gone out after all.

Photo 10.1 *Derek Hutchinson filming near the Chenega Glacier in Alaska's Prince William Sound. Any change in the tide or wind direction can cause kayaks to be crushed by drifting ice coming together.*
TOM CASKEY

Intuition

There comes a time, after all the usual checks have been made with the weather center, the coast guard, and other forecasts, when the weather is still and the clouds betray nothing. You look up, sniff, suck your teeth, and gaze about. A deep feeling of apprehension slows you down while the rest are gleefully preparing for the trip.

Take careful note of the feeling: Either cancel the trip or, if you do go ahead, be mentally alert to the possibility of the worst happening. If it doesn't, you'll be all right; but if it does, you'll be prepared.

CHAPTER 11
NAVIGATION

Derek did such a nice job with this navigation chapter, I only had to add a few updates. All of the stories in the chapter are being told by Derek.

The term *navigation* may sound rather grand when talking about kayaking, since the equipment on the deck of a sea kayaker's boat hardly turns the deck into a chart table. Yet, quite advanced trips and expeditions are undertaken by paddlers.

As basic equipment for planning a trip, the sea kayaker needs charts of the area, Ordnance Survey maps (or topographic maps from the USGS), two rulers, and a set of dividers or pencil compasses. Parallel rules are handy but not essential, as is a Sestral navigator. This is just a 360-degree protractor with a transparent plastic arm, which swings round from the center. It can be homemade quite cheaply and might prove to be helpful in laying off a course. An orienteering compass is also handy. A chinagraph pencil (grease pencil) is useful for writing on a waterproof-covered chart if the surface is glassy.

Compass

My first compass came out of a 3d lucky bag. It lay in the bottom, next to a whistle-whizzer and a "move-it-and-the-eyes-wink" colored picture of Tom and Jerry. I set this tin and cardboard navigational wonder in clear molding plastic to make it waterproof, then drilled a hole at one end

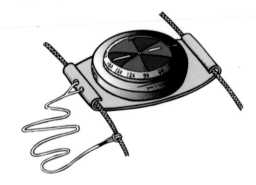

Figure 11.1 *Moveable deck compass*

for the string. Many a man has navigated farther with much less. However, a compass is hardly the thing to economize on. I now use a K-15 Suunto compass (Figure 11.1). It is luminous and the face is green, red, and black. The course direction can be read off the part of the face closest to me.

Charts

Looking at a chart should open up a wonderland of information to you. What is the direction and speed of the tidal stream? What is on the sea bottom—sand or mud? If I make bivouac, will there be a spring of freshwater? Will there be overfalls or races to fight against? All these questions should be answered when you look at your chart.

These charts contain a wealth of information for those who know how to read them. Trying to remember the many abbreviations and symbols on them is an almost impossible job, so it is

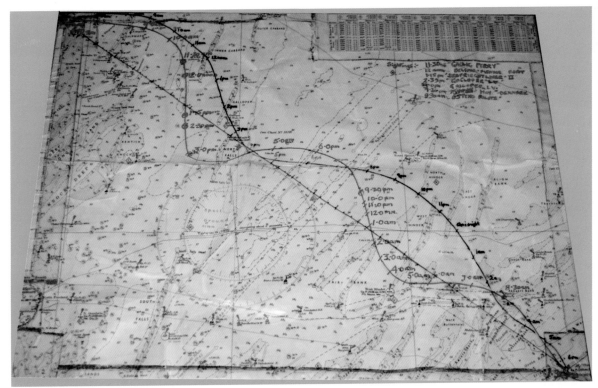

Photo 11.1 *Here is the chart Derek had on the deck of his kayak during his record-breaking successful 100-mile paddle across the North Sea (his second attempt). Since his launching point in Felixstowe Ferry, England, is at sea level with no mountains behind and his destination was Ostend, Belgium (below sea level), the only way to get there was using his compass.*

This framed chart was kept in Derek's loo, which I am sure provided him with many hours of memories and contemplation. It now sits in mine.

It is important to note that it was impossible to accurately calculate the speed of the tides, due to numerous sandbanks and varying water depths, so a straight-line bearing was chosen, 132 degrees magnetic, in blue. The thought was that every 6 hours of ebb would then cancel out the following 6 hours of flood as the trio of kayakers paddled along for over 31 hours. The actual course in red was fairly close to the planned course in black.

Derek's first attempt brought him and the other five paddlers off the coast of Dunkirk, way south of their destination. They had to be rescued by a passing ferryboat after 36 hours on the sea.
WAYNE HORODOWICH

advisable to buy chart 5011 or to get a copy of *Reed's Nautical Almanac.* (If you live in the United States, you will need to buy NOAA U.S. Chart No. 1, Nautical Chart Symbols, Abbreviations and Terms.) Certain symbols should be memorized (Figure 11.2). After all, when out at sea, the paddler cannot have a copy of *Reed's* readily at hand to thumb through at will. He has only his experience and memory to serve him. Most charts of the British Isles are now in metric, meaning that instead of the soundings being in fathoms and feet, they are in meters (1 fathom is 6 feet; 1 knot is 1 sea mile per hour; 1 sea mile is approximately 2,020 yards).

The new charts are easily recognizable due to the fact that they are colored. All these soundings are taken from the chart datum, a mark below which the tide seldom falls, which is below the level of mean low water springs.

Distances can easily be calculated from the side of a nautical chart. Just remember, "a mile a minute." Each minute is 1 mile. Use a simple string to measure your distance, and then place it on the side of the chart and count the minutes.

There are a number of waterproof, self-adhesive, clear plastic coverings on the market. It is also possible to have small sections of the chart laminated. Once covered, the chart can be

secured to the deck under the deck elastics or taped in place.

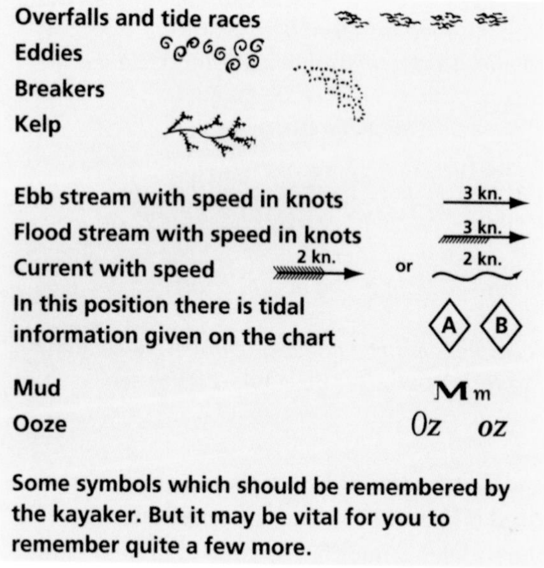

Global Positioning System (GPS)

A GPS unit can provide your exact location with respect to longitude and latitude. This is great if you have to call a rescue boat. The GPS can also provide your preprogrammed route and paddling speed. There are a number of other functions that a paddler can find useful depending on the model and make of the GPS unit. If you are interested in getting one, take a class in the use of GPS.

A paddler still needs to know how to use a compass and read a chart in order to navigate over distances and in low-visibility conditions.

Ordnance Survey Maps

Kayak expeditions should always be carried out in conjunction with an Ordnance Survey (OS) map or USGS topographic map. Campsites have to be thought out, and nearest roads for points of departure must be considered. If long trips along the coast are to be undertaken, careful thought has to be given to transport. When you finish your trip, a previously positioned minibus is a good way of getting back to the other vehicles left at the start. I remember one long crossing that meant somebody driving well over 100 miles to position the transport at the other side of the firth.

Weather conditions change for the worse very quickly. A known landing spot that permitted a seal landing or a difficult one onto rocks may on a rough day prove impossible. This will mean a long portage to find sheltered water again. The OS map will help you find the easiest route. While on the subject of escape routes on land, OS maps give post office telephones, AA and RAC boxes, youth hostels, public houses (the Englishman's

Overfalls and tide races
Eddies
Breakers
Kelp

Ebb stream with speed in knots — 3 kn.
Flood stream with speed in knots — 3 kn.
Current with speed — 2 kn. or 2 kn.
In this position there is tidal information given on the chart — Ⓐ Ⓑ

Mud — M m
Ooze — Oz oz

Some symbols which should be remembered by the kayaker. But it may be vital for you to remember quite a few more.

Figure 11.2 *Important chart symbols*

escape for many years), railway stations, and churches. After all, you never know just how bad your luck can turn out. I was once glad of a church to provide shelter for someone in an exposure bag while I waited for assistance from the mainland.

Once during an 18-mile day trip along the southern California coast above Santa Barbara, I needed four different topo maps to see the detailed features of the shore. The entire trip was a wall of sandstone cliffs with a flat beach in front of the cliffs all the way. The chart did not give enough information to pinpoint my location.

Dead Reckoning

If a kayaker knows the course he paddles and the distance he has traveled, he can use this information to pinpoint his position by what is called "dead reckoning." Did I say pinpoint? If the sea were like a lake with no wind or currents, navigation at sea would be rather like fell walking. However, conditions are never quite like that. It is extremely difficult for a paddler to guess at his speed with tides running and winds blowing. His course, even with a compass, will hardly prove consistent because of the gyrations of his kayak.

As in all things, however, practice makes perfect, or should I say *almost* perfect. After settling down to a steady speed over a fixed distance, using a good watch and with some trial and error, the kayaker can learn to work out his average speed under all sorts of varying conditions. He can then calculate the distance he should travel in a fixed time, and this will help him find his position.

Cross Bearings

With your chart in front of you, it is easy to take a cross bearing from two fixed objects on the land. Choose two objects so that after you have

taken a bearing on them, the lines drawn from them on your chart are almost at right angles. The point of intersection should indicate your position on the chart.

If you are sitting in your kayak and about to set the course with your compass from a bearing taken from a chart previously, remember that the compass you carry points to magnetic north, *not* true north. If, therefore, your bearing was taken from grid—i.e., from an Ordnance Survey map or the outer ring of the chart compass rose—do not forget to *add* the magnetic variation. This varies between 15 and 9½ degrees, depending where you are in Britain, and is printed on the rose of a chart. Remember, in the British Isles:

> Magnetic to grid—**subtract**
> Grid to magnetic—**add**

It is important to remember that your location on the globe will dictate whether you add or subtract this variation. On topo maps this variation is called declination.

If your front pocket is full of car keys, carabiners, a metal torch, a camera and exposure meter, and a load of other ironmongery, don't wonder why your compass has taken you to Cap Gris Nez when in fact you set out for the end of Brighton Pier. (For a good laugh, place your transistor radio near your compass. Watch what happens and be warned.)

Transit Bearings

The system of transits (sometimes referred to as ranges) is the oldest navigational aid in the world. Ever since men first ventured from land, sailors have set up two posts on a beach so that when they were kept in line, the seagoing craft could keep clear of unknown dangers (Figure 11.3). Any chart or indeed OS map will provide an enormous number of ready-to-use transits, such as a colliery tower in line with a pier, a wireless mast in line with a buoy, a piece of land just jutting out in front of another, or two headlands kept in line. All examples provide either a leading line for the paddler to keep on or a position line on a chart, more accurate than a bearing taken by a compass.

The sea kayaker will gain other benefits from the persistent use of transits. Once he is transit minded, he will instinctively be aware of how the tidal stream or the wind is setting his craft, even when he is some distance offshore, without taking any bearing at all. Briefly, the paddler will develop "feeling" for his position.

A bearing taken by transit is an ideal way of pinpointing (I mean it) wrecks for skin diving at a later date (if you are so inclined). You will find the exact place every time by this method, something that cannot be said about taking cross bearings with a compass.

Correcting Course

It is very easy to be carried away at sea. You can be duped into thinking that the direction you aim for is the direction you go in—far from it.

Here is what happens. In Figure 11.4 you set off from the coastguard (C) aiming for the lighthouse (L). It is 4 miles away and you are paddling at a steady 4 knots. Suddenly, a curtain of

Figure 11.3 *The paddler could look backwards and keep the pier lights in line, but will more likely line up the buoy and the headland and keep them in transit. He will see immediately any drift caused by an offshore wind. When he sees the church tower in line with the hilltop, he knows it is time to change direction. Keeping them in transit, his course will safely avoid the broken water over the reef at the entrance to the bay. The ship is using transit towers to guide it between the piers. When the transit beacons are lined up, this will tell the master to change direction towards them. He then uses these to keep him on course up the center of the channel.*

fog blots out the island. Your compass tells you to keep on aiming towards L. The fact you have overlooked is that tidal flow is from right to left at 3 knots. Result: At the end of the hour, you will finish up 3 miles to the left of the island. Even if the fog providentially clears to let you see where you are, you will still have another 1½ hours' paddle to beat up against the tide to reach the island.

The solution is to correct your direction of travel, and here is how to do it:

1. You know how fast you can paddle (well, find out then) and in what direction you actually want to travel.

2. You can estimate how much tidal flow there is and in what direction.

3. From C, mark off the tidal stream at 3 knots due west. Then, using compasses set at 4

nautical miles, draw an arc to cross the course line CL at Y. Join XY, which represents your course to steer (approximately NE). CY represents the distance you will cover in 1 hour, 2¾ nautical miles.

The course bearings are best written next to your cockpit or on the chart where you can see them. Paddle on the course for an hour at a constant paddling speed, and you should arrive at your pre-calculated position.

Buoyage and Estuaries

Figure 11.5 shows a typical arrangement of buoys in an estuary, based on the IALA Maritime Buoyage System A. Those who kayak should familiarize themselves with the buoyage system that prevails in the area where they intend to paddle. Not every country has gone over to the IALA system completely, however, and in the United States, Central and South America, the Philippines, and Japan, a certain amount of confusion is caused by the variety of traditional systems in use at present (Figure 11.6). In these areas, when entering a harbor from the seaward, the *port-hand* buoys are *black* (with a green or white light) while the *starboard-hand* buoys are *red* (with a red or white light). To anyone who is used to starboard green and port red, this can all be a little confusing.

It is forbidden to tie up to or climb onto any buoy used for navigation wherever you are in the world. When the first edition of this book was written, the fine for tying onto a buoy in the nearby Tyne Estuary was £5. Under the Merchant Shipping Act (1982) things have changed considerably, and anyone who is now convicted of the offense can face a fine of up to £1,000.

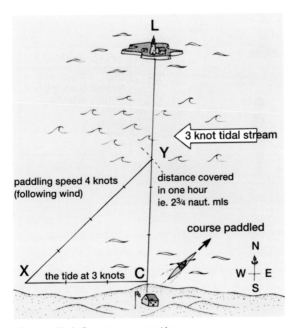

Figure 11.4 *Course correction*

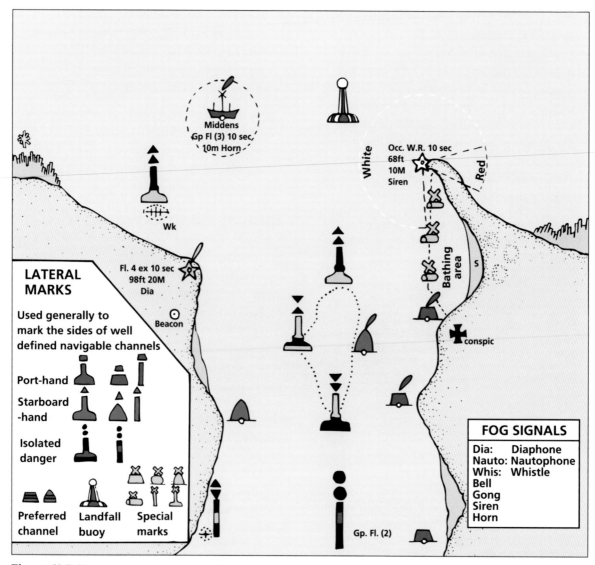

Figure 11.5 *Buoyage in an estuary, IALA System A—United Kingdom and Europe*

Take great care in estuaries and tidal rivers. Large vessels have great difficulty in maneuvering even if they do see you, which is most improbable. Beware of the upstream side of moored ships and barges. Once swept in between two moored ships, you will find they tend to squeeze against buffers, closing from about 18 inches to 6 inches. Your kayak won't stop them and neither will you (Figure 11.7). You can always tell which way the tide is setting by watching the behavior of the water around the mooring buoys. It is unwise to practice rolling in estuaries and

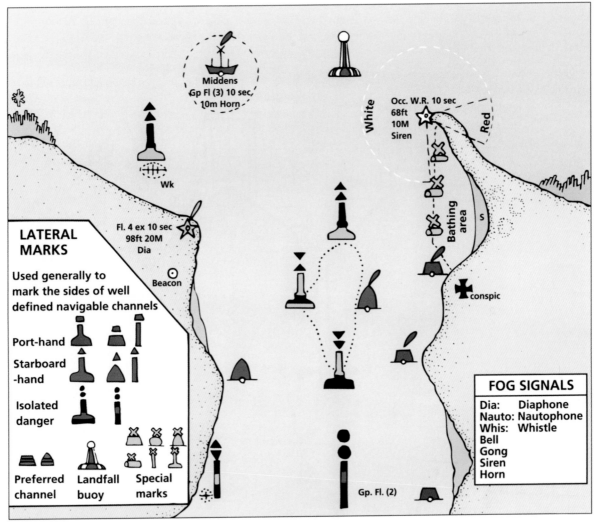

Figure 11.6 *Buoyage in an estuary, IALA System B—United States, Canada, Japan, Central and South America, and the Philippines*

tidal rivers, but if you feel you must, wear a nose clip, keep your mouth shut, and treat yourself afterwards to an antiseptic gargle. It is well to know the signals a ship will give when it alters course so that you can take evasive action if necessary.

A short blast on the hooter means it is going to starboard. Several short blasts on the hooter mean it is going to port. If you are paddling round the stern of a boat and it gives three sharp blasts, get out of the way: It is going to go astern.

Figure 11.7 *Black arrows indicate some danger spots:*
1: Crew member finds convenient rubbish tip.
2: Some of the water gushing from holes in the side of the ship may have ghastly origins.
3: The upstream side of mooring buoys could cause a capsize.
4 and 5: Two ships slowly squeezing together against buffers—a place of extreme danger.
6: To capsize in here could be quite horrific.
7: Beware of anglers and their lines.

In fog, if a vessel is moving, it will give a long blast every 2 minutes, but if it has stopped and is going to sit it out, you will hear one blast, then a 1-second gap, another blast, then a space of 2 minutes, then a repetition of the signal again.

International Collision

If you are paddling near busy shipping lanes, it will be easier to take evasive action if you know in advance what other larger vessels are going to do, especially if this entails a sudden alteration of course on their part. In all situations in which to remain on course would cause a collision, master mariners must abide by the International Collision Regulations. If you are not aware of what is happening, you may find that the captain's action is about to put his craft exactly where you are sitting in your kayak!

Meeting: Vessels that are meeting head-on alter course to starboard.

Crossing: The vessel that has "the other" crossing on its starboard bow alters course, usually to starboard, in order to pass around the stern of the other vessel.

Overtaking: The vessel that is overtaking keeps clear of the vessel being overtaken.

Narrow channel: Vessels keep to the starboard side.

Shipping separation lanes: These should be crossed as nearly as possible at right angles.

As a kayak paddler you are master of a small "powered vessel." You should therefore make yourself aware of the problems facing other watercraft and thus practice good seamanship.

Photo 11.2 *Crossing Scotland's Firth of Forth near the Isle of May. The picture was taken in June 1975 during one of the training trips prior to Derek's attempt to cross the North Sea six weeks later. It was at a time when he was experimenting with radar reflectors. He eventually came to the conclusion that loosely screwed up kitchen foil on the end of a piece of fishing rod was the simplest and best solution.* TOM CASKEY

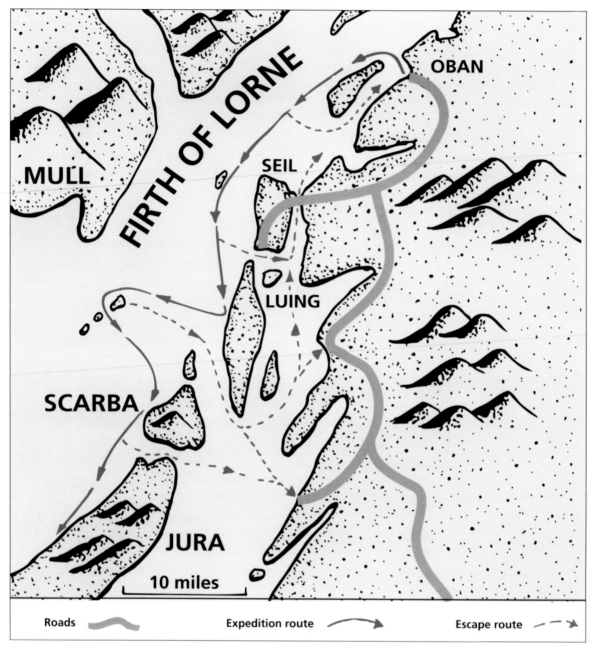

Figure 11.8 *Escape routes. The sketch map shows the route of a typical sea expedition with Oban as the base for transport and main tents. All the escape routes therefore lead either back to base, via the shelter of the islands, or to the nearest road from where someone will have to walk or hitchhike to base. Some expeditions offer a variety of escape routes by both land and sea. Some, however, offer none.*

Given the size of your kayak, it is important to remember the "law of tonnage": If it is heavier than you, get out of the way! (Photo 11.2)

Escape Routes

These should be thought of well in advance so that if conditions become unfavorable and things in general get a little tense, the leader can take his or her group out of danger into safety. Figure 11.8 shows a typical expedition. Oban is the base, the campsite having been found by an OS map. The plan is to paddle down the western exposed sides of the islands of Kerrera, Luing, Scarba, and part of Jura.

Any gale from the west will produce extreme paddling conditions but, as illustrated, there are ways back to base, which will give reasonable shelter. The routes must be worked out from a chart. If your escape route lies between two islands and the tidal stream is against you, it may be impossible to get into the sheltered water. In such a case you land in the best place you can.

A well-planned expedition should have a prearranged escape route for any given point on your route. Escape routes are not only from weather and water conditions—you should anticipate fatigue, sudden illness, injury, equipment failure, and nightfall.

Special Challenges

Fog

When I first started kayaking on the sea, very few people ventured out of sight of land. The outlook of most paddlers was very similar to that of sailors prior to the fifteenth century: It wasn't safe, and if the fog was dense, the last thing you wanted was to vanish seawards into it. If by some mischance one of those dense summer pea-soup fogs came down, it was out with the compass and grope your way back to the beach.

Be cautious by all means, but don't deprive yourself of some very interesting experiences by never attempting a trip in the fog.

Fog may be present before a trip starts or it can arrive like huge banks of moving steam while you are out at sea. It makes no noise as it creeps and envelopes everything in its path. Fog is caused when warm air blows off the land over a cool sea and cools the surface air down to its dew point. A clear sky will help the heat to radiate from the earth, and you will see that a slight breeze is needed to carry this warm air.

In really dense fog, everything appears and sounds quite different from usual. Buoys and ships take on strange shapes. One minute dogs can be heard barking miles away, and the next moment your companion's voice sounds muffled only a few yards away. You lose all sense of direction and after a while may even doubt your compass. Sometimes the sun seems to give a nice warm glow and the blue sky can be seen when you look up; the fog bank is not very high, and you may even paddle out of it. At other times it seems dark and black even at midday and there is no warm glow. This fog is high, cutting out the sun's bright glare.

If you would like to try a paddle in bad visibility, take your compass and go out a little way offshore into the fog. Don't try this in a harbor at first in case you wander into a shipping lane and get run down. Go off the beach, but not in big surf. Paddle about for 10 minutes or so and then find your way back to the beach. This will give you confidence in your compass. Then go out for about half an hour and wander around just for the thrill of it, knowing you can get back in again when you want to. Go out on a clear day and take some bearings off buoys and markers, then on the next foggy day paddle out and try to locate them. You will soon see how difficult this little exercise can be.

In fog each member must carry a compass. The chances of getting separated from your group are very great, so you may find that you can actually use the whistle that has been bleached in the sun on its rotting cord on your lifejacket all these years. I often carry a trumpet type of foghorn manufactured by the Acme firm that makes the whistles. Some handheld foghorns are driven by a can of compressed air. In dense fog don't forget you cannot see anything and—what is probably more important—nobody can see you and you will not show up on a ship's radar. If you wish to make your own radar reflector, roll up some kitchen foil into a loose ball, 6 to 9 inches in diameter. Fix it to your hat or stick it onto 3 feet of an old fishing rod and carry it upright on your rear deck. You will find it as good as anything you can buy (Photo 11.2).

Fog can make the surface of the sea very deceiving. I once set off for an island in fog with the sea like glass and no wind. I was familiar with the water and the distance involved was only a couple of miles, but after I had paddled the time it normally takes to get there, no island loomed up. It appeared it had either sunk or been towed away. I sat and wondered where I had gone wrong. Well, there is a good rule in fog: If you can't see, listen. So I strained my ears and could just hear something to the north, a rather peculiar sound I could not place. I headed towards it and soon the sky was filled with screaming, diving, swooping seabirds around the cliffs of an island. I realized what I had done. Although the water was calm and smooth, the tidal stream was running very fast. This was obvious, however,

only when I looked at the water in relation to the island it was rushing past. Out in the fog the water had appeared quite still, giving no hint that we were being swept further and further away from our destination. Remember then: Land has a sound. It may be a train, dogs barking, the sound of birds, or a combination of many things. So use your ears and listen carefully for, and be able to identify, the distinctive sounds of land.

The only way to locate something lost in fog—an island, a buoy, anything—is to use your compass and paddle a square. Paddle about 30 strokes for each side and then gradually increase the size of the box, sticking rigidly to compass bearings but, of course, remembering the drift.

One should never be surprisingly overtaken by fog. A competent paddler should be constantly scanning around them. If you see fog approaching, be sure to take a compass bearing to your destination. Really thick fog does not usually arrive without warning. There are some ways of being able to predict it. First of all, was there fog yesterday or the day before? If the answer is yes and the general weather conditions have not changed, the chance is there may well be fog today.

Look at the surface of the sea. Is it hazy and is the horizon blurred and indistinct? Is the air blowing off the land and across the cool sea? All these are sure indications of fog, and it would be prudent during the summer to pay attention to such telltale signs and to *carry a compass for even the shortest trip offshore.*

Kayaking at Night

The first time most people find out what it is like to kayak at night is usually on a late return from a day's paddle. Whatever the reason, you now find yourself in a completely different situation, so you may as well enjoy it. Paddling at night is an exciting and interesting experience, and kayaking by the light of the moon can be almost like paddling on a moonbeam.

Lights may be confusing as to their number and location. It is quite easy to misinterpret the headlights of a car as it passes over the brow of a hill near the shoreline. Don't forget that from seawards, flashing buoys are seen against a backcloth of shimmering shore lights and can easily be missed. Lighthouses always seem to look nearer at night than they really are. Sometimes you may see as many as five or six all winking and flashing different colors.

The most common type of light you will come across on your paddles is group flashing (Gp. Fl. on your chart) from a lighthouse, which is a set number of flashes repeated at a fixed interval. You can't get an accurate bearing by using these flashes, but lighthouses often have different-colored segments and in such cases you can get a bearing line as you pass from, say, the green segment to the red, since the division between the colors is shown on all admiralty charts.

At night when vessels are stationary, their lights are usually very bright. Fishing boats may have their decks floodlit. I well remember coming upon a fishing boat at about 2 a.m. out of the blackness into the illuminated area surrounding the boat and being greeted with a certain amount of alarm by the white-faced man working on the deck.

All ships—all except you, that is—must show navigation lights: white masthead lights, with the one on the front mast lower than that on the rear mast, and a red light on the port side and a green light on the starboard side. Remember that from your low position on the water the masthead

lights may look almost level. Figure 11.9 shows some interesting combinations.

A man 40 feet or more up on the bridge of a ship has a completely different view of lights and of traffic on the water than that of a kayaker. He cannot see you at all; you are completely invisible. By the time someone in the wheelhouse has made up his mind that he has actually seen your little new waterproof torch (by law you must be able to exhibit a white light to show your position if there is any danger of collision) and has then found some deck officer to make sure through his steamed-up glasses that it was a light, you are still in trouble, because he is traveling at 10 to 20 knots and is thus not likely to be able to slow down quickly. I know that when I must

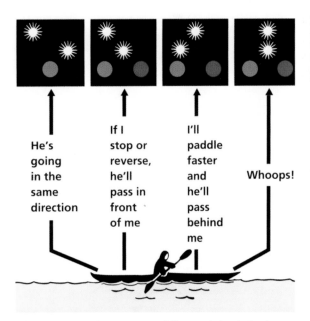

Figure 11.9 *When you paddle at night, it is the law that you are to show a white light to inform others of your position, especially if there is any fear of a collision.*

cross a shipping channel in the dark, I sit look-ing and listening for some time and then I cross at a speed that would do credit to a rather highly strung greyhound. If necessary, white or green hand flares can be fired to draw a boat's attention to your position. (Don't set off a blue one or you will get the local pilot coming out to you, and he will not be pleased!)

Probably the most important piece of equip-ment you will need and use, apart from what you normally carry, is a caver's headlamp or, failing this, a flashlight taped to your helmet. You will need this light for studying the chart and liven-ing up the sometimes feeble glow of your lumi-nous compass. However, bear in mind that some caver's lamps are not as waterproof as one would wish. You will also want another flashlight handy on the foredeck (fastened to the kayak by a cord), which will have many uses but not for warning ships of any size of your presence.

As a night navigator you will, of course, make a note of the specific lights you will encounter before setting out on a trip. For an example of what you might expect, see Figure 11.10.

Paddling at night should be tried only after you are a very competent daylight paddler. The leader must know his group and keep it small. Remember that it is one thing paddling through rough water when you can see what your paddle is going into or the speed at which the water is moving, and it is another thing entirely when you can hardly see anything.

Local Knowledge

When you read the *Admiralty Pilot*, study a tidal stream atlas, gaze long and hard at a chart, or marvel at the accuracy of the symbols that inform you of the whereabouts of rips and races, you must bear in mind that this information is set out to inform the masters of deep-draughted

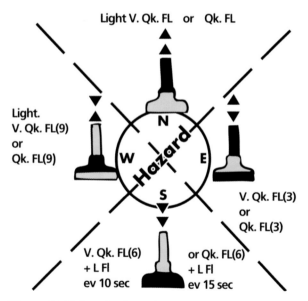

Figure 11.10 *Cardinal marks*

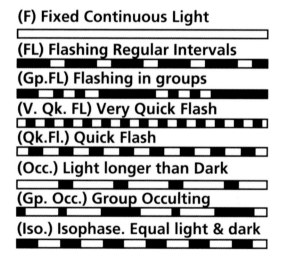

(drafted) vessels. Tiny craft like kayaks are not a priority. When you are planning your trip, therefore, remember that just because a rip or race is located at a certain position on a chart does not mean that there are no other rips or races anywhere else on the same chart—or even in the same vicinity as those already marked. There are a couple of options open to you.

First, you can draw upon your experience. Using your knowledge of water behavior, relate this to the speed of the tide, the depth of the water, and the quality of the sea bottom. Link all this with any other factors that you think relevant, and you should be able to build up a picture of what might happen at a certain location at a certain time in a particular area.

With the volume of information readily available on the Internet, gathering local knowledge is now much easier. Since you are in a kayak, you want information from other kayakers. Web searches for the kayak clubs located at your planned destination will be your best first step.

Many years ago I had the salutary experience of learning just how valuable this type of information can be. A group of us had decided to make a first crossing of the Sound of Harris. This strait separates the islands of Harris and Uist in the Outer Hebrides. There were six of us earnestly studying the chart spread out on the oilcloth-covered table of Leverbourgh's one and only cafe. We encouraged each other with the fact that the overall distance was only 20 miles, and that apart from a few rocky islets dotted about on our side of the sound, it was obviously a very straightforward open crossing.

There was a ring of confidence in the remarks from around the table.

"It all looks reasonably uncomplicated."

"The maximum speed is only 3 knots!"

"That shouldn't present any problem."

We were all dedicated ocean paddlers of considerable experience. I felt that I had studied the chart until I could have drawn it in my sleep, and surely we knew by heart the "Directions to Mariners" from the pages of the *Admiralty Pilot*. So, leaving the others to conclude their deliberations, I decided to get some fresh air.

Our brightly colored kayaks, their charts and compasses affixed to the foredecks, were now all packed and ready. They lay resting on the weed-covered rocks at the base of a stone seawall, their bows already pointing eagerly towards the mist-shrouded outline of Uist way off to the south. I went out into the wind and wandered in the direction of the kayaks.

A very old man was leaning on the low stonewall. He held a blackened pipe in his gums and he gazed contentedly out across the white-tops and into the distance. I leaned sociably on the wall, next to him. We stood together for a while before he looked at the kayaks and found inspiration. He spoke very slowly, in the strong dialect of the islands, and he seemed to weigh every word. His head was nodding as he spoke.

"Och . . . aye . . . They're bonny wee boaties you've got there!"

I needed no other opening.

"These boats are called sea kayaks and they're built especially for use on the sea."

I proceeded to expound the virtues of the sea kayak to his slowly nodding head. Eventually I paused for his reaction. His head was still nodding as he looked from me back out across the sound again.

"Aye . . . aye . . . Mind, that's a dangerous bit of water out there."

Once again my mouth went into operation ahead of my common sense.

"Oh, that's all right," I said. "We've all been paddling for a long time. We know what we're doing." (Were they vultures or seagulls circling overhead?) I reassured him that we had studied the charts, read the *Pilot,* and had got a weather forecast. He nodded his head in silence for a time, then pointed with his pipe out towards a fishing vessel about a mile into the sound.

"Ye see yon wee boaty out there?"

Yes, I could see it. He resumed his ponderous nodding, so I kept on watching the fishing boat. It appeared to be doing about 5 or 6 knots and was displaying quite a large bow wave. However, in spite of that I couldn't discern any forward movement. I made a derisory comment about what I considered was an underpowered engine.

"He's not going very fast, is he?" I said.

He nodded in agreement as he gave his reply, which was as slow and gentle as it was horrific.

"Ahh, no-o-o . . . he's going sideways!"

I ran back to the cafe and met the others emerging into the fresh air.

"Come and look at this," I said pointing to the fishing boat. "What do you think of that?"

There was a thoughtful silence as they studied the scene. I wondered who would say the magic words. Finally it was Chris who spoke.

"He's not going very fast, is he?"

I imitated the accent rather well.

"Ahh, no-o-o . . . he's going *sideways!*"

CHAPTER 12
RESCUE PROCEDURES

The information in this chapter needs to be engrained into the mind of anyone who gets on the water and goes for a paddle, but your goal is to never have to use it because you planned and trained accordingly.

As I mentioned in the "Capsize Recoveries" chapter, the term *rescue* was commonly used when Derek began sea kayaking in the North Sea in homemade equipment. If someone capsized back then (remember there was inadequate immersion clothing), it did constitute an emergency. With proper immersion clothing and quality equipment, a capsize is no big deal if the paddler is properly trained. Therefore I have reserved the term *rescue* for emergency situations.

The typical "emergency situations" one can expect in sea kayaking include: hypothermia, drowning, sudden illness, severe cuts, burns, dislocations and sprains, broken bones, concussions, dehydration, seasickness, sunburn, being adrift, and being lost. When I look at this list, it makes me think sea kayaking is a serious and risky endeavor, which should be treated with respect. Since you are putting yourself out on open ocean waters, it should be taken very seriously.

All that being said, in the thirty-five-plus years I have been paddling and leading kayaking groups on the ocean, proper planning combined with good training and sound judgment has lessened the incidents to my groups and me.

Injuries and First Aid

This is not a first-aid book. I could not do justice to proper first-aid procedures here. There are excellent books on the subject, which you should get and absorb before you get on the water. In addition, I highly recommend enrolling in a Wilderness First Responder course, since being on the ocean and doing expeditions definitely qualifies as wilderness.

When it comes to injuries and illnesses, you have a few options. You have to immediately treat (if you know how) the injury or illness. While doing that you must decide whether to call for outside help, take the person to outside help, or successfully deal with it and decide if the trip continues or ends.

As you can see, the first step is treating the injury or illness, which means being trained to do so. I can tell you if you are in a group and someone needs help and you cannot provide any help, it will haunt you long after the incident. There is a limit to how much training one can have. I am not suggesting we all become emergency physicians, but having some fundamental first-aid training will go a long way for the victim and your peace of mind.

Common Injuries and Illnesses

Following are the more likely concerns you will encounter on a sea kayaking outing, with some recommendations for them. Again, the primary reason for having this section is to make you aware of what can happen so you can research the best way to treat and deal with these issues.

Seasickness

Seasickness is mostly preventable with over-the-counter medications or preventatives. However, once a paddler gets woozy, you need to deal with it quickly. Having them splash water on their face and looking at the horizon sometimes helps ward it off.

Once they say, "I am going to be sick," quickly get them to shore, if possible. If they are ready to vomit, tell them to vomit on their spray skirt. Leaning over the side (if the kayak is not being held) could cause a capsize and a possible inhalation of water. Once the person vomits, there is a window of "feeling better." However, it rarely lasts. This person needs to be off the water. If that is not possible, a two-person tow is recommended (see the towing section later in this chapter). Paddlers who get seasick usually need to be off the water for the rest of the day. Be sure to keep them well hydrated, even though they don't feel like putting anything in their stomach. Dry heaves are worse than vomiting water.

Sunburn

Preventable! Encourage the use of SPF 30 throughout the day. Aloe ointments seem to soothe burns. Once burned, keep the area covered to prevent further injury.

Wide-brimmed hats, sunglasses, and proper clothing help minimize sun exposure. On one trip a participant, who knew better, did not put sunscreen on the top of their feet while paddling a sit-on-top. Swollen feet occurred for three days, and the participant could barely walk. Cool water compresses and elevation were the treatment we had on hand.

Cuts and Abrasions

Because of rocks, debris, barnacles, and other objects, cuts and abrasions happen on trips. Clean and dress accordingly, and change the dressings regularly. Healing on trips with regular exposure to salt water and frequent movement slows the process. Be careful of infections. Follow recommended protocols if serious bleeding occurs.

Overuse Injuries

The common overuse injury occurs at the wrist. Holding the paddle tightly is the main cause. Tell them to loosen their grip. If it is a multiday trip, I recommend putting them on a tow rope immediately. If they feel they can still paddle, tell them to do so. It is easier to tow a paddler who is helping a little than towing dead weight. Your goal is to prevent the wrist strain from getting any worse. Resting the area is what is needed.

Dehydration

Preventable! Encourage the group to drink regularly. Having a PFD with a hydration system works wonders because it keeps the water hose near the mouth.

Cold Exposure

Preventable! Dress for the conditions. However, once you are cold it presents a number of problems. First, if not reversed, the person will get colder. The colder one gets, the less they function, which makes them even colder. They need to be out of the elements, dried off, and put into dry clothes, with enough layers to keep them from losing any more body heat. Warm liquids, food, and some movement could help them generate some heat. If they are hypothermic, follow up-to-date protocols for treating hypothermia in the field.

If still on the water, try to dry the patient off and get them in better clothing if available. At the very least, get a wind shell over their torso (large garbage bag if nothing else is available) and cover their head. Keep them moving. Feed and hydrate them if possible. If they cannot stay upright, a two-person supportive tow needs to be deployed.

Heat Exposure

Usually preventable. Adequate hats and hydration will prevent heat exposure if it is just sun and outside temperature related.

Heat exposure is often caused by wearing a full dry suit on a hot day. Too many layers under the suit may also be the reason. Regularly cooling down is needed in this situation. Soaking the suit and the head is recommended. Wearing a wet cotton hat works wonders. Keeping well hydrated is essential.

Burns

Should be preventable if careful. Campfires and camp stoves are the main culprits. The most common burn is from hot water from spills. First- and second-degree burns are treatable in the field if localized. Third-degree burns can get infected easily and require advanced medical care. Read up on burn treatment.

Strains

A strain is an injury to a muscle. Strains are most likely to occur while getting your kayak to and from the launching site. Fully loaded kayaks weigh a lot. Getting kayaks on and off vehicles puts all kinds of contorted strains on the body, especially the arms and back. Two or more people should carry a kayak. Use kayak wheels if they are available. Losing your footing due to seaweed-covered rocks, slippery boat ramps, rock, or logs can also cause strains, or even worse.

Rest, mild massage, and ice can ease the pain and speed the healing process.

Sprains

A sprain is damage to your ligaments, which are located at the joints. Once you have a sprain, rest and immobilization of the area are standard protocols. Ice, compression, and elevation are also recommended depending on the sprain site (e.g., sprained ankle). Your goal is to prevent and/or minimize swelling.

Dislocations

Shoulder dislocations can occur when performing a high brace incorrectly or trying to roll incorrectly. Others joints can also get dislocated, which usually occur from falls.

You are *not* John Wayne. Do *not* yank on the victim's arm to put it right (known as reducing the dislocation). The area needs to be immobilized. If it is the shoulder, you use a sling that is secured to the body. The paddler needs medical attention a soon as possible. They will need to be towed (two-person) to shore. A dislocation is usually very painful to the victim. The main relief occurs after it is reduced.

Breaks

Falls and smashing into things can break bones. Breaks need to be immobilized, including the joints above and below the break. Getting the victim to a hospital for treatment is required.

Head Injuries

Helmets are great for preventing or reducing the seriousness of a head injury. If you are in a surf zone, around rocks, or in the water with boats bouncing around, a helmet should be worn. Since wet rocks and logs are slippery, it is standard protocol for whitewater boaters to keep their helmets on when scouting rapids. Sea kayakers should consider keeping their helmets on until they are settled in their camp. I am 6 feet 7 inches, so tree limbs around camp have been a challenge for me. Until I learn where they are, my helmet is very useful.

Head injuries can be very serious and life-threatening. Follow recommended guidelines.

Shock

Prevention and treatment for shock are the same. Read up on it so you know what to do. Once a person goes into shock, you need to get them advanced medical help.

Sudden Illness

Heart attack, allergic reactions, strokes, food poisoning, seizures, and more fall into the category of sudden illness. Obviously, dealing with these types of issues requires advanced training.

While these illnesses cannot be prevented, they can possibly be minimized depending on the illness. Having foreknowledge of preexisting conditions (medical history) can prepare you or force you to exclude a paddler from a specific trip. Having an EpiPen (for anaphylactic shock) due to bites, stings, or allergies should be considered. Proper food storage and preparation and good sanitation can reduce the possibility of food poisoning. Typical food poisoning "runs" its course in a day or two. This does not include poison

mushrooms or other forest edibles that you may unwisely wish to experiment with.

Drowning

Dealing with a drowning victim is very emotional. If they can be revived with CPR, that is great. If you are successful with CPR and they regain consciousness, even better. Otherwise, you will be dealing with a dead body.

Aside from the physical challenges of dealing with a corpse, there will be emotional challenges that need to be handled, for you and the rest of the group. The legal authorities need to be contacted. Moving and transporting a dead body needs to be done by the proper authorities. Realize a thorough investigation is going to ensue.

I am sure there are other concerns that I have not mentioned. The ones listed above are those I have had to deal with or have heard about from other guides and instructors. Again, the more training you have, the better prepared you will be in case of injuries or illnesses.

A well-supplied first aid-kit should be standard equipment on day trips and overnight trips.

Calling for Outside Help

Chapter 1 contains a full list of the different communication devices a paddler should or could carry with them when taking a trip. The more remote you are, the more farther-reaching means of communicating you will be carrying.

Day trips in urban areas usually mean you are a cellphone call from 911 and emergency response could be at the shore fairly quickly. In remote areas, help—if you can make contact—could be hours or days away. Most of the time there will be enough local boat traffic that your

VHF radio call on the emergency channel (16) will be picked up and relayed if need be. Then hold tight and wait.

When I plan a trip, I ask myself the following question for any spot along my route: "Will my communication devices allow me to be seen (day or night) and/or heard if I need outside help?" The answer all along your route is hopefully yes. If not, where do you have to paddle to in order to make contact, or what additional equipment do you need?

Although escape routes will be discussed in the "Touring and Trips" chapter, I will mention them here too. If you cannot signal for help, what is the quickest route to find help or to get off of the water? I said quickest, not shortest. You should also know the location of the nearest hospitals in your paddling location.

Judgment

I have often heard it said, "You can't teach judgment!" To be honest with you, I have said it too. After a heated discussion with other instructors at the Port Townsend Sea Kayaking Symposium, I pondered the issue on my twenty-hour drive back to Santa Barbara, California. Not only did I disagree with the premise, I realized that sound judgment can be taught. Whether you agree with me or not, please keep reading.

In short, judging is what other people are going to do with respect to your actions. Whether it is good or bad depends on their values. What we are really talking about when we say "judgment" is, what actions or non-actions were taken. Therefore, if you can train individuals in what actions to take and what situations to avoid or anticipate, you are dealing with the issues. We should not be saying "good judgment"—we should be saying "appropriate actions."

A great quote I use in my Teaching Judgment lectures is, "Good judgment is learned from experience and experience is gained from bad judgment." In essence, we learn from our mistakes. Therefore, if you train others to be aware of common mistakes, you are dealing with part of the issue. With that in mind, I highly recommend two books for your paddling library (aside from this one): *Deep Trouble* by Matt Broze and George Gronseth and *More Deep Trouble*, edited by Christopher Cunningham. These books are a review of kayaking accidents and incidents put together through the now-defunct *Sea Kayaker Magazine*. You can learn a lot of lessons from them.

After reading the first book, I made a list of the repeated mistakes from all the incidents. The most recurring mistake was stubbornly sticking to the itinerary when conditions were such that it would be better to change plans. Staying on the beach and not paddling that day would, of course, usually have prevented the incident.

I learned early on in my teaching career to not get into the situation in the first place. I trained my leader staff to anticipate a problem before it becomes one. We would then try to role-play different scenarios so they could get accustomed to taking actions or non-actions to solve the problem. The more times you have to deal with challenges, the better you get at it. Keep in mind, you will not be successful all of the time. What is most important is that you tried. The more experience you have, the more information you will have to draw upon when facing challenges.

Towing

Derek once told me the following story: "It was a cold, dark night. The place was Alaska and it was raining. My back had seized up with cramp and I couldn't move a muscle. My friends looked after me and towed me for six rain-drenched, moonlit miles. I had never been towed before and it was only then that I realized that nobody's perfect."

Whether you are leading groups or merely paddling with friends, you will soon discover that giving assistance by towing is a fact of life on the sea. It can be difficult, and over many miles it can be grueling, heartbreaking work, especially when you feel that your stamina cannot keep pace with the urgency of the situation. People rarely need towing in good conditions. Because towing in wind and spray is physically demanding, whatever towing system you use must be comfortable and efficient right from the start. Once you are in the towing situation is not the time to decide such matters as the length of the line or the position of the anchoring point.

Unfortunately, towing has gotten a bad reputation. Being towed has become a sign of failure. As a result, those who do need a tow often wait until the last minute to speak up. Yes, a towline is used to pull another paddler along who can no longer paddle. However, that is not its only function. It essentially makes two single kayaks into a tandem kayak.

If you look at two paddlers in a tandem kayak, you cannot tell which one is moving the kayak faster. Their combined power is moving the vessel. If you were to take a strong paddler and attach them to a slower paddler, their combined power would be moving the two boats connected via the towline.

Aside from pulling someone who can no longer paddle, towlines can be used for keeping groups together, keeping overuse injuries from getting worse, anchoring a recovery (Figure 2.18, Chapter 2), pulling someone out of danger, and retrieving equipment out of caves. I also use my towline to secure my boat to shore above the high-tide line.

Before the Tow

Once you have decided a tow is needed, you will need to communicate the method of tow that will be used, the responsibilities of all involved, and the signaling to and from the one(s) being towed.

The towline should be attached (clipped in) to a secure part of the kayak being towed. Through collective experience, the forward deck lines seem to work best. Too often the front toggles get ripped out. Some metal fittings on the bow are very strong but some get pulled out. Many are not large enough to allow the carabiner to connect to it.

When you clip into a front deck line, only connect to one side (Photo 12.1). Connecting to both lines does not work if the front metal anchor gets ripped out. The advantage of using

Photo 12.1 *Clipping in to a deck line for a tow*
WAYNE HORODOWICH

a deck line is the slight stretch the deck line provides. Since it give a little bit, it is less likely to snap. However, attachments do not always hold. If your first choice does not hold, move to the second.

I have yet to hear of a commercially produced towline breaking during a tow. The features of a good tow belt, which is my preferred towing system, are discussed in Chapter 1.

After you are clipped in, slowly paddle forward and let the line play out from the pouch. As the line gets pressure on it, adjust the belt as needed on your body. When ready, slowly get up to your cruising speed. The shock cord, integrated into the towline, reduces that jerking feeling. Once you are at cruising speed, you will be surprised how well you will move along. Cruising at a constant speed and maintaining the momentum save energy over the long haul.

If you have a tow belt, as recommended, you will be able to quick-release the belt if you are being dragged backwards or sideways. It also allows you to pass the belt to another paddler if you need a rest.

A tow belt should be worn if you have it, because you never know if you will need it in a hurry. Trying to get to a stored tow belt is time-consuming and risky in rough seas.

Towing Configurations

There are numerous ways to configure a tow. The following are tried and tested over years of experience and different conditions.

One-on-one is probably the one you will use most often. You are going to be pulling the person directly behind you. You use this tow if the towee can stay upright without help or is still paddling. If there are only the two of you, there are no other options.

In the one-on-one, Sea Wings (Photo 2.19, Chapter 2) could be used to stabilize the towee if they have difficulty staying upright on their own. Making a double outrigger (like training wheels on a bike) from the extra paddle and two paddle floats could also provide stability, but that setup will create additional drag.

One-on-two is what you will need if the towee cannot stay upright without help (seasick, sudden illness, injury, extreme fatigue). This is essentially a one-on-one tow but there is a second kayaker holding onto the towee's kayak to stabilize it. The job of the stabilizer is to lean over onto the towee's kayak, behind the cockpit. They also need to keep their bow as close as possible to the bow of the towee's kayak to reduce drag (Photo 12.2). This is done using their thigh and trunk muscles. The stabilizer should *not* connect to the towee's boat. They need to be free to react as needed.

Photo 12.2 *Stabilizing the kayaker being towed. The tow rope is on the kayak of the unstable paddler.* WAYNE HORODOWICH

If the drag is too much for one person to tow, add a second in either the tandem or V configuration.

A **tandem tow** arrangement has three paddlers in line, with the towee positioned last. In other words, the tower is being towed. This is a good, powerful system, with the danger of collision kept to a minimum. Towing by this method, you should be able to maintain the cruising speed of the main group. While you could add more paddlers to the front of the tandem tow, it does not really provide much net gain.

The **V, or "husky," tow** is favored by some leaders, so I have included it here. As the name implies, the paddlers who do the towing are arranged in front of the victim, rather like the husky dogs in front of a sledge. Derek once tried this in a rough sea. The tow certainly had power, but the whole affair almost finished in calamity with kayaks colliding and paddles clacking together. The biggest challenge is keeping the two towing kayaks apart and not being drawn together.

The **contact tow** is a great tow if there are only two of you and one of you cannot stay upright. The paddler who cannot stay upright rests on the bow or stern of your kayak while you paddle the both of you to your destination. You need to be able to paddle without the resting paddler's kayak interfering with your stroke.

You and your partner will need to try the following four options to see which one works best given your different boat lengths and shapes: resting on your bow, both facing forward; resting on your bow, facing each other; resting on your stern, both facing forward (Photo 12.3); resting on your stern, facing opposite each other. Regardless of your choice, the resting partner needs to keep their kayak positioned next to

Photo 12.3 *This is a "resting on stern, both facing forward" contact tow.* WAYNE HORODOWICH

yours in such a way that it creates the least amount of drag. This is something else you need to try in order to find out what works best.

Towing Challenges

It can all go wrong when conditions are bad or you have a following sea. During a tow, the kayak can either override your back deck, jab you in the ribcage, or harpoon your hull. Longer towlines are needed in some following seas to keep the kayak behind you from catching up to you. A 50-foot tow usually works, though longer may be needed in larger conditions. Off of Kaua'i I had to connect two towlines together to avoid getting run over due to the large swells coming in behind us.

As a leader, your towing capabilities should be beyond question. However, once you are linked up to another kayak in a towing situation, you cease to be an effectual leader with full control over the group. Routine towing jobs should therefore be delegated to skilled assistants.

After the Tow

As soon as you can, after disconnecting the towline from the towee's kayak, repack the line and get it ready for another use. It is amazing how many times one tow finished and I immediately needed the belt again. When conditions get rough, things seem to happen in threes.

Also recognize the good job done by all those involved in the towing, even the towee. Remember the stigma I mentioned about being towed.

Transfers

Another type of towing is called a transfer. This is moving a person who is in the water with your kayak. It is usually used when a person loses their kayak. You have a few transfer options.

The downside to transfers is the exposure time for the person in the water and the instability the rescuer feels with the extra weight of the swimmer on their kayak. This is an excellent time to be using the supportive forward sweep stroke described in Chapter 3.

Push transfer has the swimmer holding your bow with both arms as you paddle them to your destination (Photo 12.4). When you pick up speed, their body will be under your bow and their feet will rise upward. If the swimmer wraps their feet around the front of your kayak, it may reduce some drag but adds instability to you. It may not be worth the possible capsize.

Back deck transfer has the swimmer climbing onto your back deck (Photo 12.5). Nerve-racking is the best word to describe the feeling as they climb onto your boat. Their goal is to be lying flat on your back deck with their feet in the water, flared out for stability. If it does not

Photo 12.4 *Push transfer. Dressing for immersion is important because it allows this option.* WAYNE HORODOWICH

interfere with your paddling, the swimmer can put their arms around your waist.

I recommend you use the extended paddle sculling brace on the swimmer's side as they climb on your back deck. Once they are on, quickly move into a supportive forward sweep stroke.

Although the dragging legs increase drag, it is more stable than having the swimmer hooking their ankles over the stern. The advantage of this transfer over the push transfer is the victim is no longer in the water.

Photo 12.5 *While the back deck transfer works, it is not very stable, especially in rough seas.* WAYNE HORODOWICH

Single wing transfer is the same as the back deck transfer with one addition. If there is a second boater available, they come parallel to your kayak and you can use their bow to stabilize yourself as the swimmer climbs on. When you are ready to move, the second paddler (your wingman) drops back and presents his bow to the person on the back deck. The rider holds that bow near their armpit (Photo 12.6). This should keep the bow away from your cockpit so you can paddle. The wingman also paddles. This transfer is faster moving and more stable than the standard back deck transfer. The "wing" transfers were developed by "Boston" Bob Burnett.

Double wing transfer is the same as above, but it adds another kayak, if available, on the open side of the single wing. Now there are three boats paddling and the stability is fantastic, not to mention the speed (Photo 12.7). Because of the added stability, the swimmer can hook their ankles over the stern to reduce the drag in the water.

Towline submarine transfer is a "what not to do" technique. If you are thinking of just having the swimmer rest back on their PFD while you tow them with your towline, forget it. As you pick up speed, the floater begins to submerge (Photo 12.8). The faster you go, the lower they go. This is a good way to win a "Darwin Award."

Photo 12.6 *The single wing transfer*
WAYNE HORODOWICH

Photo 12.7 *Double wing transfer*
WAYNE HORODOWICH

Photo 12.8 *Towline submarine transfer, or how to drown your partner* WAYNE HORODOWICH

Hand of God

This is a capsize recovery technique that might more appropriately be called a "rescue." If a paddler capsizes and they do not wet-exit, this technique can solve the problem if done correctly and if the victim is not too big.

Paddle up to the overturned kayak by the cockpit, then lean over the hull and grab the other side (Photo 12.9). Your goal is to roll the kayak upright by pulling the outside edge and pushing down on the edge nearest you. If the submerged paddler is very large and unconscious, it may be difficult for a smaller person to get them upright. If this technique is done incorrectly, the victim's kayak may get pinned against your kayak because you only tried just pulling them over. Remember, it is a pull and push.

If you cannot roll the kayak up, you will be forced to get them out of their kayak by pulling them out. You are doing their wet exit. The person doing the extraction needs to be in the water if you want to get it done quickly. If you try to do it while staying in your kayak, you will most likely need help, which takes time to orchestrate. Remember, the victim is underwater. Drowning is likely. Brain death begins between 4 and 6 minutes without oxygen. Get them out and

Photo 12.9 *Hand of God rescue* WAYNE HORODOWICH

immediately begin mouth-to-mouth while they float on the water. Full CPR needs to be done on a solid, stable surface (land, wooden raft, or adequate-size motorized vessel). Don't even think about trying CPR on a bunch of rafted-up sea kayaks. The victim will be long dead by the time you organized the raft and got them onto it.

Deepwater Repairs

Two experienced paddlers are well out to sea, and it has been discovered that a kayak is leaking. The man from the damaged boat sits tandem on the other kayak, sculling the paddle backward and forward to steady the rescue boat (Figure 12.1). The leaking boat is hoisted across the rescue boat's cockpit, just in front of the seated paddler. If the leak is small or very gradual, the water can be drained and the boat can be righted and the trip continued. However, if necessary, a repair kit can be taken from the damaged boat or the rescuer's kayak. While the kayak is across the rescue boat, you can repair whatever needs fixing (Figure 12.2). If it is a hole, duct tape or a patch kit can be used. It is much easier to repair a seat back or a footrest because the cockpit is empty. The rescuer's paddle can be trapped against his hull by the patient's leg or secured with a paddle park.

If two kayaks participate in this rescue, the patient will get only the bottom of his legs wet. If there are more boats involved, he can lie across the decks and keep completely dry. I have seen this operation performed successfully by an experienced coach, repairing his own boat while sitting on the foredeck of the rescue craft facing a very inexperienced rescuer, who did the support sculling.

The precarious part of this technique is when the damaged kayak is being turned perpendicular to the rescue kayak. Once the damaged boat is

Figure 12.1 *Positioning the damaged kayak*

Figure 12.2 *Deepwater repair*

across the rescue boat, the stability is incredible. You may rock from side to side if the damaged boat is balanced dead center, but you cannot go over once the bow or stern hits the water. If the damaged boat is off-center, you can take a nap if you wanted.

I have used this technique for leg stretches and picnics on the open water. If you plan to cut salami and cheese on the hull, be sure it is your partner's kayak.

If you do not have a pump and the swimmer is not dressed for immersion, this could be a useful capsize recovery technique.

Worst-Case Scenarios

In the judgment section I mentioned scenario reviews as a way to improve your decision-making skills. Aside from the ones in the *Deep Trouble* books, which you can read at your leisure, here are some for you to consider and ponder. I am not going to give you definitive answers because it is time for you to think. Also, in cases like these, are there ever definitive answers, given so many variables?

Alone in the Sea

Figure 12.3 is just about as bad as it can get. You are in the water and cannot get back into your

kayak. Even worse, your kayak and paddle have drifted away. This is when I expect to hear Marlin Perkins of *Mutual of Omaha's Wild Kingdom* say, "While Jim is being surrounded by sharks, let me say a word about life insurance."

In the above situation, the length of your initial survival time will be based upon your immersion clothing. Assuming no other dangers, your ultimate survival depends on outside help. Hopefully your immersion clothing will give you enough time for help to arrive.

Your communication devices are your last line of defense. Hopefully they will work for you. If you lost your kayak, did you grab your "bailout" bag before the boat blew away? Some paddlers keep their bailout bag in the big pouch on the back of their PFD. I know some folks who tether themselves to their kayak so it won't blow away. Ed Gillette, who solo paddled from California to Hawaii, tethered himself to the kayak, especially during nature calls when he went into the water. Remember when Tom Hanks lost Wilson in the movie *Cast Away*?

Float plans are important (see Chapter 13). However, in the above scenario, by the time your emergency contact realized you were not home in time and makes contact with the authorities, you will probably be long gone. Does your

Figure 12.3 *A bad day "capsized and in the water." His orange exposure bag, filled with wind, his paddle blades with reflective tape, and perhaps even his colorful PFD with reflective tape will all help him to be seen by rescuers. This might be a good time to try your VHF transmitter/wet flares/prayer/EPIRB, not necessarily in that order. Before setting out you should have notified someone of your destination and your ETA (float plan). Help should then be on the way if you are greatly overdue. The inside of your kayak should be marked with your name, address, and phone number.*

bailout bag have a strobe light if it gets dark before help arrives?

Seas Are Too Rough for You and Your Partner

During his first North Sea crossing attempt, Derek and his friend Tom decided they would raft up and tie their kayaks together in order to make it through the night. They were exhausted, and the weather was turning foul. Fortunately, they were able to signal a passing ferry and all was well.

If you and/or your partner could not continue because the conditions were so rough, what are your options? If either of you could not go on any farther, rafting up may be your best option and then calling for help.

Another option, if one of you is strong enough to continue, is using the contact tow. If you thought I was going to say one of you goes for help, not a chance. That option is just another way of saying, "Every man for himself." When you paddle with others, there is an obligation to the group. Most of the time the group is better off when it stays together. There are exceptions, but you have collective assets when together.

If this happened in a group, do you create one big raft or go for smaller rafts? The next time you are out with a group in rough water, try both out.

You Have to Get Home

It is the last day of a two-week solo trip, and you have a six-hour paddle (in good weather) to your takeout. Then you have a five-hour drive to the airport to catch your flight. You rented your kayak. Your stretched your vacation to the limit. If you don't make it to work tomorrow, that promotion may go to someone else.

The weather is the worst you have ever seen in this area. You have been coming here for a few years now and you are familiar with the route. You also know that your camp is in a communication blind spot. I forgot to mention, the breakfast you just ate was the last of your food. The big question is, "Will that be your last meal?" In others words, "Do you take the chance in the risky conditions, or do you wait it out and be hungry and possibly lose that promotion?" What if the storm went on for two or more days? What do you do?

Do you recall my observation regarding "sticking to the itinerary"? How many tombstones read, "I wish I spent more time at work"? Did you think to bring some emergency rations for just such an occasion?

PPPPPPPP (Proper Prior Planning Prevents Particularly Poor Paddling Performance)

After running an outdoor program for twenty-five years, I firmly believe good planning and comprehensive training can significantly reduce and almost eliminate the need for being rescued during your adventure (Photo 12.10). However, the dynamic nature of the ocean and the power of Mother Nature mean there is always the possibility of everything going wrong regardless of training and planning. That is the purpose of this

chapter: to give you options that will hopefully save your life and those in the group when things go wrong.

It is impossible to plan for every contingency. Researching the mistakes others have made is not only a practical bit of education—it is the key to prioritizing your own training and planning. Again, that is why I recommended the *Deep Trouble* books. The more you learn how things go wrong, the better you can be at preventing or lessening those potential challenges.

As mentioned at the start of this chapter, both Derek's and my goal in our teachings is for our students to never need to use the information in this chapter. You need to know it, but we hope you never have to use it. We wish you well in your training.

Photo 12.10 *You are never too young or old to learn. Derek is teaching his 10-year-old grandson, Paul Hutchinson, strokes and capsize recovery techniques.* HELENE HUTCHINSON

CHAPTER 13
TOURING AND TRIPS

Once you put your kayak onto the water and leave shore, you are on a trip. It could be a one-hour paddle, a class, a surfing session, a full-day tour along the coast, a two-week trip, or a serious expedition. I am using the term *expedition* for long duration and/or distance trips that are commonly in remote areas with little or no outside rescue options readily available.

This chapter will not be dealing with expedition planning, although most of the information contained herein will be pertinent to expedition planning. Derek has a separate book on the

Photo 13.1 *4:30 a.m. on 3rd June 1976 and three kayaks lie ready for what proved a successful attempt to cross the North Sea from Felixstowe Ferry to Ostend in Belgium. Each had his own compass arrangement. During the first hours of darkness, poor Tom Caskey lost his overboard—it wasn't tied on!* DEREK HUTCHINSON

subject, *Expedition Sea Kayaking.* The North Sea crossing referenced in Photo 13.1 was a major expedition in its time. It was unsupported and covered 100 miles with an estimated travel time of 30-plus hours.

Trip Planning

Planning a trip should be more than a quick thought. "I am going to grab my kayak and go for a paddle" should not be the sum total of your planning. That being said, you will eventually get

EQUIPMENT LISTS

Day Trips

- Kayak
- Paddles (one spare)
- PFD (with knife, whistle, and nose clips)
- Spray skirt
- Paddle float and pump
- Tow belt
- Stirrup
- Immersion clothing
- Footwear
- Extra clothing layers
- Water
- Food
- Dry bags (as needed)
- Net bag (for carrying gear)
- Sunscreen and insect repellent
- Visor/hat
- Sunglasses with strap
- Compasses (deck and orienteering)
- Charts
- GPS (if you prefer)
- Extra bungee cords
- Waterproof light (night paddling)
- Radio with two batteries (plus car charger)
- Cockpit cover
- Sponge
- Signal flares
- Painter (bow line)
- First-aid kit
- Repair kit

- Kayak wheels
- Camera
- Binoculars
- Tie-down straps (also bumper ties)
- Red flag for kayak (while driving)
- Cleaning racks (for kayak)
- Cable lock (for securing kayak)

Overnight Trips

- Tent
- Sleeping bag, liner, and pillow
- Ground sleeping pad
- Camp chair
- Stove, fuel, pots, and matches
- Mug and food bowl
- Swiss Army knife and utensils
- Sponge and cleaner
- Water bottle
- Tie-downs, carabiners, and clothespins
- Tarps (one over tent and one over kitchen)
- Headlamp and extra batteries
- Tent lamp
- Sunscreen and repellants (bug and bear)
- Water filter and collapsible water bottles
- Hammock
- Pee-bottle/towel
- Toilet paper, scooper, and matches
- Shammy towel
- Journals and books
- Reading glasses
- Passport (if needed)

to a skill and experience level where the above example can be true. If so, it means you have done this trip so many times before that all of your planning has been done and now you just need to grab your equipment and go.

When you plan your first trip, there are items and concerns you will not even consider because they are unknown to you. We will try to cover many of these items.

Trip Location

The first part of trip planning is to choose where you want to go. Your destination research should include launching and landing sites, parking, permits, degree of difficulty, skill level = expected conditions, shuttles, rescue possibilities, overnight sites, and the major points of interest.

Trip Duration

The duration of the paddling portion of the trip is affected by a combination of the days out and the distance traveled during the paddle. You also need to add the travel time to and from your put-in and takeout points. Personally I see two major categories of trips: the day trip and the overnight trip. Regardless of the duration of the trip, there are standard items that are needed any time you are on the water. I consider my day trip equipment as my basic "any time on the water" necessities. For an overnight trip, I use my day trip equipment list and add to it (see "Equipment Lists" sidebar).

When I pack for an overnight night trip, the gear is the same for one night or for two weeks. The only real difference for the number of nights out is the amount of food, water, cooking fuel, and toilet paper. There might be a couple of extra clothing items too.

Itinerary

I am defining "itinerary" as your plan of travel (destinations and events) according to a timeline. While you can plan your destinations without any specific schedule in mind, I am suggesting you include a timeline, if possible, because your itinerary is the most important part of your float plan, which is discussed later in the chapter. The reason a timeline is preferred is for rescue efficiency. Since rescue personnel are at risk when they are out searching, being able to concentrate on a specific area is better for them and you if you were sticking to your timeline. However, if you are not where you are scheduled to be, the search will then encompass your entire planned route. If you go off route, rescue chances decrease.

When I write out my itinerary, it is in two parts. Part one is my timeline for getting to and from the kayaking portion of the trip. The second timeline begins at my put-in point and ends when I arrive at my final takeout point. For most trips, they are one and the same. However, you may have one-way trips that include a shuttle, in which case I include the shuttle in part one. Since land and water rescue agencies are often different, I prefer to keep them separate.

When I write out my itinerary, I try to estimate where I will be at what times. In order to do this, you need to know your regular travel speed, along with tidal flows and times. What you cannot predict is wind, which can move you along quickly or hold you in place.

Another aspect to consider is getting as much local knowledge as possible when planning your itinerary, including resources like local paddle shops in your trip area, local clubs, guidebooks (if available), and web searches.

Escape Routes

At the end of my one-month-long Outward Bound course, five of us were put together for a four-day final expedition. We were given our starting point, our final destination, and a specific mountain we had to climb along the way. It was my job as team leader to plan the route and my "escape route" at any point along my planned route.

The escape route was defined to me as, "Where are you going to go to get outside help in the quickest amount of time?" The escape route concept has stuck with me ever since then.

When I plan a trip, I have different levels of escape routes. I have the "get off the water escape routes" and the "get outside help escape routes." When conditions get bad or there is need to get off the water, but outside help is not needed, I like to know all the landing locations along my route and the pros and cons of those takeouts, which include ease of landing, freshwater availability, possible tent spaces, firewood availability, vantage points, and wind protection.

If I need outside help or need to evacuate, my primary concern is ease of landing and quickest route to outside help. It could be as simple as landing on beach "A" and climbing the hill to be in radio contact. It could also entail paddling 5 miles to beach "B" and then hiking another 6 miles to the road with the hopes of a passing car taking me the additional 10 miles to the nearest phone.

Planning your escape routes while sitting at home minimizes poor choices, which are common when trying to find an escape route when under duress while experiencing the emergency.

Local Knowledge

It is great if you can get information from others who have done the trip you are planning to do. Clubs, kayak shops, and guidebooks are great resources. Once you are at the location, it is always good to ask locals about the conditions or any other peculiarities in the area. Keep in mind that powerboaters may have good information, but kayaks can get to many places larger boats cannot. Also, powered vessel operators are not paddling against currents. They just move a lever.

Pre-Trip

Now that you have a planned trip, with an itinerary, you can begin to get ready for that trip. The first thing that I do is to create three lists: my "to-do" list, my equipment list, and my food list. Once I have my lists, I can begin checking the items off of the lists after I have completed them.

My to-do list contains the following items: check all equipment (repair and replace as needed), coordinate equipment with others on the trip (if not a solo trip), check my car racks to see if they are still functioning well, buy my food and supplies, pack as many of my storage bags (dry bags) as possible before departing the house, have all of my written resources collected (maps, guides, permits), program my car's GPS, and write out my float plan. It also includes turning off my water heater, adjusting the furnace thermostat, alerting credit card companies, setting automatic e-mail messages, backing up computers, paying bills, getting to the bank, cleaning out the refrigerator, setting light timers, putting valuables in the safe, and telling my neighbors to keep an eye on the house and to pick up mail and newspapers.

Float Plan

A float plan is a document that you can leave with a responsible individual who will use the information contained in your plan to initiate and/or provide rescuers your planned itinerary. Remember, your rescue will be initiated if you do not check in at the designated time at the end of your trip. That responsible person is usually your spouse or a close friend. It can also be an individual at the put-in point.

It is extremely important that you make confirmed contact with the holder of your float plan informing them you are back from your trip. The last thing you want to have happen is rescue personnel risking their lives looking for you while you are sitting in a pub or driving home because you forgot or neglected to check in after getting off of the water.

Food and Necessities

Since entire books have been written on camping meals, I am not going to try to compete with that information. My goal is to give you some hints and perspectives. Camping via kayak is an absolute luxury compared to backpacking because you do not have to carry all of that weight on your back. You are floating it to your destinations. All you need to do is move your kayak to and from the water, which will be discussed later.

If I go out for a one-week trip, I have enough space in my kayak for canned soups, liquid refreshments, salad fixings, bagels, and many other hydrated food items. I find bagels, tortillas, and pita bread fit well in my front hatch. Canned items provide excellent ballast if packed properly.

Trips longer than a week mean I need to pack more dehydrated food items. I want to add that many of the dehydrated food packages designed for backpacking can be quite expensive. Some are delicious, and some are not so good. Try them at home first to see if you like them. I prefer to get my dehydrated food directly from the supermarket. There are so many noodle, rice, and soup packets available that you can be quite creative for a fraction of the cost.

Before the trip I consolidate all items in ziplock plastic bags. I reuse most of them for many trips. Definitely keep your TP in a ziplock if you want it to last. I also keep a small box of matches in the center of the tube if burning TP is environmentally acceptable at my destinations.

I highly recommend keeping your sunscreen and insect repellents in separate ziplock bags. When the containers eventually leak, you will have prevented a messy cleanup and your food and gear will not get contaminated.

Lifting, Carrying, and Loading Your Kayak

The easiest way to carry your kayak from one place to another is to persuade a friend to help you. One of you holds the rear, one holds the front, and off you go. Always try to leave the awkward, heavy rear end for your friend. Even though the grab loops are designed for carrying an empty kayak, I prefer to hold under the bow and stern in case the grab loop breaks. Constant exposure to UV rays weakens many grab loops.

If you are alone, trying not to strain your back is your top priority. For a right-handed lift, stand next to the boat's point of balance. This should be an inch or so in front of the seat. With your legs slightly apart and your back straight, bend at the knees, reach down, and take hold of the coaming with your right hand, palm uppermost. Using your legs to help you lift, hoist the kayak up onto your knee and then onto your shoulder (Figure 13.1 A). Because you lift the boat slightly in front of the center, the stern will remain supported on the ground (Figure 13.1 B). Hitch the boat slightly forward until you find its point of balance and the stern pivots up. Bring the paddle up to your hand with a deft movement of your left foot (Figure 13.1 C). The kayak

Figure 13.1 *Lifting and carrying your kayak step by step*

should rest comfortably on your shoulder and be easy to carry (Figure 13.1 D).

I believe carrying kayaks for over thirty years contributed to having four herniated discs in my back. With all of this experience and wisdom, I highly recommend using the kayak wheels for moving your kayak whenever you can. I also recommend the Thule Hullavators previously mentioned as a back-saving device.

Loading onto a Vehicle

This is much easier than it first appears because you are not going to try to lift the boat all in one go.

In the absence of those roof rack cradles that have tiny roll-on wheels, you will have to do what I do and use a piece of old carpet, a blanket, or a rubber-backed bathroom mat (my favorite). You will need this layer to protect the back of your car. If you use a carpet, the pile side faces down. This is important, as the burlap backing will damage your vehicle's paintwork. The rubber-backed mat is great because the rubber does not harm the car's finish and it holds in place when the kayak is sliding on the carpeted side.

Lift or carry your kayak until you can rest the bow on the roof rack or the trunk of your car (Figure 13.2 A), then walk to the stern and lift it high in the air. Now push the kayak forward into position on the roof rack (Figure 13.2 B). Be sure to secure your kayak to the racks with non-stretch tie-downs. The straps with cam buckles are the ones most commonly used. You can cut them to size for your particular kayak and racks. If you pull too tightly on your cam straps, you can dent or crack your kayak. You want it secured, not damaged.

Securing the bow and stern to your bumpers has two purposes. First, it is backup protection in

A

B

Figure 13.2 *Loading a kayak onto a vehicle*

case your rack breaks or detaches from the roof mounts. Second, it keeps the bow and stern from swaying side to side, which can stress the rack mounts. Please remember to attach those bow and stern lines before moving your vehicle. If you drive over them, you can severely damage your kayak, racks, and roof.

Before you drive off, do not forget your piece of carpet. You can also stand on it while you get changed, but remember to brush off the sand and grit before placing it on your cart again.

Note: If your kayak is made of polyethylene, move the bars of your roof rack as far apart as possible. This is especially important in hot climates, where the heat can soften the plastic, thus causing your kayak to sag into something resembling a banana!

The Trip

The day has arrived and you are on your way. Whether it is a day trip or an overnight, your kayak is secured to the car and you have your necessary gear and directions to your launching site. You also left your float plan with a responsible individual if you are not filing it at your launch site.

At your launch site be sure to display any parking permits if required. After emptying the car, secure it for the time you will be away on your trip. A hide-a-key is a good idea if you take your keys with you on your trip

Packing Your Kayak

When packing the kayak, try to keep all the heavy gear near the center, away from the bow and stern. If the weight is at the extremities, some inertia will be produced when the kayak is turning. Reasonable care must be exercised in balancing the kayak by distributing the weight fore and aft, but it is surprising how little the trim of the kayak (how the kayak sits in the water) is affected by quite heavy loads if loaded evenly.

A small space should be left behind the seat for emergency gear (first aid, repair kit, exposure bag, and any odd items of clothing needed during the trip) and snacks. These should all be held in place by shock cord stretched across the inside of the kayak and attached to small loops glassed onto the inside of the hull. If the kayak is not fitted with bulkheads, all gear and food bags should be secured with either rope or shock cord or else stored behind inflated, tailored air bags so that they will not float out in the event of a capsize.

Some folks like to pack their kayak to be bow heavy or stern heavy, which can provide a drier ride depending on the water and wind conditions for that day with respect to their course. A heavy bow with head seas will be a wet day for the paddler. I find it best to balance the load so the design features of my kayak are most efficient.

Once a kayak is packed, it becomes very heavy. Most paddlers decide to pack their kayak right near the water if possible. If you have to move a loaded kayak from the parking lot to the water you may be moving 100 to 150 pounds. More strains occur from moving a kayak than from paddling. It is often said that getting to and from the water is the most dangerous part of kayaking (especially the driving).

If you must carry a loaded single kayak, I recommend at least two to do it. I personally prefer four if you can round them up. Using straps underneath with two on each side is a nice way to distribute the weight. I have seen six to eight folks carry a loaded tandem kayak to the water using slings. Using your tie-down straps as slings works well.

I pack my kayak by my van and use my kayak wheels to get the loaded boat to the water's edge. Once I am all ready to go (fully suited up), I roll my kayak to the water. Then I run my wheels back to the van and hustle back to the boat to launch. I do not want to crowd the launching area, especially if it is a boat ramp.

Before Launching

This is the last time to check in with yourself before you get onto the water. The check-in I am referring to is being physically and emotionally ready for the trip. Are you seaworthy? Perhaps the conditions deteriorated, you started getting a head cold, the last call with your spouse was not a pleasant one, and/or a friend called and needed your help in an emergency.

You may be physically ready to go, but emotionally you are compromised, which can lead to poor decision-making. On the flip side, you are raring to go because you have dreamt of this trip for the last ten months and you need it for your soul, but the sore shoulder or back you thought would get better did not follow your plans, which will affect your performance, especially if conditions get rough.

If you are *not* seaworthy, cancelling, postponing, or revising the trip may be the smart thing to do. Remember, sticking to the itinerary can be dangerous if you do not allow for flexibility.

Launching and Landings

How you launch and land your kayak will be dependent on the terrain and the water conditions. We already discussed surf launchings and landings. Using boat ramps in protected harbors is the easiest; however, rocky shores, docks, and mudflats can present challenges. Here are some considerations for these environmental challenges.

Cockpit Entry from Rocks

Taking care not to fall as you carry your kayak over the slippery rocks, find some water that is deep enough to float your boat clear. Watch out that the surge doesn't lift it up and settle it down on a sharp rock. Now, suppose you are positioned on the left side of the kayak (Figure 13.3).

1. Lay the paddle across the deck just behind the cockpit and across a convenient rock, thus forming a linking bridge.

2. Hook your right-hand thumb around the paddle shaft while your fingers hold onto the cockpit rim.

3. Grasp the shaft with your left hand. Keeping your center of gravity towards this hand, sit on the kayak and shaft where it meets the kayak's deck, and lift your legs into the cockpit. Straighten your legs and slide yourself onto the seat.

Figure 13.3 *Method of entry from rocks or from non-beach shorelines*

Figure 13.4 *Entry from a low dock*

4. Transfer the paddle to the front of the cockpit or a paddle park and adjust the spray cover *with the release strap on the outside.*

Note: This is also the method you would use to launch from a steep, sloping concrete ramp or steep shoreline. Keep in mind, launching straight out from a steep ramp or shore can leave you balancing with your stern high on the shore and your bow in the water with you balancing between the two. Launching sideways is a lot more stable.

Entry from a Low Dock

Get into the seated position, and merely sit on the dock. Put both feet in the center of the boat and lower yourself onto the seat, keeping all of your weight on your arms (Figure 13.4).

When disembarking, do this in reverse, but as you leave the boat and stand up, remember to hook your paddle into the cockpit in case the kayak drifts away. Many good paddlers have prized their stiff limbs from the cockpit, straightened up, and stretched with relief, only to turn round and see their boat bobbing in about 5 feet of water just out of paddle reach.

Entry from a High Dock

This launch involves climbing into your boat from a high dock. The high dock support probably needs more care than any other method of entry. You will find that the boat is too far down for you to steady it with either your paddle or hand. Personally, I always try to get someone to hold my boat when I do a high entry.

First make a little test. Sit on the edge of the dock with your legs dangling into the cockpit. If you can place the soles of your feet into the cockpit, you should be all right; any higher and you could finish up in the water.

Sit on the edge of the dock facing the bow. Prevent the kayak from drifting by placing your feet in the cockpit. Twist sideways towards the dock, keeping your weight on your hands. Roll over onto your stomach so that your behind is suspended over your cockpit. Keeping your feet in the center of the boat, bend your knees and lower yourself gingerly onto the seat. Your weight should be supported by your hands on the dock (Figure 13.5). If your kayak has a small cockpit, you will have to sit on the rear deck before sliding into the boat.

Figure 13.5 *Entry from a high dock can be tricky*

Photo 13.2 *Driftwood kayak slide*
WAYNE HORODOWICH

Getting out next to a high dock can also be tricky. I usually position myself as close to the side of the dock as possible and keep my paddle fastened to the boat. With a deft piece of balancing, I place both hands on the back of my cockpit coaming and totally unsupported, I slide out and sit on the rear deck. With the speed of light, I bring the nearest hand onto the dock for support. I then hoist my body upward and twist so that I'm lying on my stomach, all the time keeping one foot in the boat as an anchor.

Crossing Barnacle-Covered Shorelines

The challenging part of barnacle-covered shorelines is moving from the high-water line to the actual water without ripping out the bottom of your kayak. If it is day trip, carrying the kayak may be your best option. If you have a loaded kayak, you can carry it if there are enough paddlers to help you. If you are alone, you may have to load or unload your kayak by the shore with multiple trips carrying your gear over those same slippery barnacle-covered rocks.

In the Pacific Northwest, this is a particular challenge. Fortunately many of these shorelines have an ample supply of driftwood that I have used as skids under the hull so I can slide my kayak over the barnacles (Photo 13.2). Four or five pieces of wood are all you need. As you slide the kayak along, take the last skid and move it to the front. Keep the process going until you get to the water when launching, or above the high-water line if landing.

Negotiating Mudflats and Quicksand

It is well to be especially careful when exploring low-lying tidal wetlands and estuaries. Although these areas are ideal for studying nature and usually sheltered from the dangers of wind and rough water, they can present us with their own unique problems. When the tide drains from large flat estuaries and inlets, it can often leave large expanses of soft sand or leg-sucking mud of unknown depth. Whether you are launching or landing or for some reason you have been cut off from solid land and have now been forced to make a crossing, *keep together and always*

Figure 13.6 *Crossing mud or quicksand flats can be at best unpleasant, and at worst quite frightening and fatal. The thing to do is to stay together and keep calm. Some of the areas in Britain where these low-tide problems exist are the Wash, Holy Island, and the Solway Firth. In North America, San Francisco's East Bay, the Everglades, and the Knik Arm of Alaska's Cook Inlet pose similar problems.*

stay with your boat. In other words, if you have to move, *take the kayak with you*. Of course, the really sensible thing to do is to sit in your boat and wait until the tide comes back in again. But that is not always possible.

Let us suppose that you have to make your way over this kind of surface. Pull the kayak behind you so that you can use it for support if necessary. If the mud is too deep for you to walk across safely, sit astride your boat and slide it forward over the mud, making sure you stop sliding it while there is still plenty of the hull's buoyancy underneath (Figure 13.6). You'll then have to extricate your legs and hitch forward along the

kayak, before sliding it forward underneath you once again. This can be a slow business, but you will be quite safe so long as there is some part of the kayak underneath you.

If you do find yourself alone and sinking into mud or sand, you should lie across the surface and attempt to move forward by swimming as if you were doing the breaststroke.

Seal Launching and Landing

A seal launching or landing means you are launching from, landing onto, and sliding over rocks (Figure 13.7). Any time water meets rocks, you need to be cautious. I recommend only

Figure 13.7 *The Seal Landing*

skilled paddlers try this maneuver and only if it is absolutely necessary. Since your kayak's hull is not pliable like a seal's belly, it makes it difficult for your kayak to balance and/or keep from sliding on the rocks as you try to get into it or out of it.

When launching, you are trying to slide into the water. When landing, you are hoping to use the surge to move you up onto the rocks. Timing is very important. This is where plastic boats are an advantage.

Another possibility is getting out of your kayak right near the rocks and using your bow-line to keep your kayak near as you carefully climb up onto the rocks. Once you are stable, you can haul your kayak up onto the rocks.

Any time water meets the rocks, you need to be wearing a helmet. Shoreline rocks are slippery and a lot harder than your head.

Side Drop

The side drop is a method Derek included in his book, so it remains in this new edition for you adventurous souls. While it works, a miss can be painful. This is not recommend with a loaded kayak. It is a good launching method to practice in the pool.

This is what Derek had to say about the side drop:

I have used this launching technique many times and it has allowed me to launch from the decks of small boats and numerous high docks. The method is simple, although on your first "drop" I'm sure you might feel a little apprehensive. The first thing to do is position your kayak right on the edge of the pool and parallel to it. Make sure your spray skirt is on and then inch the boat sideways, a little at a time, until half your hull is hanging in space and you are almost at the point of balance (Figure 13.8). You should be positioned so that your "good" side (for strokes) is on the side of the water. This is because you will have to brace on that side when you hit the water. (In the illustration, the paddler happens to be left-handed.)

The general idea is not merely to drop into the water, but to *lift* and launch yourself out into space and get well clear of the poolside. To do this you will need some momentum. Remembering that you are at the point of balance, twist your body round and bring the blade, which is over the water, through approximately 100 degrees so that it's now well over the "land" side. Try to imagine that your body is a spring and you are tightening it by swinging the paddle round. Go through the "one-two-three" routine, and on three aggressively uncoil where the paddle sweeps *upwards* as well as *outwards*. At the same time and with the help of the paddle, you alter the point of balance by giving your body a violent hitch upwards and outwards. With any *luck,* you will land hull first and slightly over towards your "good" side. The second you hit the water, you will need to perform an instantaneous high brace (Figure 13.8). If you happen to feel a little nervous about the success of your high brace, you can always hold your paddle in the extended position.

Figure 13.8 *Launching by means of a side drop is best practiced in a swimming pool*

While Paddling

Anytime you are on the water, it is recommended that you are dressed for immersion. You should stay well hydrated and fueled. Use appropriate sun protection. Having extra clothing layers will allow you to adjust to the conditions as they change.

Paying attention to your course is important, especially in locations with lots of little islands. Before you got on the water, you should have listened to the weather channel for your location. It is wise to monitor it during the day aside from using your senses to see if the conditions around you are matching the forecast.

Choosing Landing and Camping Sites

On day trips your landing sites will usually be temporary. Since you are likely to have all the provisions you need for the day, water and even shelter may not be a concern. Remember to take into consideration that you are going to have to launch from this same location but the water height may be different. Landing through rocks on a calm day becomes difficult and dangerous when trying to launch through those rocks after the afternoon winds come up with accompanying waves.

Choosing a camping site has more requirements. Ideally you are looking for a site with water, level ground for your tent, and shelter from winds. Having good sun exposure could be helpful for drying wet gear.

Be sure to secure (tie off) your kayak well above high-tide line while you are at your campsite.

Environmental Impact

Here is where I emphasize adopting and following LNT (Leave No Trace) guidelines for your geographic area. Trying to leave a place nicer than you found it is a recommended endeavor. Visit www.lnt.org for details.

Group Paddling

The advantage of paddling with a group is the increased number of options you have with respect to capsize recovery methods and emergency situations. It also allows you to share your experience with others aside from providing companionship during the trip.

Even though a properly equipped group will have more assets when challenges arise, do not automatically assume safety in numbers. While every paddler in the group can be an asset, they can also be a liability if they are not properly equipped, not properly dressed, cannot assist in a capsize recovery, cannot handle the conditions of the day, and do not stay with the group. Therefore, it is the responsibility of each member of the group to be an asset rather than a liability. Learning and perfecting the many different capsize recovery methods puts you on the road to being an asset in a group.

When you paddle with a group, you have a responsibility to that group. There should also be explicit norms for the group. The greatest challenge to any paddling group is staying together. Using the towrope as previously discussed is a great tool for keeping a group together, but towing and other issues need to be discussed before incidents happen.

A number of years ago I posted the "Group Paddling Creed" on the USK website along with many other articles about paddling in groups and paddling solo. This creed was compiled from the typical complaints raised by group members over many years of trip reports. Use the creed to initiate a discussion with your paddling group with respect to group behavior and responsibilities.

USK'S GROUP PADDLING CREED

When I choose to paddle in a group, I realize I have a certain responsibility to the group. I understand the group members can be on the trip for different reasons. Some of my personal desires and freedoms may take second place to the needs of the group. I always have the right to paddle alone, if I so choose, rather than paddling in a group and complaining about the group. Therefore, when I paddle with a group, I will try to be an asset to that group by abiding to the following principles:

- I will paddle with the group.
- I will be on time and ready to go.
- My equipment will be properly maintained and outfitted.
- I will dress properly and wear my PFD.
- I will carry the recommended recovery and signaling equipment.
- I can do a solo recovery if I capsize.
- I can assist others if they capsize.
- I will not put the group in harm's way.
- I will communicate with the group if there is a problem.
- I will tell the group if I choose to leave the group.
- I will respect the quiet time of others.
- I will not over-techno others with my toys.

In Chapters 1 and 2, I mentioned a flotation device called Sea Wings (Photo 2.19, Chapter 2). These should be part of every guide's emergency kit in case you need to tow a paddler that is unstable.

When conditions get difficult, most paddlers focus on their personal survival first. If you paddle with a group with the expectation that the group will be there for you if it gets rough, you may be in for a rude awakening. When conditions get difficult, some paddlers are just hanging on for dear life and are unable to assist others. I personally believe a group is a collection of solo paddlers. You should be thinking, "I need to be able to take care of myself." If you do that, then you may be able to assist others. Therefore, you need to train to be a solo paddler even if you never paddle alone.

Solo Paddling

Every time I hear an instructor tell their students "Never paddle alone," I am hoping they will add a condition onto their statement, but most of the time the warning stands alone. I believe a blanket statement discouraging solo paddling is a disservice to paddlers.

Personally I love paddling alone. In fact, I encourage paddlers to learn to paddle alone, but I add conditions to my statement. I am not suggesting I would tell a rank beginner, "Go out and paddle alone." However, I do tell my beginning students, "If you are well trained, have reliable solo recovery skills, and can handle rough conditions, then paddling alone can be an acceptable risk." More importantly, solo paddling teaches self-sufficiency. If you choose to go out alone, every aspect of that paddle is your responsibility. If anything goes wrong, it is your responsibility to take care of it. If I put together my ideal group for a trip, it would consist of seasoned solo paddlers. Then I know they all bring a lot to the table when it gets rough.

If you choose to begin solo paddling, start with short trips on calm days with plenty of escape options. As your skills increase (recovery and rough-water techniques, and navigation and maneuvering skills), you can attempt rougher conditions. Any time you choose to go out on a solo paddle, you are saying to yourself, "I believe I can handle the conditions, and I am willing to take the risk and accept the consequences." Consequences can be good if you are successful. Consequences can be nasty if you cannot handle the conditions. The greatest reward of solo paddling is not a specific skill—it is a change in attitude. There is an increase in self-confidence and self-reliance. I also believe there is a greater sense of awareness in those that take solo trips.

Your goal as a solo paddler is to be able to go out and return so you can go out another day. If you go out with the attitude, "If I get in trouble, I will just call for help," you are missing the point. You should go out with the attitude, "I am prepared to be here and I am not depending on outside help to come back from my outing."

Post-Trip

Of course, you contacted the person who had your float plan when you got off the water, so a search was not initiated because you forgot to call. I just had to mention this again because it is a serious concern.

In reality, the post-trip begins when you get home. My post-trip activities include:

- Unload, clean, and store all gear (dry)
- Immediately fix any broken equipment
- Make notes about the trip for future reference
- Upload and sort my pictures
- Update my pre-trip checklists as needed
- Reflect on the trip regarding lessons learned

Now that this trip is over, you are a first-hand expert to give advice as to how to do this trip. Your equipment list is fine-tuned. Your food list is accurate. Your charts have great details added. You now have local knowledge.

When I get back from a trip, I want to have all of my equipment, lists, and charts ready to go out again. If I ever decide to do this trip again, I want to have accurate notes so I do not have to reinvent the wheel.

A good exercise is to write a detailed trip report. If you are a member of a club, you can post it for your fellow paddlers to read and envy you. You may even try to have it published in a magazine or on a kayaking website. Your experience could be useful and/or motivating to another paddler. At the very least, you have a detailed description of your adventure that you can share with your kids if they ever ask, "Have you ever done anything?"

Figure 13.9 *"Northwest Design of a Killer Whale" Original artwork by Derek Hutchinson*

CHAPTER 14
ARCTIC ORIGINS OF THE SEA KAYAK

While I would love to take credit for all of the research it took to write this chapter, I cannot. This chapter was written entirely by Derek, and it was in his very first book. Reading about the native paddlers added to my and many other paddlers' desire to enter the world of sea kayaking.

Some of the horrors that float about on our coastal waters under the name of sea kayaks bear little or no resemblance to the designs developed over many hundreds of years by the indigenous inhabitants of the Arctic. The genuine sea kayak of the Arctic was evolved by adapting a particular type of kayak to specific needs and conditions. Throughout its history it has been essentially a completely seaworthy boat in order to fulfill its primary function of being a hunter's boat.

Photo 14.1 illustrates the fierce conditions of the Arctic Ocean. The Eskimo has always had a constant fight for survival against what would seem to be overwhelming difficulties—the long dark winter, the eternal cold, and the never-ending search for food. The only element that can provide subsistence is the sea. It is from the sea that the Eskimo gets most of his food, from fish or from sea mammals such as the seal, walrus, sea otter, and whale. From these animals he also gets oil for his lamps and sinews and baleen for sewing skins and furs. The ivory and bones from

these animals, as well as from his own dogs, can be made into weapons, tools, domestic implements, and ornaments.

The only other raw material available is driftwood, which floats in large quantities down rivers like the Yukon and Mackenzie and is then spread around the seas of the Arctic along the northern shores of Russia and the coasts of Greenland. But the right type of driftwood is rare, and the scarcity of wood necessitates the retrieval of harpoon shafts while hunting and makes the kayak a highly prized piece of equipment, handed down from father to son.

The Eskimo used to hunt the whale in an open boat about 30 feet long and 6 feet wide, with a flat bottom. It was propelled by women and was named the *umiak* (the Russian word is *baydara*), or "woman's boat." Hunting the walrus and seal required a different type of boat altogether from the *umiak*, so the Eskimo developed what is probably the world's most famous single-handed craft. For elegance, grace, and austere beauty, it has never been surpassed by any other type of solo craft. Since it also boasts speed, silence, and seaworthiness, this is a true kayak, or "hunter's boat."

When the Eskimo built a kayak, the frame was constructed first. Two long planks from 2 to 7 inches wide were used as gunwales, which

Photo 14.1 *Necessity is the mother of invention—or innovation. Fridtjof Nansen and Hjalmar Johansen sailing their united kayaks over the waters of the Arctic Ocean. "There was nothing else to be done except lash the two kayaks together side by side, stiffen them with snowshoes under the straps and place the sledges athwart them, one before, one behind."* PICTURE FROM AN ORIGINAL WATERCOLOR BY OTTO SINDING FROM A SKETCH BY NANSEN, 1897; COURTESY OF ALISTAIR WILSON. QUOTATION FROM *FARTHEST NORTH*, VOL. II, BY FRIDTJOF NANSEN, ARCHIBALD CONSTABLE & CO., 1897

were secured fore and aft in a position to take the bow and stern posts. The gunwales were supported by cross members or deck beams. Lashed on top of these with seal thong was a lath, which ran down the center of the deck. Rib frames of bent wood were mortised into the gunwale planks. The kayak was then turned onto its deck. A longitudinal lath was lashed to the bottom in the center and an even number of laths, usually either four or six, secured at either side. Any slight gaps between the bent frames and the laths could be packed out by thick pieces of hide to stop the frames from distorting (Figure 14.7). The frame was then covered tightly with sealskin from which all the hair had been plucked. A small manhole was left in the deck. This was fitted with a wooden hoop coaming through which the skin was tightly stretched and tacked over with bone or ivory pins. As the skin shrank, it drew the coaming even tighter to the deck.

When finished the kayak had to be light enough to be carried by the paddler either over his shoulder with his arm inside the manhole or, in the case of some Greenland kayaks, on his head with the cockpit coaming resting against his forehead. A walk from one bay to the next might save many miles of paddling, or make the difference between launching on a lee or weather shore.

In winter the man wore a hairless sealskin jacket with a hood. This was the anorak, or "full smock." The bottom hem of this could be pulled over the cockpit coaming and lashed tightly round the hoop with a long piece of thong. Two strips of narrow bone beading 6 or 7 inches long and about ¼ inch wide were fixed by pins to the top edge of the coaming at the back. The two other pieces were fixed parallel to these but lower down (Figure 14.7). This arrangement formed a locating channel for the thong when it was wrapped around. Although the anorak was

secured in this way only at the rear of the cockpit, it is doubtful whether the hunter would be able to wrench the jacket free in an emergency, so that a roll or an assisted rescue would be his only means of salvation.

In southern Alaska and the Aleutian Islands, the hunter would wear a longer garment made from horizontal strips of seal gut, called the *kamleika* (originally this Russian word meant "fur coat"). The half-frock, another garment worn by the hunter, was more like our spray cover. It was a short skirt of sealskin tied around the cockpit rim to keep out the water, and it could also be tied under the armpits if necessary.

Native Kayaks

North Greenland/Hudson Bay Kayak

Kayaks from the far north of Greenland and certain parts of Hudson Bay have larger cockpits,

Figure 14.1 *North Greenland/Hudson Bay kayak. This kayak is rather ugly when compared with other Greenland kayaks. The wide deck is flat except for the sheer up to the large round cockpit. Note the high wooden coaming. The man appears to sit quite loosely and slumped back. The paddle, drawn to scale, is long by Eskimo standards. In the photo that inspired this drawing, what appears to be a large full dustbin is stood on the deck just forward of the cockpit; this may give some indication of the stability of this particular kayak.*

which are left unsealed (Figure 14.1). Seal gut was 3 inches in diameter, and when opened out it provided a strip 6 inches wide. Walrus gut was even wider. (Source: R. Frank, *Frozen Frontier: The Story of the Arctic*, George G. Harrap, 1964)

Hunting the walrus can be very dangerous, and if the prey turns and comes into the attack, the hunter can leave his kayak much more quickly if he is not fastened by thongs to the cockpit coaming. If the walrus slashes huge rents in the skin of his own boat, he can always seek safety on the deck of a companion's boat, thus saving himself from the wrath of the walrus, the bitter cold of the water, or death by drowning. It is almost unheard of for an Eskimo to swim. Where would they practice?

Kayaks vary in pattern and shape, each having its own distinctive seagoing qualities and style. Each kayak is also tailored to the body measurements of the individual paddler and is worn like a garment rather than just "sat in" like a rowing boat. To get into the boat the man first sits on the back deck, puts both feet up inside the kayak, and wriggles until he is firmly in the manhole. His back is jammed against one of the crossbeams protruding into the cockpit space. This means that any strain is taken on the wooden strut rather than by the wooden hoop. The hunter uses one of the curved hull frames as a footrest, and the kayak becomes rather like an extension of the man's body, responding to his every move.

Although methods of measuring may differ slightly, the system is basically the same. For instance, the King Islander makes his kayak gunwales two and a half arm spans long. The stem piece, which has a notch at the top to locate the gunwales, is the distance from the elbow to the fingertips (a cubit). The two middle thwarts are as long as the outstretched arm, including the fingers. This makes the width about 25 inches, but the flared sides bring the waterline beam down to about 18 inches.

The King Islander had to face not only the very stormy waters of the Bering Sea but also a launching problem. His walrus-gut parka (derived from the Russian word for "shirt," the Eskimo word is *cemain-ee-tik*) was secured tightly around the cockpit coaming and he and his boat were then picked up by four men and thrown into the sea. His kayak therefore had to be very strong, so just any wood was not good enough. The gunwales had to be straight-grained and matched. For the ten thwarts, natural curved pieces of wood were used, and the twenty-five- to thirty-rib frames were split from birch logs and bent by steaming. The willow cockpit hoop was an integral part of the framework. Compare this robust construction (Figure 14.12) with that of the Nunamiut kayak (Figure 14.2).

The Nunamiuts, members of an inland tribe, lived by hunting caribou in a kayak about 20 feet long. The gunwales were two spruce strips bound together at the ends by rawhide thongs. The U-shaped ribs were green willow shoots the thickness of a man's thumb, bent and then mortised into the gunwales to form the hull. The five or seven longitudinal laths were strips of birch or spruce, which did not extend completely to the stern or stem, where slender deck beams of willows were fixed, much less curved than the other beams. Even though this kayak was nowhere near as robust as its coastal cousin, it had violent usage.

The migrating herds of caribou were frightened into making river crossings at places chosen previously by the Eskimos. The women would creep up and frighten the herd towards the river.

Figure 14.2 *The death of a caribou—note the* inukshuks *in the background. Killing caribou could be a very dangerous occupation. Note how the hunter keeps hold of his paddle rather than push it under the deck thongs, as he would if he were harpooning at sea.*

Piles of stones called *inukshuks*, which at a distance looked like groups of people, were used to divert the terrified animals to the chosen spot. Once in the water the herd was at the mercy of the kayak men who paddled amongst them (Figure 14.2), stabbing them with a spear high in the rib cage to one side of the backbone, piercing the heart or lungs. The thrust and withdrawal had to be quick, or the animal would thrash about and the man could be overturned and pitched in the icy water among the surging animals.

Some tribes such as the Aivilingmiuts used a heavy kayak for walrus and seal hunting and a lighter one for lake work and caribou hunting. But the Caribou Eskimos used a kayak similar to the one illustrated in Figure 14.6 for both purposes. If they were going to hunt sea mammals, the kayak frame was covered with sealskin, whereas if caribou were to be the victims, the same frame was covered with caribou skin. The Itiumiut Eskimos also had different kayaks for inland and sea work, and it is obvious that the Eskimos came to the same conclusion as that arrived at by so many modern paddlers—that there is no such thing as a general-purpose boat for both river and sea.

A Greenland kayak equipped for hunting seals had a framework platform or tray called the "kayak stand" on the foredeck to carry a long coiled line (Figures 14.3, 14.8). One end of the

Figure 14.3 *Seal-hunting Eskimo*

line was secured to the detachable head of the hunter's harpoon, and the other end led under his arm to the back deck and was fixed to a large sealskin float which itself was attached to the rear deck in a quick-release manner. Lying on the foredeck next to the harpoon might be a lance, while underneath the kayak stand, safe in its bag, would be a rifle.

Hidden behind a white camouflage shield mounted on the foredeck, the hunter would look for the seals. As soon as he saw his prey. the hunter would paddle into range and, quickly shipping his paddle, withdraw the gun and fire. Then, gun away, he would paddle swiftly within harpoon range. The paddle would be pushed under the deck thong again and the harpoon hurled accurately and forcibly with the assistance of the

throwing stick. During the time the kayak was running free with no paddle, it might have been held on course by means of a detachable skeg. As soon as the prey was harpooned, the flotation bag was released from the rear deck. Thus if the prey was killed immediately, it would not sink, or if it was only wounded and dived, it would then tire with the drag of the inflated bag.

Baffinland Kayak

This kayak from Baffinland (Figure 14.4) looks rather ungainly with its huge thick bow and flat squat stern. The cockpit slopes down towards the flat back deck and is horseshoe shaped. Apart from the forefoot at the bow, the boat is virtually flat-bottomed. In spite of its rather unwieldy appearance, however, this kayak was reputedly

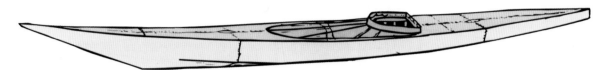

Figure 14.4 *North Baffinland kayak (length: 19 feet 3 inches; width: 24 inches). The widest part is just rear of the cockpit (20 by 18 inches).*

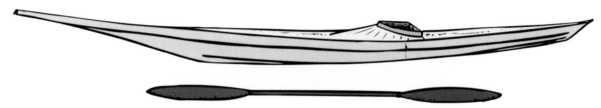

Figure 14.5 *Labrador kayak (northern). Length: 24 to 26 feet; width: 23 inches*

easy to turn, presumably sliding around over the water on its flat bottom. However, its seaworthiness in extreme conditions must be suspect because of this same flat bottom (see the section on hull shapes in Chapter 1).

The Labrador kayak is very similar to the Baffinland kayak (Figure 14.5). Like the Baffinland kayak, this also has a flat bottom and is very stable. It is strongly built, heavy, and very seaworthy. The cockpit is horseshoe shaped, flat along the back. The superb "clipper bow" is 5 feet long. To assist in the turning of this very long kayak, the *pautic,* or paddle, is 10 feet long.

Caribou Kayak

This kayak (Figure 14.6) came from the northwestern shores of Hudson Bay. Although the

caribou were hunted mainly at river crossings, they were also driven into small open-water lakes and were forced to cross narrow sea fjords.

When viewed in plan and elevation, the Caribou kayak could be compared quite closely with a modern competition slalom kayak, as it has a considerable rocker. The only real differences are the slender willowy bow and stern of the Caribou kayak and its obviously seaworthy cockpit. A group of kayak hunters paddling in amongst a herd of frightened swimming caribou needed a kayak that would turn very quickly and had a strong covering and a bow that could safely hook into the antlers of an escaping animal and divert it long enough for a companion to close in for the coup de grace.

Figure 14.6 *Caribou kayak (west Hudson Bay). Length: 18 feet 6 inches; width: 21 inches; cockpit: 18 inches diameter*

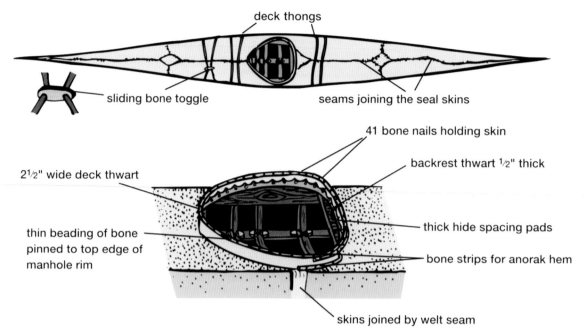

deck thongs

sliding bone toggle

seams joining the seal skins

41 bone nails holding skin

backrest thwart ½" thick

2½" wide deck thwart

thin beading of bone
pinned to top edge of
manhole rim

thick hide spacing pads

bone strips for anorak hem

skins joined by welt seam

Figure 14.7 *Whitby kayak. Plan view and detail of cockpit*

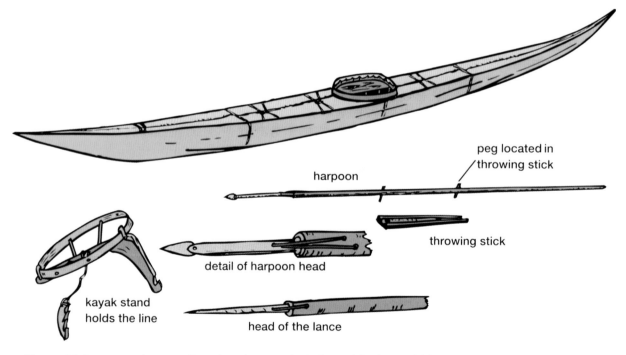

peg located in
throwing stick

harpoon

throwing stick

detail of harpoon head

kayak stand
holds the line

head of the lance

Figure 14.8 *Newcastle-upon-Tyne kayak. Length: 17 feet 10 inches; width: 16 inches*

Greenland Kayaks

Kayaks from this huge, sprawling landmass, specifically the designs from the west coast of Greenland, have influenced modern sporting sea kayaks more than any other type of Eskimo kayak. It was difficult to know which particular types would best illustrate the qualities of the West Greenland kayak. After a great deal of examining, measuring, and sketching, I chose three that best illustrate not only the superb seagoing qualities, but also the subtle local differences in design. I refer to all three kayaks by the names of the museums where they are to be found: South Shields, Whitby, and Newcastle (Figures 14.7–14.10).

It will be seen that the kayaks from South Shields and Whitby have extremely high sterns. There were very good reasons for this. When the hunter approached his quarry from downwind, the high stern would act as a kind of rudder. This meant that the kayak would continue to travel

forward, held straight and true, while the hunter, shipping his paddle, could fire his rifle or throw a harpoon. The bow and stern of the Newcastle kayak are less exaggerated and much lower than the other two, but the hull aft of the cockpit is very narrow, rising gently to a low, slim stern.

All three kayaks are rather straight-sided and almost flat-bottomed. It seems incredible that an adult male even of Eskimo proportions could get into any of the cockpits, since the width of all the hulls is only 16 inches at its widest part and the internal measurements at the cockpit can be as small as 15 inches. Legroom is no less of a problem. The South Shields kayak has only 6 inches from the deck thwart in front of the cockpit to the bent frame at the bottom of the hull, into which a man must squeeze his feet, legs, and thighs. It is hardly surprising that modern manufacturers when trying to imitate Eskimo designs have had to make considerable modifications to accommodate the European man.

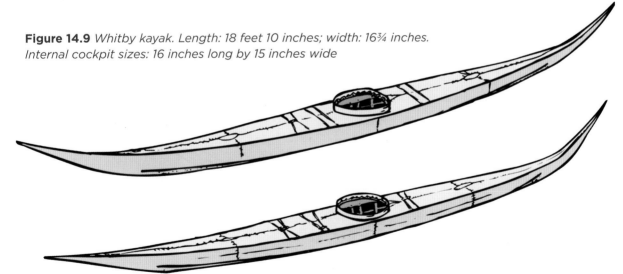

Figure 14.9 *Whitby kayak. Length: 18 feet 10 inches; width: 16¾ inches. Internal cockpit sizes: 16 inches long by 15 inches wide*

Figure 14.10 *South Shields kayak. Length: 17 feet 6 inches; width: 16 inches; round cockpit size: 16 inches*

Figure 14.11 *East Greenland kayak. Length: 19 feet 6 inches; width: 20 inches*

East Greenland Kayak

This differs in design from the other Greenland kayaks illustrated (Figure 14.11). Its length—usually 18 feet but up to 20 feet—and its long, low clipper bow and long, low stern make it a very fast hunting machine, with little for a beam wind to catch. As with all Greenland kayaks, the primary function was to carry a man while he hunted seal in sheltered waters amongst ice flows or fjords.

In design it was not really meant for the use to which sporting paddlers now put it. Paddling into a steep head sea in any kind of wind would be a wet, chilling, and dangerous business. Because its lines embody speed and slender grace, the design has been used as a basis for some modern kayaks of a similar type. The really rough-water kayaks, however, are those from the Aleutian and Alaskan areas.

Early King Island Kayak and Kotzebue Sound Kayak

Both these kayaks are outlandish, perhaps even quaint in appearance, but no less seaworthy because of it. The bow of the early-type King Island kayak (Figure 14.12) would rise beautifully to short steep seas, while the steeply pitched deck would quickly shed heavy water breaking over it. Like the more modern King Island kayak, it was paddled with a single-bladed paddle, except when the double-bladed paddle was used for speed during hunting.

It is interesting to view the similarities of the Mackenzie Delta kayak (Figure 14.13) and the King Island kayak even though there is considerable distance between the two locations.

The Kotzebue Sound kayak (Figure 14.14), with its low freeboard and flat deck, would be constantly awash in anything but a reasonably

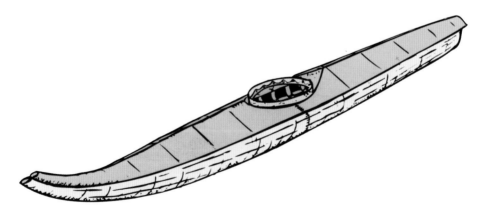

Figure 14.12 *Old design from King Island. Length: 15 feet 4 inches; width: 25½ inches*

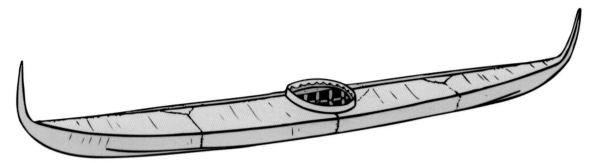

Figure 14.13 *Mackenzie Delta kayak. Length: 19 feet 6 inches; width: 20 inches*

Figure 14.14 *Kotzebue Sound kayak. Length: 17 to 18 feet; width: 18 inches*

calm sea, although I cannot imagine any water gaining access to the kayak via the manhole. With this tremendous amount of buoyancy amidships coupled with the flat deck, its rolling qualities can only be guessed at. Fast hunting-paddling was done with a double blade.

Kayaks of the Aleutian Islands

Any account of Eskimo kayaks would be incomplete without a mention of the *baidarkas* (Russian for "kayaks") of the Aleutian Islands, which have some of the most dangerous waters in the world (Figures 14.15, 14.16).

To hunt the whale and the sea otter, the Aleuts used a narrow two-manhole *baidarka* 21 feet long by 23 inches wide. It was very shallow, and in cross-section the bottom was round and therefore very difficult to keep upright.

The Koryaks are the indigenous people who live on far east coastline of Russia. The Koryak kayak (Figure 14.17) was used on the calmer waters along the coast.

Figure 14.15 *Aleutian Islands kayak. Length: 17 feet 9 inches; width: 20 inches*

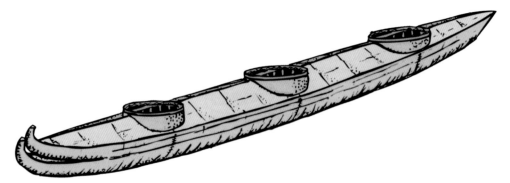

Figure 14.16 *Three-manhole* baidarka, *southern Alaska and Aleutian Islands. Length: 25 feet; width: 30 inches. The Eskimos used a two-manhole* baidarka *21 feet long by 23 inches wide. The three holes were a Russian idea; the middle one was used for transporting a passenger or carrying supplies.*

When hunting the sea otter the Eskimos formed themselves into groups, from a few pairs to perhaps a hundred on the water at one time. The front man in the kayak used a spear, while the man in the rear cockpit maneuvered the kayak with a long double-bladed paddle. The flotilla would move quietly along in a line until

Figure 14.17 *Koryak kayak. Length: 9 feet. The Koryaks were a gentle people. There was no comparison between them and the daring sea kayakers of the Aleutian Islands. However, this kayak was used on the sea but only on calm water. The small wooden hand paddles are fastened to the cockpit coaming by seal thongs. This kayak would probably maneuver rather like a modern swimming pool kayak. Note the thwart that acts as a back support.*

someone saw an otter on the surface. He would raise a paddle in the air to warn the others and then paddle to the sea otter's last position on the surface of the water before its dive, where the rest of the group would form a large circle around him (source: Harold McCracken, *Hunters of the Stormy Sea*, Oldbourne, 1957). As soon as the sea otter resurfaced, the nearest hunter paddled towards it, giving the animal no time to fill its lungs. This happened repeatedly until the duration of the dives got shorter and shorter. The hunters would then close in and the animal could be speared.

If the wind was violent and the air filled with rain and spray, a tired sleepy animal might lie on the top of the kelp beds, its head hidden under the floating seaweed. In such a case the hunters could stealthily approach close enough to strike out and kill the unsuspecting creature with a wooden club.

Perhaps the greatest conquest of all for the kayak hunter was the killing of a whale. Once these huge mammals were sighted, only the bravest and most experienced hunters with the strongest and heaviest and sharpest of harpoons would dare take to the water. Paddling out amongst the feeding school, the hunters would select the small calves for their attention. To force the harpoon—tipped with aconite poison—deep enough into a whale for a kill, the men would have to position themselves about 10 to 15 feet away, and then throw the harpoon with the full force of the throwing stick, aiming for a point just below the huge dorsal fin (source: ibid.). On feeling the pain, the whale would explode into thrashing violence, its flukes waving high above the hunters before crashing down and churning up the water (Figure 14.18). It would not be unknown for the whale-hunting Eskimos to be killed by "the hand of God," the name given in the Azores to these giant tails that would crash down onto the whaling *canoas* (source: Trevor Housby, *The Hand of God: Whaling in the Azores,* Abelard-Schuman, 1971). With any luck, however, the *baidarka* would maneuver clear of the injured whale and also of any enraged bull or cow swimming near.

The Aleuts might have been hunting the whale to this day had not greedy, vicious men

Figure 14.18 *Whale hunting from a* baidarka

thousands of miles away taken a hand in their destiny and altered their way of life forever. In 1725 Vitus Bering, a Dane, led a Russian expedition of geographic exploration to Siberia and the north Pacific coast. Survivors from this ill-fated venture took sea otter pelts back to Russia, which excited the Russians so much that they sent other expeditions to obtain more furs. Many of the men who elected to go could see fortunes for themselves on the horizon. They were the human dregs of Siberia, pirates with no moral code or thought for human life. Their code of conduct was ruled by the knowledge that punishment for crimes was nonexistent: "God is high above, and the Czar is far away" (source: McCracken, *Hunters*). These were the *promyshleniki,* the professional hunters. By murder and intimidation, the native Eskimos, the Aleuts, were taken hostage, enslaved, and forced to hunt the sea otter until it almost vanished from the area.

The Russians then had to turn their attentions farther afield, as far south as the coast of California. While the *promyshleniki* traveled in the comparative comfort of large boats called *shitikas,* the Aleuts were forced to paddle their *baidarkas* over distances that can only be described as appalling. (Because of the shortage of materials and tools, the Russians built their boats from roughly shaped timbers fastened together by hide thongs in the absence of nuts, bolts, and nails. Thus sewn together, *shi-it,* Russian for "to sew," became *shitika.* Some of the early models literally fell to pieces only a few miles from land, drowning the crew.)

In the summer of 1783, a veritable armada of large boats with scores of accompanying Aleut hunters set off from Unalaska for Prince William Sound, a distance of over 1,000 miles across storm-swept open sea. Fear of the *knout* (whip)

and the knowledge that their wives and daughters were on board the *shitikas* kept the Aleuts paddling night and day at about 10 miles per hour, unable to stop, sleeping in the kayaks by turns, unable even to relieve themselves properly. Journeys such as these, with fear of stragglers or the sick being shot (source: ibid.), must have been a nightmare and reflect no credit on the colonizing Russians of the eighteenth century. It is fortunate that the *baidarka* with its bifid stem was probably the finest sea kayak in an area of fine kayaks and that the Aleuts were brilliant sea kayakers.

The three-manhole *baidarka* (Figure 14.16) invented by the Russians to carry a passenger or goods was much larger than the two-hole hunter's boat. The single-manhole boat could also be used for seal hunting, while the clumsy family *baidarkas* could carry dogs, children, furs, wife, meat, nets, and all the other luxuries of life. What faith in their husband's kayaking ability these women must have had in order to huddle happily inside the claustrophobic hull. The order of packing and distribution of the cargo (dogs with meat, wife, or children?) can only be wondered at.

It is sad to think that many of the kayak and hunting skills described in this chapter are dying out or are already a thing of the past. The whaling carried on by the Aleuts died forever during the hundred-year Russian tyranny. The King Islanders no longer live on their rocky island but are now housed on the mainland and display their kayak skills mainly to impress the tourists. The Danish government is doing good work in encouraging the Greenland Eskimos to maintain and preserve their culture and way of life, but even many of their kayaks are now built with canvas and joined with nails. Fortunately, nails don't rust in the cold, dry atmosphere.

The Eskimo is no longer dependent on his own skills for survival, and the kayak, the hunter's boat, sadly may soon be gone forever. However, it is to be hoped that designers will preserve the tradition of the Eskimo kayak even if in fiberglass, and that people will be encouraged to learn to handle what must surely be the most demanding yet the most rewarding boat in the world.

Eskimo Paddles

At one time my idea of a typical Eskimo paddle was like the Newcastle paddle in Figure 14.19, which is from West Greenland. These paddles displayed a high degree of workmanship, with bone beading to stop the sides of the blade chafing

and bone ends made from the shoulder plate of a dog. Although some of the paddle looms (shafts) from this area were rectangular in cross-section, the majority I have seen have been oval, giving a firm, comfortable, and positive hand grip. However, Eskimo paddle designs are almost as numerous as the kayak designs themselves.

Quite a number of paddles have some kind of anti-capillary groove or ring. Water constantly running down the loom onto the hands could be more than uncomfortable in freezing temperatures with a wind blowing, even if mittens were sometimes worn. The function of these anti-capillary devices is a little different from that of the onetime popular drip rings, which were used in the older European type of kayak before the adoption of spray covers. The idea behind these

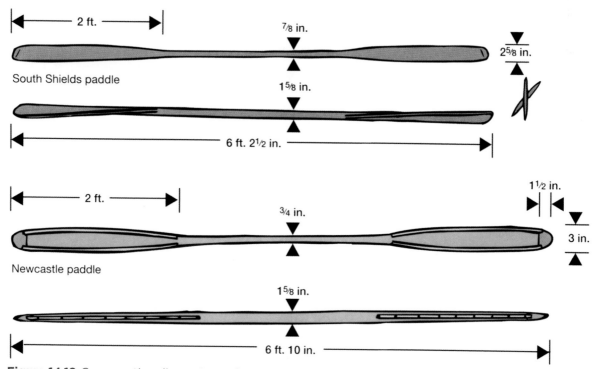

Figure 14.19 *Comparative dimensions of West Greenland paddles (not to scale)*

rings was to stop water running down the loom, down the arm, and then dripping uncomfortably off the elbow, thus entering the large cockpit and then onto the knees and into the boat.

In Figure 14.20 the North Labrador paddle has shaped pieces to shed the water at the extremities of the loom. It was probably a very satisfactory arrangement. The Aulatseevik paddle seems to be the ultimate in Eskimo paddle comfort. In a photograph I have seen of this, all the wide sections appeared to be bone sheathing an oval wooden interior. The hands were positioned in the space between the wide center piece and the first bobbin; next came another drip ring to stop any stray drops of water which may have

escaped the efficient-looking anti-capillary curve at the beginning of the blade. This Rolls-Royce of paddles was photographed lying across the cockpit of an Eskimo kayak, the interior of which was lined with what appeared to be white polar bear fur. The owner of this outfit was obviously a man who valued his creature comforts—I know the feeling well.

The most distinctive feature of the Labrador paddle is its length (Photos 14.5, 14.6). It is hardly surprising, of course, that a boat of up to 26 feet should need a large paddle 10 feet long. An even longer paddle was used by the Nunamiut tribe, whose kayak has already been described. In front of the cockpit, a forked piece of willow

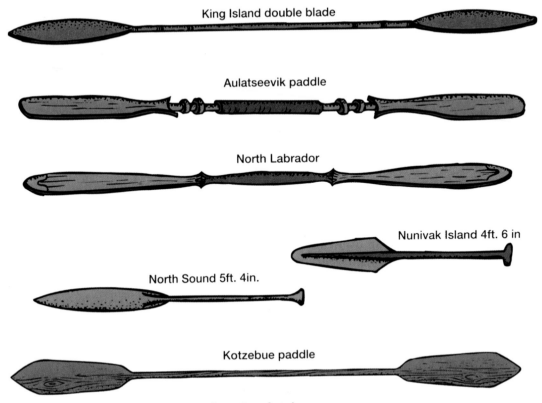

Figure 14.20 *Eskimo paddles showing diversity of styles*

Photo 14.2 *"Eskimos in Kayaks—Mackenzie Delta." In my eyes this is the most graceful of all the skin boats. Although this kayak formed the inspiration for one of my own early designs, I have never been able to discover why the bow and stern were so fine and yet turned up so acutely.* PHOTOGRAPH BY ERNEST BROWN, IN The Search for the Western Sea BY LAWRENCE J. BURPEE, ALSTON RIVERS LTD., 1908

or alder tree was used as a pivot for the almost 20-foot-long paddle, which was hewn from spruce log (source: Nicholas J. Gubsen, *The Nunamiut Eskimos: Hunters of the Caribou*, Yale University Press, 1965). Spare paddles were sometimes carried by the hunters, especially those who used single- and double-bladed paddles, such as the Eskimos of Alaska and some of the offshore islands, although I have never heard of Greenland Eskimos carrying spare paddles.

When the Eskimo gripped a double-bladed paddle, his hands were positioned about four hand-widths apart. This is quite close compared with modern practice, but anyone who tries to paddle in freezing conditions and wants to keep his hands dry without drip rings will find the Eskimo hand position practical. How the Koryaks (Figure 14.17) managed with their little hand paddles is not known to me. I've often wondered if through the years they developed extra-long arms.

The Eskimo never used a feathered blade. Various theories have been put forward as to why this should be. Some say the blade is so narrow that the retardation caused by a headwind is hardly noticeable. The reason may, however, be much simpler: He may never have thought of it.

While investigating the various kayaks, I was surprised to see, lying in the cockpit of the South Shields kayak in storage at the local museum, a

Photo 14.3 *Two people do not always need two cockpits—and is that a dog on the rear deck? In this picture by an unknown photographer, a man and woman share a Nunivak Island kayak. Boats from this area were deep and buoyant. The remainder of the paddler's family might possibly be carried inside the hull. Care had to be taken that small children were not put at the same end as the dogs. In the event of a capsize, it was possible for a single occupant to withdraw inside the body of the kayak.*
SMITHSONIAN INSTITUTE PHOTO 34, 358-B

paddle that was feathered at 45 degrees for a left-handed paddler (Figure 14.19). This may sound strange, considering the blades are of course flat, but it is extremely difficult to manipulate this paddle while trying to paddle right-handed. The loom is oval and has no twist along its entire length. Only the paddle blades themselves twist gently along their length, finally setting themselves at 45 degrees to each other at the end.

Photo 14.4 *The nonstop distance you can paddle in a single kayak is limited to the number of hours you can stay awake. This is not the case with a double kayak, in which it is possible to sleep. This model of an Aleutian two-manhole* baidarka *was made for me by Sergie Sovoroff of Nikolski. The rudder was a Russian innovation.* DEREK HUTCHINSON

Photo 14.5 *"Labrador Eskimo and Kayak." Note the length of the paddle and the "drip rings." These huge kayaks were up to 24 feet long and had a beam of 23 inches. They were never rolled by their occupants, and in the event of a capsize, the paddler would need assistance from a companion in order to get back into his boat.* FROM *AMONG THE ESKIMOS OF LABRADOR* BY S. K. HUTTON, MB, CHB VICT., SEELEY, SERVICE & CO. LTD., 1912

Photo 14.6 *"Labrador Eskimos Ready for the Seal Hunt"* FROM *AMONG THE ESKIMOS OF LABRADOR* BY S. K. HUTTON, MB, CHB VICT, SEELEY, SERVICE & CO. LTD., 1912 (PHOTOGRAPHY: MORAVIAN MISSIONS)

Photo 14.7 *Aloysius Pikongonna at Nome, with the equipment used at King Island for hunting walrus or seals* BOB AND IRA SPRING

Photo 14.8 *Eskimo spearing a "sea unicorn" (narwhal), circa 1896. Note the feathered paddle.*

Photo 14.9 *Harpooning and retrieving a walrus could be fatal to the paddler.*

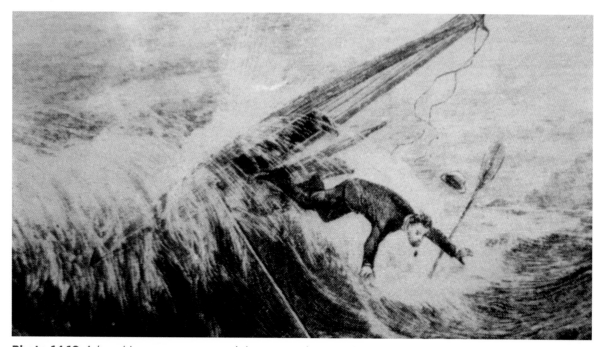

Photo 14.10 *A breaking wave can wreak havoc on the untrained paddler.*

Photo 14.11 *Modern custom-built replica of original one-hole* baidarka *taken from Atka on the Aleutian Islands. For those romantics who hanker after the "old" days, there are now a growing number of craftsmen who will build for you an original design in the traditional manner. In this beautiful model by R. Bruce Lemon of Idaho, the frames are lashed together with waxed polyester instead of sinew. The skin is made from dead 14- or 26-ounce nylon instead of the skin of a dead seal. This cover is then sewn together with braided nylon.* R. BRUCE LEMON

Photo 14.12 *This hunter from Nunivak Island is using a throwing stick and wearing the familiar wooden wedge-shaped hat. When the need arises, he can bend his head forward and effectively shield his face from windblown spray. In the event of a capsize, he could either withdraw into the cockpit, breathe the air inside, and wait for a companion to twist him upright or attempt to roll upright. Similar to the Toksook paddle mentioned earlier, the paddle is willow leaf in shape. The spine down the face of the blades is the key to its efficiency.* EDWARD S. CURTIS, COURTESY OF THE UNIVERSITY OF WASHINGTON LIBRARIES

Figure 14.21 *"Paddler with Spirit Mask"* ORIGINAL ARTWORK BY DEREK HUTCHINSON

CONCLUSION

This is the conclusion Derek wrote for the fifth edition of this book:

The whole coast of Britain, with its many islands, is suitable for sea kayaking expeditions that can open the door to adventure, thrills, and discovery and to many strange and beautiful experiences.

It would take another book to recount the tales I have to tell. There is room here only to make passing reference to a few incidents—the pleasure of observing in all seasons the gray seals of the Farne Islands; the beautiful and eerie night trip around the Fames when the phosphorescent plankton illuminated our wake with myriads of stars, and hundreds of birds flapped around our heads without uttering a single cry; the extreme tension during the paddle through fog across the

Photo C.1 *A kayak is the ideal vehicle for carrying camping equipment. This campsite is on Heather Island, Alaska. Left to right: Chris Jowsey, Derek Hutchinson, and Tom Caskey. The Columbian Glacier is in the background.* ALISTAIR WILSON

Firth of Forth for the Isle of May and the tremendous feeling of elation when we realized our compass work had been accurate; the hilarity of finding that all discussion about pitching our tent to face the sunrise, the sunset, or the prevailing wind had been an ironic waste of time, when we lay under the charred, flapping remnants after someone had set fire to it while making the coffee; the incredible satisfaction of overcoming everything the sea could throw at us, the freezing cold, the pounding waves breaking on reefs, the huge Atlantic swell, the lashing fury of a Force 8 gale, and, to add to the confusion, a 7-knot tidal stream cutting across our path as we slogged our way across the Sound of Harris to the coast of North Uist.

Since the earlier editions of this book were written, my kayaking has taken me to other countries and coastlines. I have looked into the eyes of a killer whale and felt the mist of its breath on my face. I have watched an iceberg leave the face of a glacier in silence and fall 300 feet to the sea and seen the approaching wave, only to hear the roar of the calving ice seconds later (Photo C.1). I have enjoyed the antics of sea otters and manatees and observed turtles and alligators at very close quarters. And all from the seat of my kayak.

To those of you who are just starting to enjoy paddling on the sea, I say: Take your kayak and first discover the world on your own doorstep. Remember that although the backdrop may be familiar, the sea itself is always changing and will never be the same.

To others I can now say, twenty years later, and with even more conviction, that kayaking on the sea is not just for the young; it is for the young in heart and the adventurous in spirit who want to fly with the wild swans.

If Derek was still with us, I believe he would add the following to this conclusion. I was with him after he taught his very last class, and I asked him what he was feeling. Little did he know that cancer was already eating away at his body. This was his reply:

I had an incredible life as a result of sea kayaking. I felt I gave it my all. As I hang up my PFD for the last time, I have a combination of feelings. Sadness in knowing I will never again be sitting in my kayak and feeling the motion of the sea. Satisfaction for having made a difference in the lives of so many other paddlers. Joy for the many adventures. Gratitude for the wonderful people I met along the way. I am sure I will be longing to once again venture onto the sea when I take my morning walks on the banks of the North Sea. I hope others will take to the sea in their kayaks to experience all the sport has to offer.

In September of 2010 Derek and I went for a paddle on the North Sea (Photo C.2) not knowing it would be his last time on those waters, which were his favorite. As I reflect on Derek's contribution to the world of sea kayaking and my

Photo C.2 *I hope to see you on the water!*
WAYNE HORODOWICH

relationship with him, I feel grateful for all he has given the sport, the lessons he shared, and most of all the desire for adventure he instilled in generations of paddlers all around the world because he wrote that first book.

I am sure Derek is looking down from above saying, "My sea kayaking life has concluded, but I hope it is just the beginning for all those who choose to take a chance and try their hand at sea kayaking."

CONVERSION TABLE

Note: All units of measurements in the text are imperial. The following may be useful for conversion into metric.

10 millimetres	=	1 centimetre	=	0.395 inch (in.)
10 centimetres	=	1 decimetre	=	3.94 inches (in.)
10 decimetres	=	1 metre	=	1.094 yards (yd./yds.)
10 metres	=	1 decametre	=	10.94 yards (yd./yds.)
10 decametres	=	1 hectometre	=	109.36 yards (yd./yds.)
10 hectometres	=	1 kilometre	=	0.621 miles

A kilometre is approximately five-eighths of a mile

1 inch (in.)	=	2.54 centimetres		
1 foot (ft.)	=	30.48 centimetres		
1 yard (yd./yds.)	=	3 feet (ft.)	=	0.914 metre

1 square centimetre	=	0.155 square inch (sq. in.)
1 square kilometre	=	0.39 square mile

1 kilogram	=	2.205 pounds (lb.)

BIBLIOGRAPHY

Abbot, R., *The Science of Surfing*, John Jones Cardiff Ltd., 1972.

American Red Cross, *Canoeing*, 1956.

Automobile Association, *Book of the Seaside*, Drive Publications, 1972.

Barret, John, and Yonge, C. M., *Collins Pocket Guide to the Sea-Shore*, Collins, 1970.

Birket-Smith, Kaj, *The Eskimos*, Methuen, 1959.

Bowen, David, *Britain's Weather, Its Workings, Lore and Forecasting*, David and Charles, 1969.

British Canoe Union, *Canoeing in Britain*, magazine back copies since 1963.

———, *Choosing a Canoe and Its Equipment*.

———, *Coaching Handbook*.

———, *The Eskimo Roll*.

Broze, Matt, and Gronseth, George (authors), and Cunningham, Christopher (editor), *Sea Kayaker's Deep Trouble: True Stories and Their Lessons from* Sea Kayaker *Magazine*, International Marine/Ragged Mountain Press, 1997.

Byde, Alan, *Beginner's Guide to Canoeing*, Pelham Books, 1973.

———, *Living Canoeing*, A & C Black, 1969.

Clark, Mike, *Canoeing*, Canoeing Press, magazine back copies since 1965.

Cock, Oliver J., *A Short History of Canoeing in Britain*, BCU, 1974.

———, *You and Your Canoe*, Ernest Benn, 1956.

Cunningham, Christopher (editor), *Sea Kayaker's More Deep Trouble: More True Stories and Their Lessons from* Sea Kayaker *Magazine*, International Marine/Ragged Mountain Press, 2013.

Dempsy, Michael, *The Skies and the Seas*, Ginn, 1966.

Gubsen, Nicholas J., *The Nunamiut Eskimo: Hunters of the Caribou*, Yale University Press, 1965.

Harrington, Richard, *Face of the Arctic*, Hodder and Stoughton, 1954.

Housby, Trevor, *The Hand of God: Whaling in the Azores*, Abelard-Schuman, 1971.

Houston, James, *The White Dawn*, Heinemann, 1971.

Ingstad, Helge, *Land Under the Pole Star*, Jonathan Cape, 1966.

Keatinge, W. R., *Survival in Cold Water*, Blackwell Scientific Publishers, 1969.

McCracken, Harold, *Hunters of the Stormy Sea*, Oldbourne, 1957.

McNaught, Noel, *The Canoeing Manual*, Nicholas Kaye, 1961.

Mawley, Robert and Seon, *Beaches: Their Life, Legends and Lore*, Chiltern, 1968.

Mowat, Farley, *The Desperate People*, Michael Joseph, 1960.

———, *People of the Deer*, Michael Joseph, 1954.

Murray, W. H., *Islands of Western Scotland*, Methuen, 1973.

National Geographic Society, *The National Geographic Magazine*, June 1956, vol. 109, no. 6.

Newing, F. E., and Bowood, Robert, *The Weather* (A Ladybird Book), Wills and Hepworth, 1962.

Pemberton, John Lee, *Sea and Air Mammals* (A Ladybird Book), Wills and Hepworth, 1972.

Pilsbury, R. K., *Clouds and Weather*, Batsford, 1969.

Proctor, Ian, *Sailing Wind and Current*, Adlard Coles, 1964.

Pryde, Duncan, *Nunaga: Ten Years of Eskimo Life*, MacGibbon & Kee, 1972.

Reed's Nautical Almanac, Thomas Reed.

Robertson, Dougal, *Survive the Savage Sea*, Elek Books, 1973.

Rodahl, Koare, *Between Two Worlds*, Heinemann, 1965.

Ross, Frank Xavier, *Frozen Frontier: The Story of the Arctic*, George G. Harrap, 1964.

Ross, Dr. Helen, *Behaviour in Strange Environments*, Allen and Unwin, 1974.

Sawyer, J. S., *The Ways of the Weather*, A & C Black, 1957.

Searl, F. H. L., *The Book of Sailing*, Arthur Barker Ltd., 1964.

Shenstone, D. A., and Beals, C. S. (eds.), *Science, History and Hudson Bay*, Department of Energy, Mines & Resources, Ottawa, 1968.

Skilling, Brian, and Sutcliffe, David, *Canoeing Complete*, Nicholas Kaye, 1966.

Spring, Norma, *Alaska: The Complete Travel Book*, Macmillan, 1970.

Staib, Bjorn, *Across Greenland in Nansen's Track*, Allen and Unwin, 1963.

Sutherland, Charles, *Modern Canoeing*, Faber and Faber, 1964.

Tegner, Henry, *The Long Bay of Druridge*, Frank Graham, 1968.

United States National Museum Bulletin No. 230, *The Bark Canoes and Skin Boats of North America*, Adney and Chapelle, 1964.

Watts, Alan, *Wind and Sailing Boats*, Adlard Coles, 1965.

Whitney, Peter Dwight, *White Water Sport*, Ronald Press Co., 1960.

Zim, Herbert S., *Waves*, World Work, 1968.

INDEX

ABOUT THE AUTHORS

Derek C. Hutchinson

Derek Charles Hutchinson was born at 10 in the morning on June 30, 1933. When he was eighteen months old, his mother died and his father disappeared. He was adopted and raised by his maternal grandmother.

Derek grew up during the air raids of World War II in the playgrounds provided by Adolf Hitler. The bombed-out buildings were his personal amusement parks and the unsafe, precariously suspended floors his trampolines. He felt he was on a treasure hunt, every day down by the sea, sifting through debris that was washed up on the shore.

As a boy, he had a classical education at a private school in northern England. Derek told me, "I know it must have been a good school, because we were flogged with unfailing regularity." After finishing his first round of schoolwork, he became an indentured apprentice in the shipyards in the north of England, working as a plumber and a pipefitter. He then spent two years in the British army, serving in the 15th/19th Kings Royal Hussars stationed in the UK and Germany.

After the army, Derek studied craft and design for five years at South Shields Marine and Technical College. He spent two more years studying silversmithing and jewelry making at Newcastle College of Art and Industrial Design. He attended Durham Technical College for two years, where he gained a technical teacher's training certificate. With this training Derek taught craft, design, and technology at Gateshead School for twenty-four years before retiring in 1985 to devote all of his efforts to the sport of sea kayaking.

During his earlier years he married his sweetheart Helene on October 17, 1953, and they had three children: Clive, Graham, and Fiona. After over fifty years of marriage, Helene passed away in 2004.

On October 10, 2012, at 4:12 p.m., Derek died peacefully in his sleep surrounded by loved ones. He often joked that he wanted to go in his sleep just like grandpa, instead of the passengers screaming with terror as grandpa drove off the cliff.

The above paragraphs are the basic facts about Derek, but they do not do justice to the man. Derek had two lives. In South Shields he was known as a man who was always full of life, a loyal friend, a talented man, and usually the life of the party. Around the rest of the world Derek was known as the "Father of Modern-Day Sea Kayaking." Derek's friends in the UK knew he had a reputation in kayaking circles, but most did not realize that he had directly affected hundreds of thousands of paddlers around the world. He wrote the first book on sea kayaking and at least a dozen more, some of which have been translated and distributed internationally. He designed seventeen different kayaks, was featured in numerous videos, led record-breaking expeditions, achieved Senior Coach status with the BCU (the highest level), and taught classes and lectured internationally. It was amazing to read the hundreds of tributes that poured in from around the world after Derek's passing was announced online.

Derek was an adventurer. In 1976 he was the first man to cross the North Sea (100-mile nonstop trip) in a single kayak along with Dave Hellawell and his very dear friend Tom Caskey. At

Here is Derek performing his signature move. CAROL T. HARRIS

the time it was the longest attempted distance in single sea kayaks, but the greater feat was staying awake for that length of time on the water. Going to sleep was not an option. That North Sea expedition earned Derek a place in the *Guinness Book of World Records*. He also led expeditions to the Aleutian Islands, Prince William Sound, and numerous places around the UK and the west coast of the United States.

That wanderlust, hunger for adventure, and love of the sea lived within Derek all of his life. His first adventure happened in South Shields on the northeastern coast of England when Derek was four and his friend Alan was three. Derek's grandfather made him a wheelbarrow. One fine day Derek, as expedition leader, took Alan and the wheelbarrow from Pollard Street down Ocean Road all the way to the beach. The two young adventurers spent the day sifting through the sand and the rocks for little treasures. When the sun started to get lower in the sky, Derek thought it was time to head home.

As the two young lads headed back up Ocean Road, a black car stopped beside them. A man with a pointed hat stepped out of the car and said, "Are your names Derek and Alan?" Derek replied, "Yes they are." The constable then said, "Your grandma and your mother are worried about you." Their expedition ended with a wonderful ride in the back of the police car to the worried arms of Derek's grandmother and Alan's mother.

The people who knew Derek fell into three categories: those who loved him; those who hated him; and those who wanted to hate him, but couldn't help but love him. When Derek presented his strong opinions with his dry British humor, some people judged him as insensitive and cold. In truth he was a very caring man who drove his students hard because he wanted them to be the best they could be.

Derek believed you should try your best in anything you do, and he was successful at nearly everything he put his mind to. In addition to kayak design, Derek's creative talents lent themselves to photography and painting. He also created numerous pieces of jewelry as an artist and silversmith.

Those who knew Derek appreciated his sense of humor. He was a showman in every sense of the word and knew how to capture an audience with just his charm and wit. He was usually the center of attention in most gatherings. Believe it or not, Derek would have butterflies in his stomach before he would get in front of any group whether to teach or tell his tales.

Given Derek's worldwide following, the tributes received after his passing, and the turnout at his memorial service, the evidence is clear: Derek made an incredible difference in the lives of others.

Wayne Horodowich

Wayne Horodowich was born in Brooklyn, New York, in June 1950. He spent the first eighteen years of his life living in the projects and attending public schools. At 6 feet 7 inches, Wayne was recruited to play basketball through high school and then in college as a center for CCNY. He originally went to college to be an engineer, but he discovered his true passion the summer between his first and second year when he worked as a basketball instructor for a summer camp in Pennsylvania. That passion was, and still is, teaching.

When he returned to college the following semester, Wayne changed majors to become a physical education instructor, to the dismay of his father. His dad came around after Wayne received a master's degree from the University of Oregon and taught anatomy and physiology at UC Santa Barbara. After four years of teaching at UCSB, he decided to return to the U of O to finish the work he began on his doctorate in biomechanics. However, life challenges got in the way. In 1980 Wayne accepted a career-changing job at UCSB as the director of the Outdoor Program. Since he was an Outward Bound graduate (mountaineering program), a certified scuba instructor, experienced rock climber, downhill skier, avid backpacker, and certified EMT, Wayne felt confident he could do the job.

Little did he realize that running the Outdoor Program, later named Adventure Programs, would change his life. During the first few years, he spent more time in his sleeping bag than in his own bed. He kept adding different activities to the program offerings. Since UCSB is located right on the Pacific Ocean, starting a sea kayaking program was a natural. Using one of the whitewater kayaks intended for the guides to use on flat-water canoe trips, Wayne started paddling along the coast. He had no knowledge of rescues or stroke technique, and he had a hard time paddling in a straight line. He could not paddle beyond the kelp beds because when he capsized, he had to swim to shore. He tried to learn to roll from a book, with a 50 percent success rate. He then came across a sea kayaking book in the local chandlery by some English guy named Derek Hutchinson. The book became Wayne's bible and this unknown individual became his guru. Wayne purchased eight sea kayaks for the program, and his career as a kayak instructor began.

At that time, the American Canoe Association (ACA) did not have a sea kayaking program, so there was no US certifying agency for sea kayaking instructors. Wayne networked and shared information with other self-proclaimed instructors on the West and East Coasts. He found this type of sharing invaluable. He attended sea kayak symposia and eventually became a featured presenter and instructor at symposia around the country. He also solidified an instructor exchange program for TASK (Trade Association of Sea Kayaking). Even though he did receive his ACA Sea Kayaking Instructor Trainer and Whitewater Instructor ratings, aside from his four-star rating from the British Canoe Union (BCU), Wayne realized he was paying others to tell him what he already knew, so he put his resources into instructor exchanges.

While still directing Adventure Programs, Wayne went back to school at UCSB to get a second master's degree in experiential education because of all the team-building work he was doing at the Challenge Ropes Course he built for the program. This additional training changed the way he taught all his outdoor classes.

Campus Point at UCSB is a famous Southern California surfing spot. Wayne would regularly take his whitewater kayak out at lunchtime and dodge the board surfers on the waves. He regularly competed in kayak surf competitions and had the honor of being the captain of the US Surf Kayaking Team at the World Championships in 1991 in Thurso, Scotland, and in 1993 in Santa Cruz, California. The medals above his desk are reminders of that platinum experience.

Wayne first met Derek Hutchinson when the Father of Modern-Day Sea Kayaking interrupted a presentation Wayne was doing for his kayaking peers because he took exception to Wayne's explanation. A few years later, Derek told Wayne that their friendship was a testimonial to the

Wayne Horodowich CREDIT USK LIBRARY

younger man's ability to endure adverse and impossible challenges.

Over the years Wayne's path would cross Derek's and eventually they became close friends. They taught numerous clinics together and spent long hours on the road as Wayne drove his van from class to class up and down the west coast of the United States.

The greatest public compliment Derek ever gave his friend was: "Wayne is a perfect example of shining mediocrity." His smile was ear to ear when he said it.

In 2000 Wayne started the University of Sea Kayaking to promote sea kayaking education, with hundreds of articles on sea kayaking. He also produced an award-winning video series on sea kayaking education. The result was overwhelmingly positive, which meant he was now teaching clinics from Alaska all the way down to Mexico, across the US, and in the UK. His greatest joy was being asked to teach the Outward Bound instructors for the Baja program. Having been an Outward Bound student, he was honored to give back to the program.

In 2005 Wayne took an early retirement at age 55, after directing Adventure Programs for twenty-four years. During that time he had personally trained and guided a few thousand paddlers and trained close to one thousand college students to be trip leaders and instructors. He relocated to the Pacific Northwest about 10 miles north of Seattle, Washington. Since retiring from UCSB, he has produced more videos and continues to teach kayaking, write articles, and find time for his own adventures.

During their last paddle together, Derek confided in Wayne that there was no one else in the world he trusted more to have beside him on the water.

Wayne brings his decades of experience, personal anecdotes, and the wisdom he learned through his friendship with Derek to the new edition of this book.